I0896428

Wilfried Raussert

'What's Going On'

How Music Shapes the Social

INTER-AMERICAN STUDIES
Cultures – Societies – History

ESTUDIOS INTERAMERICANOS
Culturas – Sociedades – Historia

Volume 26

Wilfried Raussert

'What's Going On'

How Music Shapes the Social

Wissenschaftlicher Verlag Trier

Copublished by

UNO University of New Orleans Press

'What's Going On':
How Music Shapes the Social /
Wilfried Raussert. –
(Inter-American Studies | Estudios Interamericanos; 26)
Trier: WVT Wissenschaftlicher Verlag Trier, 2021
ISBN 978-3-86821-811-4
New Orleans, LA: University of New Orleans Press, 2021
ISBN 978-1-60801-199-5

SPONSORED BY THE
Federal Ministry of Education and Research

The project, on which this book is based, has been funded by the German Federal Ministry of Education and Research (Bundesministerium für Bildung und Forschung, BMBF). The responsibility for the content of this publication lies with the author.

Cover Image: "Prince Mural with Woman, Denver, CO" © Wilfried Raussert
Cover Design: Brigitta Disseldorf

Library of Congress Cataloging-in-Publication Data
Names: Raussert, Wilfried, author.
Title: 'What's going on' : how music shapes the social / Wilfried Raussert.
Description: [First] | New Orleans : University of New Orleans, 2021. | Series: Inter-American studies ; 26 | Includes bibliographical references.
Identifiers: LCCN 2020044533 | ISBN 9781608011995 (paperback)
Subjects: LCSH: Music--America--Social aspects. | Music and identity politics. | Music and tourism. | Music museums. | Music--Historiography.
Classification: LCC ML3917.A63 R38 2021 | DDC 306.4/842097--dc23
LC record available at https://lccn.loc.gov/2020044533

Publisher: WVT Wissenschaftlicher Verlag Trier, Postfach 4005, D-54230 Trier, Bergstraße 27, D-54295 Trier, Tel. 0049 651 41503, Fax 41504, www.wvttrier.de, wvt@wvttrier.de

Copublisher: University of New Orleans Press, 2000 Lakeshore Drive, Earl K. Long Library, Room 221, New Orleans, LA 70148, United States, 504-280-7457, unopress.org

CONTENTS

1 Music and the Social (Introduction)

What's Going On
(Marvin Gaye)

Bruno Latour is one of the first critics in the twenty-first century to articulate the 'crisis' of the social. Stressing the "many … contradictory cartographies of the social" (2005, 34), Latour highlights the interaction between human and nonhuman actors in making social connections and raises questions about the interrelationships between plural socialities. Latour favors a "sociology of associations" (34). A similar critique of Durkheimian or Marxian reductive "sociology of the social" (34) is present in contemporary music sociology. For instance, Tia DeNora claims that "music is active within social life" (2000, 3). Hence, the meanings of music "may be constructed in relation to things outside it," and "things outside music may be constructed in relation to music" (3). Georgina Born, with a nod to Will Straw's theory of musical scenes, makes a strong argument that "music necessitates an expansion of previous conceptions of the social" (2012, 266). In her reading, "music creates its own diverse socialities, animates new imagined communities, refracts wider social identity formation, and partakes in late capitalism's multi-polar cultural economy" (267).

Daniel J. Levitin reminds us of the omnipresence of music when he lists human reunions and encounters such as "weddings, funerals, graduation from college, men marching off to war, stadium sporting events, a night on the town, prayer, a romantic dinner, mothers rocking their infants to sleep and college students studying with music as a background …" (2007, 8) in which music play a pivotal role. We may add music's role in the cotton fields in the American South, modern working spheres, shopping malls, and museums (8). Indeed, music is part of the fabric of everyday life. With the rise of modernity a strange division between performers and listeners emerged that overshadowed a historical presence of music as a basic human activity and condition in which all members of a community participated. Contemporary rituals like karaoke and sports hymns in soccer stadiums publicly perform the closure of the above gap. Music penetrates all strata of public life. Music is home entertainment. Music is a spiritual force in religious contexts around the globe. As contemporary mall culture shows, it is also the bedfellow of commodity and market strategies that want to sell. Music is present in social and political movements as a mode of inspiration, reflection, a chant for action, and a tool for propaganda. It functions as a model and inspiration for artistic endeavors from literature to film to multi-media performance arts. Music has become immaterial heritage culture and a driving force in diasporic, subaltern, alternative, and mainstream identity politics, be they on a local, regional, national, or global scale. It is notable that music frequently assumes a seismographic function and transmits to a larger public the presence of social crisis through the act of performance. Since music appeals to all human senses, it carries the potential to push affective politics and sensitize its audience to social conflict, crisis, and injustice. It is the mix of affective, cognitive, and kinesthetic response to music that makes music a powerful medium to express, narrate, and reflect the social.

Jay Schulkin and Greta B. Raglin emphasize that "[m]usic is often functional because it is something that can promote human well-being by facilitating human contact, human meaning, and human imagination of possibilities, tying it to our social instincts" (2014, n. pag.). Most people today have access to music. The development of the recording industry and innovation in distribution technology have revolutionized the means through which music infiltrates all levels of the social. In regards to community- and nation-building it is important that we keep in mind that music is a powerful social player. Beyond verbal communication, music facilitates human bonding and communication. It takes a crucial role in creating and maintaining individual, group, and national solidarity. Music fosters physiological, cognitive, emotional, and behavioral responses.

Music also functions as inspiration, action-stimulation, trigger of emotions and reflections, and therapeutic tool. On an individual and collective level, music forms the social by promoting bonding via sound and rhythm. It performs and narrates the social in its extension in dance and lyrics. Jill Suttie points toward a conceptualization of music as social and existential force of human survival:

> For much of human history, the only way to experience music was live – there were no recordings allowing us to share music outside of perfor-

> mance. Since music had to involve contact with others (e.g. coming together for a concert), it provided a net of physical and psychological safety that may have helped our early ancestors – and may still help us – to survive. (2016, n. pag.)

Music is arguably among the most primal and basic elements of culture. For some critics its function equals that of language as a fundamental form of human communication. American poet and thinker Henry Wadsworth Longfellow even called it "the universal language of mankind" (1835, 4). With a nod to critics like Susan Hallam (2008), I argue that there is an intimate and permanent relationship between music and society, and music and the social. Music creates, changes, and reflects the social.

This book begins from the premise that we are living in an age in which the social is in a continuous process of reinvention. It is also grounded in the assumption that music is a perennial key player in the processes of reinventing the social since music holds the power to stimulate and transport visions of change through its appeal to all human senses. I believe that visionary flight and action-impulse interact and fuse in music more easily than in any other cultural expression. Since it is one of our most basic forms of expression and communication beyond cognitive and language barriers, it lends itself to performing, expressing, and creating the social in multiple spheres.

The book traces music's presence in various social realms and cultural fields of production. Less concerned with analysis of music and musical expressions per se, it intends to illustrate how deeply music from the Americas has infused social, cultural, political, and economic practice in the twentieth and twenty-first centuries. The first chapter unfolds the intersection of music and identity politics; the second chapter addresses the role of music in social movements and their political and economic contextualization; the third chapter explores music's presence in commodity and tourist culture; the fourth chapter looks at music in the context of museum culture and heritage politics; the fifth chapter traces music's presence in artistic media like literature and the visual arts, while the sixth and final chapter approaches how music as social force is reflected anew in contemporary music documentary. The intention behind this book is to open the reader's eyes to music's omnipresence in our social life beyond the *muzak* sound in shopping malls, the background music in bars and restaurants, and the spatially marked distance of music from the audience in exclusive concert halls. It further wants to illustrate how music from the Americas keeps reinventing the social within and beyond the American hemisphere.

Music not only seems the most ubiquitous art form today, but is arguably also the most propelling art medium in crossing boundaries aesthetically, geographically, politically, and ideologically. Throughout its history, popular music has negated clear dividing lines and, in addition, has repeatedly proven capable of transforming itself despite its entanglement in mass and commodity culture. And, in reference to the latter, one may state that in the age of internet, MP3, P2P technologies, and the frequently envisioned death of the music industry, popular music once more paves the way for new modes of cultural production, distribution, and reception. The access to music online may be read as a further process of democratization in the sphere of cultural production and distribution. Not only does this shift open venues for composer and musicians to reach large audiences online, locally, regionally, nationally, and transnationally, but it also changes aspects of agency and power in the production and control over "culture."

1.1 Music in the Americas

From the late nineteenth century with the global success of spirituals to the twenty-first century with the global expansion of rap, music from the Americas has taken the world by storm, to a large extent shaping global culture. Youth cultures and countercultures continue to draw upon musical expressions from the Americas to form new identities, express new communal ties, shape new body languages, and voice political dissent. While musical flows frequently follow multi-dimensional directions, the presence of jazz, reggae, and rap around the globe suggests a hegemony of afro-descendent musical forms from the Americas. Many of the musical flows travel south-north and north-south and form inter-American musical webs that find their expressions among others in less marketed musical forms as well, such as fandango, calypso, and kaiso jazz. Others have shaped dance cultures like the Charleston, mambo, salsa, rap, and reggaeton and have created a whole new music industry for entertainment.

The utopian imaginaries at the very foundations of 'America' in the Northern and the Southern hemispheres seem to shape the social and political directions of music in the Americas. Hence, juxtapositions of utopia and dystopia, hope and disillusionment, vision and lament characterize many musical expressions from blues to rock, from protest songs to *nueva cancion*, from soul to rap. Music and politics unfold a complex interrelation that makes it difficult if not impossible to separate entertainment from political mission, artistic expression from commerce, action-orientation from pleasure. The Americas, so it seems, provide a particularly rich terrain for such a complex – at times conflictive and explosive – mix. Long standing communal indigenous forms, newly emerging afro-descendent cultures, and the fusion of them with musical traditions from around the globe have brought forth a rapidly expanding and diversifying field of music made in the Americas.

1.2 The social and social movements

A hemispherical approach serves as a good starting point to rethink the social in the Americas in new ways, challenging the postmodern assumption that the social is dead. Writing in 1996 about the destruction of the European social welfare state, sociologist Nikolas Rose claimed the death of the social (2008, 85). While the destruction of the social welfare state and its generalized social cleavages were also a fact for the neoliberal decade of the 1980s – from Reaganomics to the Chicago Boys in Chile under Pinochet – there has also remained a popular notion of inventing the social. This argument is based on the historical assessment that utopian social imaginations are woven deeply into both Latin American and North American societies. In addition, the collectivization of the 'convivencia' claims among Latin American groups and the 'community' politics in North American history require us to rethink what the "social" and "social coexistence" mean in the American hemispheres (cf. Kaltmeier and Raussert 2019).

The renewed importance granted to social narratives in contemporary times is also sustained by two closely connected social developments: the present eruption of grassroots and social movements in the Americas that resist neoliberal globalization – from Occupy Wall Street to the Black Lives Matter movement – and the popular movements backing the leftist governments in Latin America in the 2000s. These movements also challenge the social status quo of systems of domination. Most notably, this rings true for protest movements against Donald Trump's election and presidency in the United States and the Black Lives Matter movement, as well as protest movements against exclusion and for recognition and redistribution in Latin American and Canadian indigenous movements. These dynamics illustrate the social's high sociopolitical volatility through the contrast between utopia and dystopia (Kaltmeier and Raussert 2019).

The call for rights of indigenous people, the fight against racial discrimination and oppression of gay and lesbian cultures, and demonstrations against the eviction and deportation of undocumented migrants have catalyzed a new wave of diverse and frequently interconnected social movements across the Americas. These movements have inspired and been inspired by new musical forms such as calypso, salsa, reggae, folk, rock, punk, funk, soul, and rap. Frequently, movements such as the Civil Rights movement, the Black Power movement, the Black Lives Matter movement, the Chicano movement, and the Dreamers' movement have brought music to the streets, public places, conflicted territories, and cultural centers to support their efforts in resistance politics and new community-building processes.

Furthermore, music as a community-building medium goes beyond entertainment and cultural consumption. Several music projects emphasize participation, tear down walls between artistic stage and public space, and dissolve boundaries between performer and spectator. The boundaries between cultural production and social movements eventually blur. Religious, ethnic, environmental, and women's movements have been a major contributing factor to breaking with traditional concepts of the social, as well as inducing change. With respect to music, one may think of Chican@ Punk and Alice Bag and their engagement in the women's movements, or El Vez and his politicization of Elvis Presley songs in the context of recent immigration movements that redefine the social from marginal and subaltern positioning (cf. Raussert 2017).

The anniversary of more than three decades of the HIV/AIDS epidemic recently inspired filmmakers and musicians not only to commemorate the somber occasion but to cherish activism in the face of tragedy and recall loved ones with a series of documentaries recounting the early days of the epidemic, including United in Anger: A History of Act Up, 30 Years from Here, and How to Survive a Plague. Certainly, one of the most salient and enduring aspects of United in Anger, for example, is its invocation of music about HIV/AIDS that captured a moment and defined an era, which transports the viewer to those nascent days of Act Up. Experimental gay artists and supporters including the Pet Shop Boys and Cyndi Lauper addressed the epidemic in song even as the Reagan Administration dragged its feet in acknowledging the issue. Dionne Warwick and Friends performed together to raise money for AIDS research as early as 1985, while 1990 saw the release of the popular, queer-positive *Red, Hot + Blue* benefit album.

Alongside such movements, new narrations of cultural creation and production of knowledge are being currently introduced, which push contemporary concepts of the social to their limits. Among Latino communities in the U.S. and Central American or South American countries, post-territorial narrations of the social have emerged that reach beyond nation-state projects. Concepts such as society, community, state, and nation are too narrow and specifying to do justice to the "fluidity of the social" (Bauman 2000, 25).

In the field of cultural production, practice, discourses, narrations, and performative acts typically appear quite different than they do in social movements. In music, innovations in style, rhythm, and musical authorship bear little resemblance to the social, cultural, and political demands, protests, and forms of organization in social movements. Yet, despite these differences, both cultural production and social movements have the self-reflexive capacity to detect conflicts and breaks in the sphere of the social and to articulate them to a broader public. In doing so, music weaves the social ties between different groups and enables social movements' identity formation. In diachronic terms, music narrates stories of the past and serves as a cultural memory of movements. Music is also a vehicle for constructing identities and creating political imaginaries that shape social movements, political projects, and geopolitical imaginaries. According to George Lipsitz, popular music functions as a "vital repository for collective memory" (2007, vii). Whether or not they view themselves as historians, songwriters frequently provide "alternative archives of history" (xi) emerging from the artist's experience, memory, and vision. Besides these active community-based forms of memory, we also see today a push to regulate formats of memory by institutions such as the UNESCO Convention for the Safeguarding of Intangible Cultural Heritage, an organization that has produced numerous initiatives to recognize musical traditions as cultural heritage. In Germany, grassroots and union songs of the worker's movement have been declared heritage. In the Americas, the cultural expressions – especially the songs – of the Afro-American Garifuna in Belize, Honduras, and Guatemala have been declared Intangible Cultural Heritage of Humanity, as well as Afro-Cuban rumba, tango in Argentina and Uruguay, samba in Brazil, marimba in Ecuador and Colombia, and reggae in Jamaica.

1.3 Traveling sounds

The study of music offers a unique lens with which to focus various debates in cultural studies, media studies, literary studies, history, sociology, and anthropology that try to come to terms with issues of shifting identities and agency, new ethnicities, intercultural exchange, processes of commodification, and transnationalization in times of globalization. Additionally, it permits critics to look at "the status of popular culture and audiovisual media at the beginning of the twenty-first century" (Miklitsch 2006, xviii), to explore dynamics and tensions between aesthetics and politics, art and entertainment, and production and reception in contemporary popular-cultural studies. Music seems to be not only the most ubiquitous art form today, but the one that most forcefully promotes the crossing of aesthetic, geographic, political, and ideological boundaries.

Why choose music as a field of exploration to come to terms with cultural and social spheres in the Americas? By its very nature music appeals to a variety of human senses simultaneously. Music, through the interweaving of melody, harmony, and rhythm is able to circumvent cognitive and language barriers more easily than other media. And in terms of both physics and geography, sounds travel fast, thanks to a broad range of transmitters: e.g., the singing of a parent to a child, radio distribution, concerts, televised performances, video music channel distribution, CD and DVD productions, and, most recently, the distribution of music on the internet. Being part of the social, the economic, and the political, music displays a high adaptability, not only to different transmitters but also to different media, as its presence in theatre, museums, film, the shopping mall, and the internet illustrates.

Music has shaped the social in local and global contexts. Because of its presence and importance beyond closed tribal, communal, religious, and national boundaries, music can be defined as an aesthetic expression that has always been closely linked with cultural heritage, cultural change and exchange, transculturation, and migration. Music shapes the social and is produced by the social at the same time. It helps us "to trace old and new maps and histories of people in transit" (Clifford 1997, 2).

Music travels within society, transgressing class, racial, gender, and age boundaries, and travels transnationally. Music uses different routes to travel: some of these routes start in the diaspora and return to an actual or imaginary homeland, while others take their origin in a specific regional or national space to reach out to multiple diaspora communities around the globe. Salsa, for instance, emerged in Cuba, reached its first heyday in New York, and was then reimported in the Caribbean and other regions of Latin America. Whereas most Caribbean music grew out of African roots in times of slavery, soukous music in the Congo can be seen as an African adaptation of Latin American rumba, the latter having been a staple of colonial radio broadcasts during the rumba craze of the 1940s and 1950s. Flows between the Old and New World follow multiple patterns. While there are some studies on African American ragtime's role in engendering a distinct South African jazz sound (Kelly 2012) and on reggae's impact on the African continent (McNee 2002), the transatlantic flow between the African continent and Jamaican popular music did not end with the cultural absorption of reggae in Africa in the late 1970s and 1980s either. Today, Jamaican reggae and dancehall are among the most popular music forms in many parts of Africa. Along with hip-hop, techno/house, and African sounds such as kwaito and zim, reggae and dancehall are major elements in the vast lexicon of African dance rhythms. Klezmer music emerged from Jewish diaspora communities in Europe, flourished in the Jewish diaspora in the United States between the 1880s and the 1930s, disappeared almost completely from the European scene in the era of Nazism and Stalinism, and celebrated a comeback in the United States in the mid-1970s, eventually returning to Europe as an American import in the 1990s (Slobin 2003, 290)

Music ethnologists have revealed that music has played a significant role in religious and later social and political contexts in all cultures around the globe (Canaris 2005, 35). Since the 1970s and 1980s we have witnessed increasing scholarly attention to the links between music and social groups. From an initial interest in the connections between class affiliation and musical preference, music scholars have expanded their analytical concerns to include issues of race, gender, age, ethnicity, culture, and counterculture. This larger focus on the interrelation between music and various aspects of identity made the 1990s "a watershed in the cultural study of music" according to John Shepard, and these concerns remain at the forefront of music studies today (2012, 75). With a nod to critics like Wolfgang Welsch (1993, 198), I see in the art of music a spearhead function that creates models for identity formation beyond local, regional, and national constraints. As Hans J. Lietzmann (2005) argues, music and politics unfold their meanings and effects only within communal contexts in close interaction with the public. Whereas politics is expected to bring order to chaos, music is allowed to embrace chaos and 'signify' upon it creatively (Raussert 2008, 16). As such, music represents an open discourse that provides ground for experimentation, innovation, and model-seeking processes outside the restraints of the social, political, and legal systems (58–59).

Because of all this potential, music has repeatedly succeeded in overcoming national as well as nationalistic boundaries. This is true for the emergence of classical music and jazz alike. Nineteenth-century Vienna represented the multicultural location for the emergence of a classical/romantic music that fused different local, regional, and national music styles and became popular world-wide even in the heyday of nationalistic thought and feeling (Rösing 2002, 23), just as polyglot New Orleans in the late nineteenth and early twentieth century became the setting for the emergence of jazz, a musical form combining African, African American, and European musical styles and elements in spite of racial segregation in the American South. While various musical genres keep crossing national and continental boundaries today, pop music – through its close link to fast-traveling sounds and images – functions as an ideal means of communication between cultures. Although pop music frequently lacks clear contours, critics like Gabriele Klein and Malte Friedrich remind us that exactly this may be an advantage for communication beyond fixed ethnic, racial, social, cultural, and economic boundaries. According to their affirmative view, the "glocal" communities of pop are linked through music and image. They create alliances because they manage to connect people beyond national and continental borders. Precisely because the diasporic pop community refuses to be pinned down to fixed paradigms, it provides alternative models to nationalistic and racist attempts to enforce ethnically homogeneous communities (2003, 98).

In sum, to analyze the emergence of the social, this book considers the social as a process, something always in a state of becoming (Deleuze and Guattari 1987). The special significance of music for the social consists in its ability to connect persons, artifacts, and occurrences with each other in new ways. In doing so, music plays a particular role in upheavals and revolutions, linking the day-to-day world to such movements (Selbin 2010).

It is music's close relationship with everything social that inspired the writing of this book, which looks at music in context. Music's utopian and dystopian potential has paved the way for its leading role among the arts to successfully cross the gap between entertainment and the social, leisure and the political. The chapters highlight music's presence in various contexts: politics, tourism, heritage culture, documentary film, literature and the arts, and identity politics. The idea is to illustrate that the Americas are indeed "sonic Americas" and that music is the ideal point of departure for remapping the social in its various sonic facets. The idea is not to point out the social functions of music but rather to trace music's presence in, and shaping of, the social.

Works cited

Bauman, Zygmunt. 2000. *Liquid Modernity*. Cambridge: Polity Press. Print.

Born, Georgina. 2012. "Music and the Social." In *The Cultural Study of Music: A Critical Introduction*, ed. Martin Clayton et al., 261–274. New York: Routledge. Print.

Canaris, Ute. 2005. *Musik//Politik. Musik und Projekte zur Musik im politischen Kontext*. Bochum: Kamp. Print.

Clifford, James. 1997. *Routes: Travel and Translation in the Late Twentieth Century*. Cambridge: Harvard University Press. Print.

Deleuze, Gilles, and Félix Guattari. 1987. *A Thousand Plateaus: Capitalism and Schizophrenia.* Minneapolis: University of Minnesota Press. Print.

DeNora, Tia. 2011. *Music in Everyday Life*. Cambridge: Cambridge University Press. Print.

Hallam, Susan. 2008. "The Power of Music," July 10. https://musicmagic.wordpress.com/2008/07/10/music-in-society/.

Kaltmeier, Olaf, and Wilfried Raussert. 2019. "Introduction." In *Sonic Politics: Music and Social Movements*, ed. Olaf Kaltmeier and Wilfried Raussert, 1–18. New York/London: Routledge. Print.

Kelley, Robin D.G. 2012. *Africa Speaks, America Answers: Modern Jazz in Revolutionary Times*. Cambridge: Harvard University Press. Print.

Klein, Gabriele, and Malte Friedrich. 2003. "Globalisierung und die Performanz des Pop." In *Popvisionen. Links in die Zukunft*, ed. Klaus Neumann-Braun and Axel Mai, 92–114. Frankfurt/Main: Suhrkamp. Print.

Latour, Bruno. 2005. *Reassembling the Social: An Introduction to Actor-Network-Theory*. Oxford: Oxford University Press. Print.

Levitin, Daniel J. 2007. *This is Your Brain on Music: The Science of a Human Obsession*. New York: A Plume Book. Print.

Lietzmann, Hans J. 2005. "Politik und Musik. Gemeinschaft und Differenz." In *Musik und Projekte zur Musik im politischen Kontext*, ed. Ute Canaris, 48–73. Bochum: Kamp. Print.

Lipsitz, George. 2007. *Footsteps in the Dark: The Hidden Histories of Popular Music*. Minneapolis: University of Minnesota Press. Print.

Longfellow, Henry. W. 1835. *Outre-Mer: A Pilgrimage Beyond the Sea*. Vol. 2 of 2. New York: Harper & Brothers. Print.

McNee, Lisa. 2002. "Back from Babylon: Popular Music Cultures from the Diaspora, Youth Culture, and Identity in Francophone West Africa." In *Music – Popular Culture – Identities*, ed. Richard Young, 231–247. Amsterdam: Rodopi. Print.

Miklitsch, Robert. 2006. *Roll Over Adorno: Critical Theory, Popular Culture, Audiovisual Media*. Albany: State University of New York Press. Print.

Raussert, Wilfried. 2008. "Introduction: Traveling Sounds: Music, Migration, and Identity Formation." In *Traveling Sounds: Music, Migration, and Identity in the U.S. and Beyond*, ed. Wilfried Raussert and John Miller Jones, 9–23. Berlin: LIT Verlag. Print.

—. 2017. "Retuning Hegemonic Pop Culture: El Vez's Citation Practices." In *The Routledge Companion to Inter-American Studies*, ed. Wilfried Raussert, 178–186. New York/London: Routledge. Print.

Rösing, Helmut. 2002. "Populäre Musik und Identität. 8 Thesen." *Heimatlose Klänge? Regionale Musiklandschaften. Beiträge zur Popularmusikforschung* 29/30: 11–34. Print.

Rose, Nikolas. 2008. "The Death of the Social." In *Governing the Present*, ed. Peter Miller and Nikolas Rose, 84–113. Cambridge: Polity. Print.

Schulkin, Jay, and Greta B. Raglin. 2014. "The Evolution of Music and Human Social Capability." *Frontiers in Neuroscience*. https://www.researchgate.net/publication/266575555_The_Evolution_of_Music_and_Human_Social_Capability.

Selbin, Eric. 2010. *Revolution, Rebellion, Resistance: The Power of Story*. London: Zed Books. Print.

Shepard, John. 2012. "Music and Social Categories." In *The Cultural Study of Music: A Critical Introduction,* ed. Martin Clayton, Trevor Herbert, and Richard Middleton, 69–79. London/New York: Routledge. Print

Slobin, Mark. 2003. "The Destiny of 'Diaspora' in Ethnomusicology." In *The Cultural Study of Music: A Critical Introduction*, ed. Martin Clayton, Trevor Herbert, and Richard Middleton, 284–296. London/New York: Routledge. Print.

Suttie, Jill. 2016. "How Music Bonds Us Together." *Greater Good Magazine*, June 28. https://greatergood.berkeley.edu/article/item/how_music_bonds_us_together.

Welsch, Wolfgang. 1993. *Ästhetisches Denken*. Stuttgart: Reclam. Print.

2 Music and Identity Politics

The politics of popular music are strongly shaped by music's capacity to form affective alliances that cross lines of class, gender, nationality, race, and sexuality. Hence music plays a crucial role for both individual and group socialities on a short-term basis and identities on a long-term basis. Music's social mediation is embedded in practice and performance, distribution and reception, market circuits and other forms of institutionalization. While not necessarily related in every instance, performed socialities, imagined communities, and social identity form an important triad for the emergence of identity and identity politics within and beyond institutions (Born 2012, 266–267; Straw 1991, 374–384). Like identity in liquid times (Bauman 2006), these categories are in process, often contested, and frequently interrelated. With the emergence of new market circuits, including SoundCloud, Spotify, YouTube, and other forms of new media music distribution, individual musical expression is publicized, and the interrelation between subject and the social is intensified. The chapter at hand traces music's relation to various identity concepts and processes of transculturation and transformation, with examples from twentieth century and twenty-first century music to show various flows and entanglements of sonic identity politics in the Americas.

2.1 Entangling and entangled music-produced identities

The music of Arsenio Rodríguez expresses multiple affiliations to cubanidad, latinidad, and blackness, while at the same time embracing and acknowledging distinct differences. His work permits one to approach music in the Americas and the Latino/a input on U.S. American Popular music from a transcultural perspective that takes both a descriptive and critical position. It allows us to reflect upon links beyond nation and culture, "the always-already-traversed border in between being and becoming American" (Pease and Wiegman 2002, 19). Such a perspective is ideally suited for engaging with strategic crossroads where the national meets the transnational and with the ongoing constitution of "America" and "Americas" from a dialogical point of view.

The complex glocal webs underlying the construction and performance of identity shine through Rodríguez's musical production. As composer and performer he was responsible for crucial developments in some of Latin music's most important genres: son montuno, mambo, and salsa in the 1930s, 1940s, and 1950s. He not only developed an African playing style in his Afro-Cuban music compositions, but also created musical compositions closely tied to race, class, and cubanidad. Throughout his career he never ceased to emphasize the African roots of Cuban music and continuously combined his black musical aesthetics with antiracist struggles. In July 1969, Rodríguez performed in a program at the Festival of American Folklife in Washington D.C. that was titled "Black Music through the Languages of the New World." Introducing his music at the festival, he asserted the black roots of his compositions:

> Good afternoon ladies and gentlemen … I am Arsenio Rodríguez, the composer of many songs, principally African, which you have heard. I composed all of those afros that you used to hear Miguelito Valdés sing, "Bruca Maniguá," "Fufunando," and "Adiós Àfrica," Xavier Cugat recorded, and many songs which are sung all over the world, all of which have an African influence from my heritage. (qtd. in García 2006, 17)

Rodríguez's music first became audible within the context of the afrocubanismo cultural movement of the 1930s. Both his music and his identity he based upon a transnational Afro-diasporic perspective. In effect, he "affirmed his African heritage and Cuban identity as coexistent yet distinct rather than as mestizaje or synthesis," as David Garcia explains (2006, 12). Rhythmically, Rodríguez drew upon tango-congo-rhythmic patterns for introduction, verse, and bridge sections, and a basic son rhythmic structure for the afrocubanos's concluding section. In his lyrics he always attempted to fuse the musical-lyrical with the political. Hence, a salient feature of his afrocubanos (afrocuban songs) is the textual representation of black slaves and nineteenth century plantation life via the use of bozal speech, an Africanized form of Spanish, and through the presentation of conventional black character types found in Cuban popular theatre. The latter had become popular in the minstrel-like portrayals of black people in nineteenth century Cuban bufos, or comic theatre, and bore the signs of black difference and inferiority. In redeploying dominant signs of blackness, Rodríguez engages in what African American critic James Snead labels "repetition with a difference"; the parody of parodied blackness then becomes a political tool as well as marketing strategy in which the composer becomes an agent in his music's distribution. Homi Bhabha's theory of stereotypes in colonial discourse asserts the stereotype's general "condition of ambivalence," which, according to him, is responsible for the currency of racial stereotypes and their continuous replication across time and cultures (1994, 94–96). Using racial signifiers in classifying new musical forms can work in a number of ways. Although their use may frequently function as a gatekeeper of racial supremacy, they may also be used as a marketing strategy to introduce the strange and exotic through an act of familiarization. When artists and producers resort to signifiers of black difference to introduce an art form to a larger audience, they can draw on stock responses of historically coded and recoded images of racial stereotypes. By emphasizing, exaggerating, and thus parodying current stereotypes, a process of familiarization sets in that makes that which appears strange and exotic paradoxically familiar. While such a cultural practice runs the risk of reinforcing stereotypes, it may well propel a successful intrusion of new "exotic" art forms into dominant popular culture. Rodríguez indeed employs a parody of a parody, a process that ironically enables him to both infuse mainstream cultural industry with his artistic products and to mock dominant racist ideologies at the same time (cf. Gates 1988, 100–106).

In his popular songs such as "Bruca Maniguá" this strategy exposes the double structure of public success and cultural critique. While the black character types in the opening verses of his afrocubanos recall the conventional images of minstrel tradition, in the bridge section of the songs a transformation occurs in the voice of the protagonist, whereupon he expresses his critical and confrontational stance explicitly, verbally attacking the oppressor. What Rodríguez situated in the transcultural flow of Latin Popular music was a border-crossing, transnational way of critiquing racism against black people. In "Aquí como allá" [It's the same Here as It is Over There], a song that he recorded in Havana in 1950, he indirectly references the racial bigotry he experienced in the American South. In the verse section he gives that experience a transnational twist, however, pointing out the transnational history of slavery and racial discrimination in reference to Africa, Brazil, Cuba, Haiti, New York, Argentina, Mexico, and Venezuela. While traveling many a road that black slaves had travelled before, Rodríguez's embrace of African roots provided ways of relocating and reconnecting musical traditions from the Americas. His emphasis on the conga drum as a major rhythmic component – the conga drum "signifying stereotypes of African primitivism," as David Garcia reminds us (2006, 22) – and, in particular, his utilization of an all-white Orquesta Casino de la Playa to perform afrocubanos reveal that Rodríguez spread his music across boundaries to claim a new agency in propelling and selling black musical forms, mocking the white appropriation of Cuban-black music in clubs in Buenos Aires, New York, and Havana in the late 1930s, and infusing mainstream culture with an empowered black agent's cultural critique.

It is the intersection of music, cultural politics, and their transnational relations that surfaces again in the history of popular music in the Americas and reminds us that it is our task as critics to come to terms with transculturality in the context of power relations if we want to comprehend the complex processes of multidirectional cultural exchange that characterize the production, distribution, and reception of music and its related impact on identity politics. Rodríguez's compositions perform entangled sonic histories and can only be grasped if we see music as inseparable from transnational politics of agency, access to production, and reception. While such an investigation may surprise us with unexpected commonalities within the Americas, it will always also guide us to see 'American' diversity dialogically. In Rodríguez's music, Cuban identity is performed as interconnected with Latin America at large and Afro-diasporic identity politics throughout the Americas.

2.2 Black power and black diasporic identity circuits

Transversal flows characterize the ways in which music and identity have travelled as not-so-strange bedfellows from colonial times to the present. Arguably one of the most powerful manifestations of the comradery between music and identity occurred with the spreading of funk and soul as a sonic political voice in the second half of the twentieth century. Against the historical backdrop of the tumultuous 1960s and early 1970s, when the Civil Rights and the Black Power movements not only shook the foundations of white supremacy in the United States but advanced anticolonial black struggle throughout the Americas and other parts of the globe, musical expression turned into a major medium for spreading political messages (Steinitz 2019). Referring to the diffusion of black cultures and politics during that epoch, Thomas Fawcett writes about new identitarian links between African American and Afro groups throughout Latin America and the Caribbean that travelled via music – funk and soul – in particular. As he puts it, "the globality of soul and funk music […] shows that music can create linkages between distinct groups of the African diaspora" (n. pag.). He emphasizes that "soul and funk music linked distinct communities of the diaspora despite the potential barriers of linguistic and cultural differences" (Fawcett 2007, n. pag). "Fans and musicians alike adopted elements of the soul aesthetic – such as the afro hairstyle," he asserts, "in a show of solidarity and as an implicit protest against the status quo" (n. pag.).

Commenting on black musical expression in the Americas, Roger D. Abrahams reminds us that the various expressive forms have a strong link with location and stories of origin. He lists "the Cuban Habanera, the Samba of Rio, Reggae and Kingston, and the Mississippi blues" as examples of powerful ties between music and specific places. At the same time, however, these genres reach beyond place to the entire globe. They "are also recognizably vernacular inventions that achieved a place in the transnational entertainment industry rather than providing the kind of cultural reflexiveness that leads to the formation of a patria" (Abrahams 2001, 99). What Abrahams suggests is the diffusion of a larger black imaginary in market circles beyond the boundaries of nation-states. As he concludes, "These musics, and the peoples identifying themselves through them, knit together the entire region, even as they advertise local cultural invention to worldwide popular audiences" (99). What emerges is a vision of black Americas far beyond the US South: "It is a region which not only includes the Caribbean and the U.S. South, but many coastal outposts in South America on both the north, east, and west coasts, and many areas of the latifundium of Central America, including Mexico, Belize, and Costa Rica" (99). Afro musical expressions, hence, have affected both geopolitical as well personal identity politics in the Americas. Describing the impact of funk and soul for black liberation throughout the Americas, William L. Van Deburg writes in *New Day in Babylon* that "[t]ranscending the medium of entertainment, soul music provided a ritual in song with which blacks could identify and through which they could convey important in-group symbols" (1992, 205). As

Van Deburg puts it, music turned into an agent of empowerment and change: "Music was power and considered to be supremely relevant to the protracted struggle of black people for liberation. To some it was the poetry of the black revolution" (205). Soul songs such as "To Be Young, Gifted, and Black" by Nina Simone, "We Got More Soul" by Dyke and the Blazers, and in particular "Say It Loud (I'm Black and I'm Proud)" by James Brown turned into hymns for the struggle of black liberation throughout the Americas and other sections of the globe concerned with anti-colonial struggles. Beyond black communities in the Americas and Africa, these musical expressions fueled youth culture movements, subcultural resistance, and countercultural movements, transgressing nations, ethnicities, and class boundaries on a global scale.

2.3 Citation practices and fluid identities between North and South

Music travels fast; the social in contemporary times is fluid, and identity changes from context to context, time to time, according to Bauman (2006). One way to follow transformations of identity and meaning is by looking at citation practices in contemporary music. Certainly sampling in the hip hop scene comes to mind first. Another example, which illustrates the South-North flows and interrelation of identity politics, can be found in the music by El Vez. Citation, put simply, means borrowing, appropriating, displacing, and relocating parts of an original. It is fair to say that citation permeates all fields of social and cultural practice. It can be part of the art world, the economy, and academia. While the practice of citation is an act of copying, it does not necessarily produce a copy. What it frequently creates is a new field of meaning – of connotation, allusion, and reference. Citation is thus a cultural practice of appropriation that leads to something new in a different context. With a nod to Walter Benjamin, Rüdiger Kunow points out that citing a text means interrupting a context. This reveals a certain unruly and challenging aspect of the practice of citation. In postcolonial and decolonial criticism, in particular, the act of citing bears reference to the inside of a culture and a new context outside its constituents. In Kunow's words, "citation is both located and movable, sedentary and open to employments at other sites" (2001, 252). As he continues to explain, "citation constitutes a double move: to the inside, to core constituents of a given culture, and to an outside, to a new context" (252).

The citing agent here is Robert Lopez, a.k.a. El Vez, the Mexican Elvis. El Vez is a contemporary Chicano artist born in the U.S.-Mexican borderlands. His practice of citation can best be described as multimedial. It illustrates that citing reaches beyond language and print culture. It involves text, sound, image, clothing, and gesture. His citational practice, I argue, serves a double function. On the one hand, it allows him to promote his own performance by re-selling the familiar. On the other, it permits him to defamiliarize the already known by creating new samplings and remixes. These are characterized by sudden breaks and transitions that challenge "the hegemony of 'white' American pop culture" (Kunow 2001, 251). El Vez's music and performance is aimed at entertaining but also calls for defiance and resistance. In his songs canonized sounds of the popular music world intermingle with new political messages. As a versatile Elvis Presley impersonator, he draws upon the icon's recognition effect. Citing Presley classics such as "Suspicious Minds" and "In the Ghetto," his songs borrow from the canon of American pop culture. His lyrics, however, are citations with difference, translation, and variation. Particularly in the context of the New Immigrant Movement, his music has gained fresh political momentum. El Vez's musical citations of pop classics such as "Suspicious Minds" and "Power to the People" (Lennon) use the mask of entertainment to criticize recent U.S. border and immigration politics. In his musical citations, El Vez keeps walking a fine line between popular music's success story and music's potential for rebellion. While his sampling and remixes are reminiscent of other contemporary music strategies used in rap and reggaeton, they also express a specific mind of cultural bricolage at work.

It is important to note that El Vez cites from various traditions of social activism. The art of his citation involves the creation of new stage personae. For example, CD covers, concert posters, and stage costumes function as a matrix for El Vez to make cultural references: to the Zapatista movement in Chiapas, to Che Guevara and the Cuban Revolution, to the Chicano Movement of earlier decades, and to the Black Power and anti-Vietnam movements in the 1970s, to mention but a few. He dresses and poses as "Zapatista warrior Marcos" and as a Latin "Muhammed Ali." The broad range of stage personae that he assumes illustrates his eclectic and transnational approach to resistance politics in the Americas. He borrows from African American, Chicano/a, Cuban, and Mexican protest cultures. In addition, El Vez always makes clear that he sings and speaks for the dispossessed (Raussert 2017). While he cites a broad canon of pop music, including the works of Paul Simon and David Bowie, it comes as no surprise that the figure of Elvis Presley is key to his interpretation of pop music. Many of his Elvis Presley performances pay tribute the King of Rock 'n' Roll's working class roots and routes. Presley in many ways embodies the story from rags to riches, having moved from a shotgun house in Tupelo, Mississippi, where he lived as a poor child, to his luxury home Graceland in Memphis, a hallmark of U.S. American cultural heritage tours today. But as the early reception of Elvis Presley in the American South demonstrated, the radio audience took his voice for a black one. Hence the success of Elvis Presley goes beyond commercial and popular success. Even today it remains a quintessential example of musical expression that blurs ethnic and racial lines. As Eric Lott puts it, Elvis Presley "dismantled ... racial music" in his "cultural conquests" (1993, 103). Moreover, Elvis Presley's legendary pelvis movement meant a radicalization of white male body movement and introduced new forms of stage performance linking expressions of voice and body. These examples also illustrate why manifold types of citation in El Vez's art are important: they involve shifts in naming and body appearance. In conclusion, "naming is … also potentially a strategy of subversive mimesis" (139), a strategy that finds its musical voice in El Vez's entertaining and provocative song collages.

2.4 Zooming in: diaspora, ethnic, postethnic, and postblack dimensions of sonic identities

Following the above exploration of entangling and disentangling forms and flows of music and identity, one can assume that performativity serves as a primary basis for reinventing both identity and social relations. Ethnomusicologists, anthropologists, and cultural studies investigators have repeatedly referred to a close link between music and processes of identity formation, be they national, regional, ethnic, youth-cultural, or simply individual. With reference to the Latino impact on American popular music in the first part of this chapter, I will address questions of shifting ethnicities in the context of music migration. In his essay "Cultural Identity and Diaspora," Stuart Hall juxtaposes postmodern views of identity with the yearning to authenticate one's cultural history, discussing how this desire plays out in an emerging diasporic Caribbean cultural production, particularly in cinema. With reference to recent cinematic productions, Hall points out that cultural identity is conceived "in terms of one, shared culture, a sort of collective 'one true self,' hiding inside the many other, more superficial or artificially imposed 'selves,' which people with a shared history and ancestry hold in common" (Hall 1992, 393). As he elaborates in his foundational essay, cultural identity does not rely upon the notion of a unified history but rather embraces the fact that identities are constantly on the move, are always in a state of becoming, and are forever producing and reproducing themselves through the "continuous play of history, culture, and power" (393). Current debates about the politics of cultural difference within the context of fundamentalism and global terrorism have directed critics' attention toward the necessity to renegotiate the processes of identity formation in times of globalization and multiple migrations. While ethnicity remains one of the key tropes for asserting and defining identity, ethnic affiliations are also challenged in times of individual delocations and relocations. Contrasting concepts of ethnicity (Barth 1969), postethnicity (Hollinger 1995), and transethnicity (E Pluribus Unum Research Group 2009), therefore, have emerged and are negotiated in current debates on how ethnic identities oscillate between stasis and fluidity (Bauman 2006, 61–69). Norwegian anthropologist Frederik Barth maintains that "cultural differences can persist despite interethnic contact and interdependence" (295). While Barth shares the belief of critics such as Hollinger that the possibility of changing affiliations exists, Barth sees controlling patterns at work that limit individual choice. He thus concludes that ethnic boundaries persist despite the flow of human beings across borderlines. He also maintains that ethnic boundaries frequently are the very foundation upon which social systems are built and sometimes closed. Here one should add that ethnic identity and boundaries are repeatedly instrumentalized in ideological, political, and (para)military acts of ethnic cleansing. While Hollinger's conception of postethnic identity focuses on the crossing of borderlines, thus emphasizing elements of transgression and choice, Barth discusses aspects of interaction that occur at the very borderline of ethnic interaction. He takes into consideration that ethnic interaction often takes place between mainstream and marginal groups. According to him, agents respond to ethnic encounters in different ways. For some individuals of marginalized groups to reach incorporation into the dominant group is the highest goal. Others accept their minority status and attempt to act culturally, politically, and economically within sectors tolerated by mainstream society. Finally, Barth refers to the element of resistance when he points out that a third group of individuals claim their ethnic identity to organize new patterns of social action for forbidden sectors (303–308). Barth develops a spectrum of ethnic interaction that reaches from the acceptance of a low-rank outsider's position via the assimilation of minority groups to ethnically infused new movements in politics and the arts. Here we return to music: we can locate all dimensions of Barth's spectrum in the history of African American musical forms, in particular. In addition, we naturally have to add that the African American musicians, as well as music companies, have assumed powerful positions as agents not only in blackening the Americas but also in blackening the world (Raphael-Hernandez 2004).

The theory of postethnicity, as developed by David Hollinger, defines individuals as cosmopolitans who can belong to multiple groups simultaneously and adopt different elements from various groups they partly belong to, so that they can shape their identities accordingly. Ideally, group associations are both voluntary and fluid, and the individual is capable of choosing which of the various groups to affiliate with, depending on the context and situation. Willy de Ville's choice to stylize, pose, and present himself as a Latino musician in the rock and fusion music of the 1980s represents one such example from the world of music. Postethnicity considers identities as self-constructed and dynamic. What is essential is the basic assumption that identity can be formed out of optional possibilities. As Juanita Tamayo Lott explains, "Race and ethnicity among major group members may become optional identities over time and by situation" (1998, 91). Hollinger too emphasizes identity construction by the individual. Whereas the individual cannot choose his or her skin color and country of birth, Hollinger stresses that each individual can decide how much emphasis is put on these aspects within the process of identity formation. According to him, "the identities people assume are acquired largely through affiliation, however prescribed or chosen" (1995, 7). He describes the postethnic outlook as a perspective that includes both the multiplicity of the individual's group affiliations and the realignment of those affiliations across several identities. Viewing postethnic identities as essentially democratic, he maintains that "postethnicity prefers voluntary to prescribed affiliations, pushes for communities of wide scope, recognizes the constructed character of ethnoracial groups, and accepts the formation of new groups as part of the normal life of a democratic society" (116).

While Hollinger's concept appears idealistic, utopian, and certainly elitist, the concept of "transethnicity" suggests a more process-oriented, reciprocal conception of mobilizing, multiplying and restabilizing the idea of ethnicity. Transethnicity suggests a multidirectional process in which identities oscillate between phases of fluidity and stasis, a complex process that embraces moments of de-ethnification and re-ethnification as well as moments of transcending ethnic fixation in times of multiple migrations and constant border crossings. Music genres have long demonstrated their capacity to cross ethno-cultural boundaries; one finds in the white rapper Eminem an apt, albeit controversial, example of transethnic identity politics in the realm of popular music. Clearly, Eminem riffs on the fluidity between whiteness and blackness at the same time as he self-consciously exposes his entanglement in cross-cultural processes of musical borrowing and adaptation that have characterized the history of much of popular music. "I am the worst thing since Elvis Presley/To do black music so selfishly/and use it to get myself wealthy" (Miklitsch 2006, 8). As Robert Miklitsch points out, Eminem's "performative contradictions, snarled up as they are with Eminem's whiplash flow and mad lyrical skills, are also what makes him so compelling a figure … Eminem's angry rapping highlighted on songs like 'White America' reflects these not-so-United States in all their sound and fury" (8). Eminem's case reveals that behind postethnic and transethnic identity processes we cannot help but notice the entanglement of ethnicity in the context of commodity culture.

Another example of the complexities of transethnic identity formation is the emergence of Latina/Chicana punk in Los Angeles in the 1970s and 1980s. With a nod to Michelle Habell-Pallán, this chapter argues that the new directions punk took in the Latina/Chicana context changed punk styles and perplexed identity politics within the diverse Latina groups in California. For some rebellious Chicanas, 1970s punk served as a liberating sonic mechanism, and the punk scene served as an emancipatory social space. "A new feminist Latina/Chicana consciousness emerged from the encounter between Latin female voices and punk culture. Social critique via campy humor became a trademark of Latina/Chicana performances in East L.A., Hollywood, the Westside, and cities in Mexico" (Habell-Pallán 2008, 25). With the fading of the 1960s Chicano youth movement, and with the rise of institutionalized multiculturalism, the sonic expressions of Chicanas like Teresa Covarrubias and Alice Armendariz Velasquez confounded easy categorizations of ethnic culture, social norm, and gender identity. Idiosyncratic and eclectic in performance, dress, and voice, they broke all the rules while integrating the non-conformist style of their rebellious Pachuca foremothers. "Transgressing the social norm, these punk musicians repudiated behaviours and identities imposed on them by the male dominant culture, Chicano communities, and their conservative familial traditions" (27). The examples of Teresa Covarrubias and Alice Armendariz Velasquez also highlight the problematic, at times highly conflictive relationship between individualist and collective identity politics within non-mainstream groups.

In the current age of political correctness, neoliberal markets, and neo-conservative, chauvinist, and racist backlash, debates around concepts like "Post-blackness" and "new blackness" reveal the identitarian problems that can occur when individualist and collective interests clash. "Post-blackness" and "new blackness" are manifestations of a broader trend in late twentieth- and early twenty-first-century black cultural production towards the consideration of new definitions of blackness in the post-civil rights era. Although, as Paul C. Taylor argues, specific concepts such as "post-soul," "post-black art," "new blackness," and "post-race" each have their specific definitions, they all should be understood "as different names for the same complex reality" (2007, 625). In Jonathan M. Touré's *Who's Afraid of Post-Blackness: What It Means to Be Black Now*, "Post-Blackness" is the label used to describe new black identity patterns that embrace diversity, fluidity, and experimentation (Kennedy 2011). "Post-Blackness" means being rooted in but not limited by blackness. "Post-Blackness," in Touré's individualized utopian thinking, blossoms because of its limitless, open-sourced, and endlessly adaptable nature. This conceptualization poses a threat and challenge to earlier collective identity politics within organized and institutionalized – and at times highly regulated and restrictive – politics of black being and resistance (Marcus Garvey, Elijah Muhammad). It also reveals the tensions and dialectics between individual liberty and collective advancement faced by contemporary activists and musicians such as Kendrick Lamar. With his 2015 album *To Pimp A Butterfly* he fueled ongoing debates about individual choice and collective responsibility within and beyond the Afro communities. The album's second single, "The Blacker the Berry (The Sweeter the Juice)" elicited both praise and criticism over its engagement with police violence and its theme of black self-hatred, which many interpreted as victim blaming. The song comes to a climax in an ironic reversal. On a meta-level the song's outward focus on racist and oppressive social conditions turns inward to inquire into the singing voice's self-declared "hypocrisy" due to lamenting the violent death of young black men while celebrating his roots in a Compton community branded by gun violence. The song's release sparked competing arguments as to whether Lamar was returning to a familiar conservative politics of respectability by invoking the specter of black-on-black crime to erase white supremacy. However, Lamar's confession of his own hypocrisy appears to be a performative act that does not annihilate the structural critique of the lyrics. Instead, it highlights the growing tension between "new blackness"'s emphasis on individual empowerment and the acknowledgment of structural confinements. Lamar's song also exposes how such tensions manifest through the attempt to construct connections between the insecure and fragmented present and a collective past principally imagined through the dominant iconography of the Civil Rights Movement. In this conception of black identity, nostalgia for the collective and courageous work of the Civil Rights Movement becomes dominant. Lamar's respectability politics seem to privilege self-directed action to oppose racism. His individualist stance doesn't deny institutional foundations or racism but favors the individual agent in opposition to larger grassroots movements. Richard Iton assumes that Post-Ferguson protest music reflects a reemerging "integrationist/nationalist cleavage" within black politics (2008, 23). Nevertheless, as Fernando Orejula emphasizes, "at protest rallies and marches, the 'We gon' be alright!' chant is performed in the style and cadence and African American English vernacular delivered by Lamar's original recording" (2018, 1). Again, it is situation and context that decide which direction identity politics will take.

2.5 Las Krudas (Cuba), Chocquibtown (Columbia), Janelle Monáe (USA): creating new sonic networks and expanding twenty-first century sonic identity politics

While Lamar's song reveals the tension between individualist and collectivist stances in black identity politics, it seems fair to say that in contemporary times, overall, a new wave of black music voicing translocal identity politics stretches from the U.S. to Cuba and Columbia, among others. Whether directly related or associatively connected to the recent Black Lives Matter movement that has spread throughout the Americas, numerous artists and groups are helping to push new black identity politics between individual expression and group affirmation, acknowledging and negotiating individual, local, regional, and national differences. Looking at flows between Cuba and the U.S., we find in the U.S.-(formerly Cuban-)based band Las Krudas Cubensi a good example of what it looks like to queer race and identity politics within an increasingly inter-American music map. Queerness frequently serves as a repository for alternative identity politics. Queer expands from sexuality and connotes "the ways that race, ethnicity, postcolonial nationality, crisscross with these and other identity-constituting, identity-fracturing discourses … the fractal intricacies of skin, migration, state" (Sedgwick 1994, 9). By its very nature, queerness challenges the limits of heteronormativity and confronts hegemonic constraints. As Eng, Halberstam, and Munoz put it, "queer [challenges] the normalizing mechanisms of state power to name its sexual subjects" (2005, 1)

Founded in 1999, the queer hip hop band Las Krudas Cubensi consists of Odaymara Custa, Olivia Prendes, and Odalys Cuesta, who developed their music in street performances. Although still expressing protest within the aesthetically and politically sanctioned framework of the Cuban Revolution, they nonetheless pushed for an expansion of nationally sanctioned identity politics. Through lyrics and performance style they voiced their protest against racism, sexism, and homophobic discrimination in Cuba and the U.S. As queer black women they were also cofounders of the first black lesbian organization OREMI in 1996, challenging the Castro government by pointing out inequalities at the intersection of race, gender, and sexuality within Cuban society (Roth 2016, 104–105). Performing in Cuba, Mexico, Russia, and the U.S., among others, they spread their political mission of raising consciousness about domestic violence, gender violence, racism, homophobia, and hegemonic beauty ideals on an international scale. Residing in Texas since 2006, they continue situating their queering of identity within an overall identification with Cuban and Caribbean upbringings; however, they chose the U.S. as a locus of enunciation, specifically Austin – a hotspot of alternative music production that offered better access to marketability than they previously had enjoyed. They continue inter-American dialogues, principally with the Cuban artist and activist communities by common performances and regular exchange. Their act of queering identity politics shines through in their linguistic mixing of Spanish, Creole, and English, their references to diasporic Afro-Cuban heritage and the strong presence of black women in Afro-diasporic musical expression, and their constant struggle against sexism in mainstream hip hop. The new media serves them to bypass certain music industry control and censorship. Using alternative media channels online, they work outside the major U.S. and global music industry to spread their version of Cuban hip hop and their queer identity politics, always calling attention to power inequalities within society, cultural industry, and political movements in current times of global female migration and labor diffusion. Just as groups like Mono Blanco in Mexico and Quetzal in the U.S. have helped Fandango networks expand across the Americas, Las Krudas Cubensi, with their inter-American dialogues, are expanding and diversifying contemporary alternative hip hop networks, calling on people to rethink the social.

Arguably the first hip hop group from Columbia to address black identities in a Columbian cultural context, Chocquibtown, formed in Cali, incorporates black voices, bodies, and graffiti street art in their music videos. Representative of an overarching Afro-Latin approach to black identity politics, their music fuses diverse black musical expressions that have emerged in the Americas. Latin jazz merges with hip hop, reggae, reggaeton, salsa, and Afro-Colombian folk music. Recently, electronica has become an additional style added to their black fusion music. The group's first two albums, *Somos Pacífico* (2006) and *Oro* (2010), were backed by the singles "Somos Pacífico" and "De Donde Vengo Yo," the latter song winning a Latin Grammy in 2011. "Somos Pacífico" inscribes Afro Latina identity in a broader Pacific-Columbian context and functions as an anthem of belonging and peaceful integration. Informing their work is a mission to transform U.S. based hip hop through local and regional musical expression. While a global black awareness is an essential part of the self-presentation of the group – e.g. in their extensive world tour in 2010 – the band continues to emphasize the importance of local bonding. Accordingly, they take hip hop out its common urban contexts and address issues of land, environment, and coastal maritime in rural Colombia. They also maintain strong ties with their original community in Chocó on the Columbian Pacific coast, where they function as role models for an emerging youth culture. Their music, lyrics, and interviews reveal that their black identity politics are driven by a complex understanding of the social, beyond purely issues of race. The band's lyrics demand more inclusion for Afro-Colombians in Colombian society and in Latin America as a whole. They criticize the absence of Afro-Columbian culture from radio and television. They openly address institutionalized racism in Columbian society and link it to similar situations in other Latin American cultures. Denouncing racism and racial exclusion, the lyrics, however, consciously avoid forms of direct accusation so as not to close doors to a desired integration. Regional, ecological, and racial awareness join hands in songs such as "Oro" and "De Donde Vengo Yo," which address the extractivism and exploitation of Chocó's natural resources, leaving nothing for the region's primarily black inhabitants (Hernandez 2011). The latter song won the band a Latin Grammy in 2011 (Contreras 2011). The band's third album, *Eso Es Lo Que Hay* (2011), was nominated in 2012 for Album of the Year. This example shows that there are growing alternative networks of recognition within the culture industry that enhance new identity politics and social consciousness beyond mainstream thinking. This development is part of a global capitalism that also, as Anne Garland Mahler reminds us, "facilitates the creation of networks among grassroots movements, yielding transnational, resistant political imaginary" (Garland Mahler 2018, 244).

Queering identity politics, Janelle Monáe announced her embrace of bisexuality and pansexuality in a Rolling Stone interview in April 2018. She also expanded on her all-embracing identity politics in an interview with Stephen Colbert in his Late Show on July 20th 2018. Having already pushed the frontiers of Afrofuturism in her earlier albums, she released a queered form of Afrofuturism with her 2018 album *Dirty Computer. Dirty Computer* is a mixed-media, audio/visual concept album that tells a near-future narrative set in a totalitarian society. The album is full of self-reflexive moments and highlights Monáe's quest for self as an ongoing process, yet one full of self-assertion. She herself plays an outlaw figure rejected from society because her internal circuit board has been corrupted. Monáe's albums have continuously revisited Fritz Lang's 1927 science-fiction master narrative *Metropolis* and re-conceptualized the android struggle to escape enslavement. Monáe's Afro-futuristic aesthetic includes an exploration of contemporary issues of race, class, gender, sexuality, and politics in a science-fiction setting. Her futuristic approach, though, has not prevented her from linking past with present and reacting in the here-and-now toward recent manifestations of racism and sexism. Monáe has repeatedly participated in Black Lives Matter events during her tours. Her single "Hell You Talmbout" responds to the playing down of black death in U.S. media with the repetitive voicing of its victim's names and provides a major "thematic soundscape" to new musical activism within the Black Lives Matter movement, as is further discussed in the chapter on music and politics (Orejuela 2018, 3). Monáe's audiovisual musical projects walk a tightrope between individual and collective resistance, with a dose of science-fiction self-reflexivity. In her 1984 essay "A Cyborg Manifesto," Donna Haraway presented a thesis that the cyborg – "a cybernetic organism, a hybrid of machine and organism, a creature of social reality as well as a creature of fiction"; a "creature in a post-gender world" – is how equality will be gained (1994, 83). Monáe's alter ego and android persona, Cindi Mayweather, is Haraway's cyborg equivalent, a posthuman, genderless creature that has a fluid being without boundaries or limitations.[1] In the emotion picture for *Dirty Computer* Monáe places her android metaphor into a posthumanist narrative that allows her, for the first time so it seems, to fully

1 http://www.dazeddigital.com/music/article/39679/1/janelle-monae-visual-aesthetic-evolution.

express her identity as a pansexual black woman within her art.[2] An important hallmark of Afrofuturism is that it strategically employs the spectacle of a consciously othered state of blackness – often through metaphors of alien beings and androids. While Monáe's vision tends to oscillate between utopia and dystopia in most of her albums, *Dirty Computer* explicitly presents the power of transformation. In *Dirty Computer* Monáe and her alter ego, Cindi, merge into one person: a queer black woman absolutely convinced of her own positioning within difference and the power she has as an all-embracing agent.

In the interviews with *Rolling Stone* and during Colbert's *Late Show*, Monáe celebrated an all-inclusive Americanness deploying the patriotic use of the social. "Don't try to take my country, I will defend my land/I'm not crazy, baby, no/I'm American," she sang.[3]

Referencing her album, Monáe insisted, "Humanity says that we are full of bugs and viruses because of our very existence, whether it be you being a part of the LGBTQIA community, being a black woman, being a minority, an immigrant, the marginalized. It speaks to what it means to say our bugs and viruses are attributes; we don't need to be reprogrammed or deprogrammed – we're fine how we are. We too are American" (n. pag). Deploying an innovative fusion of Afrofuturism and queer patriotism, Monáe reveals in her music that even in the most radical musical practice the social and identity are nonetheless marked by traditions that need constant supervision and adjustment.

As the examples from the contemporary music scene show, music, more than ever, continues to be crucial for performing relational identity politics, frequently first to the self, then to a group, and eventually to networks of social and cultural empowerment on an abstract and larger scale. While recognizing the limits of reach, the contemporary examples from Cuba, Columbia, and the U.S. demonstrate how music in contemporary youth and pop culture persists as an expressive and performative medium that creates identity and identitarian relations through sonic, rhythmic, kinesthetic, and cognitive bonding. More than ever, too, the bonding power of music depends on performativity and connectivity.

---

2 https://www.vox.com/2018/5/16/17318242/janelle-monae-science-fiction-influences-afrofuturism.

3 https://www.rollingstone.com/music/music-news/watch-janelle-monae-perform-americans-talk-science-fiction-on-colbert-702307/.

How connectivity occurs remains framed by context, situation, and the constellation between performer and audience. While music circuits continue to be heavily shaped by music industries' power hierarchies, the flows, as this chapter illustrates, increasingly emerge from different loci of enunciation and crisscross the Americas in often unexpected ways, fostering forms of identitarian bonding and new social alliances between individuals, groups, and larger communities seemingly far apart, thus creating sonic maps of inter-American and global identitarian relatedness within difference.

Works cited

Abrahams, Roger D. 2001. "Afro-Caribbean Culture and the South: Music with Movement." In *The South and the Caribbean*, ed. Douglass Sullivan-Gonzaléz and Charles Reagan Wilson, 97–126. Jackson: University Press of Mississippi. Print.

Barth, Frederik. 1969. *Ethnic Groups and Boundaries: The Social Organization of Culture Difference*. Bergen: Universitetsforlag. Print.

Bauman, Zygmunt. 2006. *Liquid Times: Living in an Age of Uncertainty*. Cambridge: Polity Press. Print.

Bhabha, Homi K. 1994. *The Location of Culture*. London: Routledge.

Born, Georgina. 2012. "Music and the Social." In *The Cultural Study of Music: A Critical Introduction*, ed. Martin Clayton, Trevor Herbert, and Richard Middleton, 261–274. London: Routledge. Print.

Butler, Judith, and Athena Athanasiou. *Dispossession: The Performative in the Political*. Cambridge: Polity Press, 2013. Print.

Contreras, Felix. 2011. "ChocQuibTown Speaks Out On Racism In Colombia." *National Public Radio*, February 10.

"E Pluribus Unum?" ZiF Research Group. *Ethnic Identities in Transnational Integration Processes in the Americas*. Bielefeld University (2008–2009).

Eng, David L., Judith Halberstam, and José Esteban Muñoz. 2005. *What's Queer about Queer Studies Now?* Durham: Duke University Press. Print.

Fawcett, Thomas. 2007. "The Funky Diaspora: The Diffusion of Soul and Funk Music across the Caribbean and Latin America." http://lanic.utexas.edu/project/etext/llilas/ilassa/2007/fawcett.pdf.

García, David. 2006. *Arsenio Rodríguez and the Transnational Flow of Latin Popular Music*. Philadelphia: Temple University Press. Print.

Garland Mahler, Anne. 2018. *From the Tricontinental to the Global South: Race, Radicalism, and Transnational Solidarity*. Durham: Duke University Press. Print.

Gates, Henry L. Jr. 1988. *The Signifying Monkey: A Theory of African American Literary Criticism*. New York: Oxford University Press.

Habell-Pallán, Michelle. 2008. "Vexed on the Eastside Chicana Roots and Routes of L.A. Punk." In *Vexing. Femal Voices from East L.A. Punk*, ed. Pilar Tompkins and Colin Gunckel, 25–29. Claremont: Museum of Art. Print.

Hall, Stuart. 1992. "Cultural Identity and Diaspora." In *Colonial Discourse and Post-Colonial Theory*, ed. Patrick Williams and Laura Chrisman, 392–403. New York: Columbia University Press. Print.

Haraway, Donna. 1994. "A Manifesto for Cyborgs: Science, Technology, and Socialist Feminism in the 1980s." In *The Postmodern Turn. New Perspectives on Social Theory*, ed. Steven Seidmann, 82–97. Cambridge University Press. Print.

Hernandez, Camilo. 2011. "Afro-Colombian Rappers Vie for Grammy." *San Diego Union Tribune* online edition, February 4.

Hollinger, David. 1995. *Postethnic America: Beyond Multiculturalism*. New York: Basic Books, 1995. Print.

hooks, bell. 1992. "Eating the Other: Desire and Resistance." In *Black Looks: Race and Representation*, 19–30. Boston: South End Press. Print.

Iton, Richard. 2008. *In Search of the Black Fantastic: Politics and Popular Culture in the Post-Civil Rights Era*. New York: Oxford University Press. Print.

Kennedy, Randall. 2011. "The Fallacy of Touré's Post-Blackness Theory." *The Root* online edition, November 8. https://www.theroot.com/the-fallacy-of-toures-post-blackness-theory-1790865279.

Kunow, Rüdiger. 2001. "American Studies as Mobility Studies: Some Terms and Constellations." In *Re-Framing the Transnational Turn in American Studies*, ed. Winfried Fluck, Donald Pease, and John Carlos Rowe, 245–264. Hanover: Dartmouth College Press. Print.

Lott, Eric. 1993. *Love and Theft: Blackface Minstrelsy and the American Working Class (Race and American Culture)*. New York: Oxford University Press. Print.

Lott, Juanita Tamayo. 1998. *Asian Americans: From Racial Category to Multiple Identities (Critical Perspectives on Asian Pacific Americans)*. Walnut Creek: Altamira Press. Print.

Miklitsch, Robert. 2006. *Roll Over Adorno: Critical Theory, Popular Culture, Audiovisual Media*. Albany: State University of New York Press. Print.

Musser, Jamilla Amber. 2017. "Gender and Queer Theory." In *A Companion to Critical and Cultural Theory*, ed. Imre Szeman, Sarah Blacker, and Justin Sully, 244–254. New York: John Wiley & Sons Ltd. Print.

Orejuela, Fernando. 2018. "Introduction." *Black Lives Matter & Music: Protest, Intervention, Reflection*, ed. Fernando Orejuela and Stephanie Shonekan, 1–13. Bloomington: Indiana University Press, 2018. Print.

Pease, Donald, and Robyn Wiegman, eds. 2002. *The Futures of American Studi*es. Durham: Duke: University Press. Print.

Raphael-Hernandez, Heike, ed. 2004. *Blackening Europe: The African American Presence*. London: Routledge. Print.

Raussert, Wilfried. 2017. "Retuning Hegemonic Pop Culture: El Vez's Citation Practices." In *The Routledge Companion to Inter-American Studies*, ed. Wilfried Raussert, 178–186. New York: Routledge. Print.

—. 2011. "Ethnic Identiy Politics, Transnationalization, and Transculturation in American Popular Music: An Inter-American Perspective." *Cornbread and Cuchifritos: Ethnic Identiy Politics, Transnationalization, and Transculturation in American Popular Music*, ed. Wilfried Raussert and Michelle Habell-Pallán, 1–26. Trier: WVT, Tempe: Bilingual Press. Print.

—, and Christina Seeliger. 2011. "'What Did I Do To Be So Global and Blue?' Blues as Commodity: Tourism, Politics of Authenticity an Blues Clubs in Chicago Today." In *Selling Ethnicity: Urban Cultural Politics in the Americas*, ed. Olaf Kaltmeier, 41–53. Farnham: Ashgate Publishing. Print.

Roth, Julia. 2016. "Translocating the Caribbea, Positioning Im/Mobilities: The Sonic Politics of Las Krudas from Cuba." In *Mobile & Entangled Americas*, ed. Maryemma Graham and Wilfried Raussert, 103–123. New York: Routledge. Print.

Sedgwick, Eve K. 1994. *Tendencies*. London: Routledge. Print.

Snead, James A. 1981. "On Repetition in Black Culture." *Black American Literature Forum* 15:4, Black Textual Strategies, Vol. 1: Theory (Winter): 146–154. Print.

Steinitz, Matti. 2019. "'Calling Out Around the World.' How Soul Music Transnationalized the African-American Freedom Struggle in the Black Power Era (1965-1975)." In *Sonic Politics. Music and Social Movements in the Americas*, ed. Olaf Kaltmeier and Wilfried Raussert, 88–107. New York: Routledge. Print.

Straw, Will. 1991. "Systems of Articulation, Logics of Change: Communities and Scenes in Popular Music." *Cultural Studies* 5.3: 368–388. Print.

Taylor, Paul C. 2007. "Post-Black, Old Black." *African American Review* 41.4: 625–640. Print.

Touré, Jonathan M. 2011. *Who's Afraid of Post-Blackness?: What it Means to be Black Now*. New York: The Free Press. Print.

Van Deburg, William L. 1992. *New Day in Babylon: The Black Power Movement and American Culture*. Chicago: The University of Chicago Press. Print.

3 Sonic Politics from Above, Below, and Within Market Circuits

3.1 Prelude

Discussing Chuck Berry's "Roll Over Beethoven," Peter Wicke writes that "popular music appears for the first time within a cultural system of reference which allows it to become a fundamental experience" (1990, 11). Even more successfully than the historical avant-garde, Rock 'n' Roll dissolves "barriers between the formerly separate spheres of art and everyday life" (11). Wicke's claim suggests that popular music is a powerful agent capable not only of traversing various musical genres but also of penetrating public and political spheres. The border crossing he refers to is only one in a series of noticeable iconoclastic moves in the development of popular music in the twentieth and twenty-first century. Repeatedly, we encounter moments when high and low culture meet, in which barriers between genres, schools, and attitudes dissolve. Robert Miklitsch provides us with lasting examples:

> Although the performance of Gershwin's *Rhapsody in Blue* at Whiteman's "Experiment in Modern Music" is an especially rich example of the fission produced when high and low culture meet, there are other moments of revolution and counter-revolution that testify to the tangled history of American popular music. Thus in the world of popular music, Gershwin would go on to compose, in addition to the scores for films such as Minnelli's *American in Paris* (1951), the opera *Porgy and Bess* (1935), while Duke Ellington, some twenty years after the first performance of *Rhapsody in Blue*, would premiere his *Black, Browne, and Beige* (1943) at Carnegie Hall. (2006, 66)

As Miklitsch illustrates, music, in its tangled histories, cuts across different cultural spheres.

Music is also clearly a global player, as it traverses national and continental boundaries faster than any other art form. It moves within transnational economic, cultural, and political circuits and forms an important asset of translocal and global community-building. But does globalization via music constitute a smooth, homogeneous, and ideologically unified process? We should be careful not to overestimate music's utopian potential; nevertheless, its political significance has been recognized by governmental institutions, grassroots movements, and the music industry alike. By comparing various means by which music is politically mobilized, I point out differences and conflicts between actors in musical production, ideological differences within global circuits, and recent intersections between government, grassroots strategies, and spectacle culture within the music industry. This chapter compares different positions of agency and distribution, namely from above, below, and within music industry circuits.

In U.S. government-sponsored programs such as The Jazz Ambassadors and The Rhythm Road, music's capacity as political messenger is mobilized from above; political power structures with national interests in global politics guide the funding and distribution of "American" musical expression cross-culturally. Both projects emerged in moments of national crisis: The Jazz Ambassadors program was launched in response to anti-Americanism(s) during the Cold War Period, and The Rhythm Road project attempted to compensate for the country's loss of global prestige during the post-9/11 Bush Administration.

It is evident that the production, diffusion, and reception of music have profoundly changed since the 1950s. Contemporary media such as youtube, blogs, and the internet have led to more individualized and democratized forms of production and distribution. Directly related to these changes is the distribution of music as a political messenger from below. As part of the larger contemporary phenomenon of globally spreading grassroots movements, The Pleasant Revolution Tour by the traveling band The Ginger Ninjas and the Fandango sin Fronteras movement are two striking examples of how music is produced in translocal communal contexts from the people, for the people. Both projects respond to transnational and global issues at stake today. Whereas The Pleasant Revolution Tour addresses environmental issues and promotes alternative forms of (urban) mobility, The Fandangos sin Fronteras movement challenges U.S. American border and immigration politics and cherishes the building of translocal communities.

Contemporary musical protest from contemporary celebrities such as Kendrick Lamar, Beyoncé, Alicia Keys, Ruben Bladés, and others in the context of award ceremonies, national sports events, and global protest marches demonstrates that sonic politics also emerge from within the circuits of the music industry, which functions as channel and profiteer of sonic protest as spectacle. Cultural, political, and economic flows cross and complement each other leading to overlapping, at times conflictive entanglements of creative musical expression, sincere political protest, and the pursuit of popular success and fame in the world of music.

By using 'sonic cosmopolitics' as an umbrella term to describe the transnational music flows I am conceptually less concerned with what Daphne Brooks, in reference to the legendary African American entertainers Nina Simone and Eartha Kitt, calls "sonic cosmopolitanism" (2011, 113), defined as the vocal creation of "the very sound of 'the worldly' and the limitless traveler" (113). Rather, this chapter explores the politicization of music as a local and global community-building force. All forms of mobilizing music that will be addressed in this article generally go beyond purely national frameworks. So the chapter's point of departure corresponds to the new engagement of music studies with "geography" beyond concepts such as place, locality, and nation (cf. Krims 2012, 140).

3.2 Sonic cosmopolitics from above

The U.S.-sponsored Jazz Ambassadors tours to the Middle East, Africa, and Asia, launched in the 1950s during the Cold War period, and the contemporary The Rhythm Road project, launched in 2005 by the State Department's Bureau of Educational and Cultural Affairs, represent programs of musical mobility and cultural diplomacy organized and sponsored by governmental institutions. At their heart is an actor network based on a vertical, top-down strategy. Put simply, government officials set the political agenda, and government-sponsored cultural workers become the mediators between government officials and the musicians sponsored for touring. The overall aim is to produce political influence through cultural contact. As State Department initiatives, both projects have aimed at celebrating U.S. cultural production as a means of establishing a positive influence over, or at least better connections with, regions and countries in the world that have had skeptical, critical, or even antagonistic attitudes towards U.S. foreign policies – policies often considered part of "empire building," to borrow a term from Amy Kaplan. But while race and colonialist politics marked the framework of the Jazz Ambassadors programs, particularly in the Cold War 1950s and 1960s, it seems that cultural conflicts fueled by Samuel Huntington's notion of the clash of civilizations (2004, 192, 273) and the Bush Administration's global war on terror provide the political context for the contemporary The Rhythm Road: American Music Abroad's endeavor to improve U.S. America's public image abroad. The urge to launch this new project surfaced after the country's devastating global image loss in the aftermath of the Iraq War, a war we know now was justified with lies. Interestingly enough, the latter government-sponsored program coincides with current grassroots movements in its egalitarian approach to cultural difference and diplomacy.

As I argue, such music projects partake in larger processes of democratizing the world within and beyond Western liberalist meaning. Recent discourse on cosmopolitanism proposes a more open-minded view of cosmopolitan thought that steps into dialogue with other visions surrounding the term. With a nod to critics like Appiah, I use 'sonic cosmopolitics' to challenge both elitist and purely universalistic notions of the term cosmopolitanism and argue for "cosmopolitanism from below" as an alternative to "cosmopolitanism from above." According to Amanda Anderson:

> Cosmopolitanism … typically manifests a complex tension between elitism and egalitarianism. It frequently advances itself as a specifically intellectual ideal, or depends on a mobility that is the luxury of social, economic, or cultural privilege. … At the same time, the cosmopolitan identification with the larger sphere of the world, or with humanity, or with standards assumed to transcend any locale, is ostensibly inspired by the deep-seated belief in the humanity of all, wherever positioned. (1998, 268)

I should add that conceiving cosmopolitanism from a "below" perspective makes room for contradictions, dynamics, and conflicts. It also changes and encourages dialogue not only among different conceptions of cosmopolitanism as a philosophical world view and a political project, but also among different ideas about the cosmopolitan individual and his or her cosmopolitan disposition(s) or political engagement beyond a local and national level. "Cosmopolitan democracy," according to Danielle Archibugi,

> helps to capture the idea that the international order is becoming increasingly democratic in the sense that there are many chains of negotiation,

> multilevel and multi-sited interconnections among population segments, and the expansion of many kinds of exchanges. (qtd. in Blau 2001, 64)

Such conviction clearly opposes ideas of imperialist forms of globalization present in various political, economic, military, and cultural discourses. Hence the question arises of how far such a form of expansion can be perceived as democratic and/or how such a democratic vision could be implemented. Can we make utopia real and ever peacefully share planet Earth? As critical thinkers we would have to answer quite frankly: most likely not. But as humans we are also always driven with the desire to make things better in social, economic, and political terms. Torn between utopian belief and dystopian disenchantment, we still need to ask: What do people mean when they talk about democracy and freedom as universal? Furthermore, we may want to investigate what role "sonic cosmopolitics" occupies in this context.

The historical Jazz Ambassadors project offers a good point of departure. After all, it embodies a variety of tensions and contradictions at work in the entanglement of music with politics. We might ask ourselves, for example, how in the 1950s President Eisenhower could hold on to segregationist politics at home and still put jazz and African American jazz musicians on a pedestal as cultural ambassadors. How did jazz musicians like Louis Armstrong and Dizzy Gillespie cope with the modernist paradox of being members of a discriminated racial group on the one hand and internationally acclaimed and celebrated musicians on the other? Different liberation narratives clash when we attempt to answer these questions. While The Rhythm Road project, the second State Department program in music diplomacy now run by Jazz at Lincoln Center, was in full swing, on April 4, 2008, Meridian International Center in Washington, DC inaugurated the photographic exhibition Jam Session: America's Jazz Ambassadors Embrace the World to look back and honor jazz musicians such as Louis Armstrong, Dizzy Gillespie, and Duke Ellington for their cultural work as Jazz Ambassadors during the 1950s, 1960s, and 1970s.

Developed in collaboration with University of Michigan professor Penny M. von Eschen and drawn from collections around the United States, the presentation brought together for the first time in history more than 100 images capturing memorable scenes from jazz tours to 35 countries and four continents (Sandberg 2008).

The traveling exhibition has functioned as a mobile archive to commemorate the jazz tours that began in 1956 with Dizzy Gillespie and his orchestra's engagement as Jazz Ambassadors playing in Latin America, Southern Europe, and the Middle East. The tour involved meetings with governmental representatives, local communities, and artists, and was designed to spread the gospel of American freedom and democracy as a counterforce to Soviet communism during the Cold War period. Other musicians were to follow, such as Benny Goodman and his band, who traveled to East Asia in 1958, and the Dave Brubeck Quartet that toured Eastern Europe, the Middle East, and South Asia. Louis Armstrong and the All Stars hit the front pages of newspapers around the world playing numerous concerts in Africa in 1960 and 1961, and Armstrong was celebrated as black cultural and political voice by African communities and politicians alike. Two years later the Duke Ellington Orchestra crisscrossed the Middle East and South Asia – a tour that marked the beginning of a decade of journeys for one of the most influential jazz composers and bandleaders of the twentieth century. Numerous other jazz musicians, including Miles Davis, Clark Terry, and Sarah Vaughan, performed on a global scale as cultural ambassadors and musicians alike. These mobile and musical forms of cultural diplomacy initiatives continued under the direction of the State Department until 1978.

What was the political context and what were the politics of liberation at stake during the emergence of the Jazz Ambassador tours? The struggle for Black freedom had moved to the center of American domestic and international politics, and the global appeal of jazz music shown by the success of Dizzy Gillespie, Louis Armstrong, and others had put African American musicians in the spotlight of attention. The global appeal of jazz was due on the one hand to the individual talent and presence of Louis Armstrong and Dizzy Gillespie, but jazz had also already established itself as syncretic art form emerging out of multicultural cross-overs, and would continue to do so (e.g. Dizzy Gillespie's fusion of Latin American rhythms with earlier jazz forms or Miles Davis' fusions of jazz and rock). Hence, jazz as a musical expression sonically embodied the continuous process of crossing, bridging, and negotiating cultures.

While government officials, cultural workers, and the press may not have been aware of jazz's multicultural complexity, the success of jazz tours by Armstrong, Ellington, and Gillespie in Europe had provided sufficient evidence that the music had the ingredients to 'cross national boundaries.' So, in 1956, Gillespie, a rebellious bebop jazz musician, somewhat ironically embarked on the first government-sponsored jazz tour of the Middle East with the aid of the President's Emergency Fund (von Eschen 2004, 1). Looking at Louis Armstrong's involvement in the Jazz Ambassadors as a case study helps us shed more light on the complexity behind the politics of liberation. Historically, the struggle for civil rights in the U.S. coincides with African colonial independence movements in the 1950s and 1960s. And Armstrong's involvement is multifaceted since he consistently repositioned himself as a New-Orleans based black musician, African American spokesperson, critical commentator, and apolitical entertainer, leading to public views of him that ranged from musical genius to African celebrity to Uncle Tom entertainer. As Daniel Stein reminds us:

> In the mid-1950s, Armstrong became known as Ambassador Satchmo, a public figure that afforded him a new political platform. The primary function of Jazz Ambassadors was to present themselves and their music on international tours sponsored by the State Department with the objective of exporting a democratic image of America into regions of the world in which the Soviet Union sought political influence. (2012, 231)

We need to take into consideration that the state-sponsored politics of liberation were politically, economically, and culturally motivated. Democracy, free trade, and individual freedom of expression were fused into a package of 'feel good' foreign diplomacy. However, the politics of liberation were complicated by a number of factors, among which were the racist internal politics within the U.S. that contrasted sharply with the official support of black independence movements on the African continent. Lyrically mocking that "No commodity is quite so strange as this thing called cultural exchange" (von Eschen 2004, 81), Jazz Ambassadors like Armstrong and Brubeck themselves repeatedly called attention to the ambiguities, contradictions, and bigotry within the State Department's mission of spreading the U.S. gospel of democracy through jazz, and thus exposed the tensions within the involved actor network. The State Department adopted views of jazz as the sound of individual freedom and social equality, an attitude that could easily be supported through references to the earlier rejection of jazz by totalitarian regimes in Germany, Russia, and Spain as a threat to state order and discipline. But for musicians such as Armstrong, the politics of liberation involved more complex issues having to do with racial exclusion at home, demeaning roles in film, dependency on the pressures of sponsoring (Pepsi Cola), and attacks by black radical intellectuals. Hence for Armstrong his music became politicized through contextualization, and he wavered between the outspoken enraged African American citizen and the success-oriented popular music genius and entertainer. As Penny von Eschen reminds us:

> The collaboration in the Real Ambassadors (a jazz musical revue and collaborations between the Brubecks and Armstrong performed to critical acclaim at the Monterey Jazz Festival in 1962) offered Armstrong material that was closer to his own sensibility and outlook. And while Armstrong had often managed to rise above racist material by the sheer force of his artistry, the production allowed him a chance to make a statement about a life-long struggle for control over his own representation. … For Armstrong, freedom remained an aspiration, not an achievement. (2004, 89)

Taking place during the most turbulent period of the Civil Rights movement in the early 1960s, the Real Ambassador revue at the Monterey jazz festival expressed the State Department tours' complex and contradictory politics, which lay "at the intersection of the Cold War, African and Asian nation-building, and the U.S. civil rights struggle" (von Eschen 2004, 79). The tours were further complicated by shifting alliances and tensions between the cultural workers of the foreign-service personnel and the musicians such as Gillespie, the Brubecks, and Armstrong. While some cultural workers shared the musicians' views of music as a way to bridge cultures, nations, and races, others shared the racial views of President Eisenhower and his segregationist allies (80). Amid such tensions Armstrong continually repositioned himself from a public to a private political agent. As Daniel Stein rightly points out:

> Armstrong's at times superficial disengagement from political action – 'his professed unwillingness to dive into politics' – is counteracted further by the stories he repeatedly told about his experience with racial segregation, which usually end with the affirmation of his music's power to reach across the racial divide. (2012, 245)

Hence Armstrong's cosmopolitics emerge at the intersection of storyteller, musical genius, and conflicted public political figure. It is the autobiographical mode that becomes his primary political tool, while the music remains the central cathartic and liberating expression of his private and public self. His role as musical ambassador also provides a striking example of the ways in which popular music, throughout its history, has negated clear dividing lines and, in addition, has repeatedly proven capable of transforming itself despite its entanglement in mass and commodity culture. Clearly, Armstrong, Ellington, and Brubeck had star cult status at the time they embarked on their tours as Jazz Ambassadors, and this allowed them to raise their individual and at times dissident voices to foster their idiosyncratic understanding of community-building.

3.3 Sonic cosmopolitics from below

The Pleasant Revolution

In which ways are 'sonic cosmopolitics from below' different then? Musical Grassroots movements like the Fandango sin Fronteras and The Pleasant Revolution Tour by the rock fusion band Ginger Ninjas are recent alternative networks that critics like David F. García and Arjun Appadurai classify as flows or scapes in times of heightened globalization (cf. García 2006, 95–107; Appadurai 1996, 25 ff.). Interestingly enough, though, while they partake in the globalized transnational patterns of cultural exchange between the U.S. and Mexico that are frequently digital and/or virtual, they also resort to 'slowed-down' forms of mobility. Thus, they intensify communal contact such as dancing at the border, walking across it, or, in the case of the Ginger Ninjas, traveling from the U.S. to Mexico by bike to promote 'alternative-archaic' forms of transportation, energy production, and performance. Both projects unite music with political concern, and both work through local as well as virtual networks based on horizontal actor network strategies. Music by the Ginger Ninjas or by music groups from Fandango sin Fronteras like Quetzal can primarily be accessed via youtube and other internet sites, local radio, and occasionally CD. Quetzal also recently established its own record label, demonstrating that these movements look for independent forms of fundraising, music-making, and community-building. They embody cross-overs of music and musical heritage awareness, as well as of local and translocal community politics that arise from grassroots movements and aim at spreading new alternative forms of community building. They appropriate sections of the mass media for their communal uses to disseminate music and information. As Martín-Barbero points out:

> The efficacy and social significance of mass media do not lie primarily in the industrial organization and the ideological content, but rather in the way the popular masses have appropriated the mass media and the way the masses have recognized their identity in the mass media. (qtd. in Avant-Mier 2010, 1)

The Ginger Ninjas' Pleasant Revolution Tour belongs to the many growing local grassroots movements that have recently become transnational in scope. That grassroots movements as contemporary manifestations of Appadurai's flows have finally achieved global presence has become visible in the worldwide media coverage of the Occupy Wall Street/Occupy Oakland/Occupy Frankfurt protests against laissez-faire capitalism in metropolises around the globe. While this protest movement responds to the global crisis of money and market systems that seem to have lost all aspects of transparency and control, other grassroots movements with diverse social concerns but less media attention have increasingly crossed national boundaries in recent decades. As Srilatha Batliwala points out in "Grassroots Movements as Transnational Actors: Implications for Global Civil Society":

> The past two decades witnessed the emergence of a new range of transnational social movements, networks, and organizations seeking to promote a more just and equitable global order. With this broadening and deepening of cross-border citizen action, however, troubling questions have arisen about their rights of representation and accountability – the internal hierarchies of voice and access within transnational civil society are being highlighted. The rise of transnational grassroots movements, with strong constituency base and sophisticated advocacy capability at both local and global levels, is an important phenomenon in this context. These movements are formed and led by poor and marginalized groups, and defy the stereotype of grassroots movements being narrowly focused on local issues. They embody both a challenge and an opportunity for democratizing, legitimizing, and strengthening the role of transnational civil society in global policy. (2012, n. pag.)

When the Ginger Ninjas traveled from California to Palenque, Mexico in one of their tours as part of this larger eco-political project called The Pleasant Revolution Tour, the fact that they transported all instruments and amplifiers by bike set their form of traveling distinctly apart from exclusively elite or aesthetic notions of touring the world, often characterized by class privilege and the ability to travel and 'consume' the cultures of the world. In a youtube clip the Ginger Ninjas mockingly compare the use and costs of energy during their global music journey by bike with the costs of the Rolling Stones' tour in 2007. While certainly getting to know Mexican people and Mexican culture(s) is on the band's agenda, their major conceptual frame is the synthesis of alternative forms of mobility with music and audience interaction to promote new translocal communities and networks. During their gigs in Chapala, Guadalajara, Morelia, and other locations, they set out to connect California-style ecological awareness with the rapidly growing Mexican movement of ciclismo in order to create a transnational ecological – or, if you will, 'ecocosmopolitan' – awareness of finding new ways of encountering the other within and outside one's community. The now weekly manifestations by the ciclismo movement in cities such as Guadalajara and Mexico City correspond transnationally to the Ginger Ninjas' aim to promote biker mobility on a global scale (Batliwala 2012, n. pag).

Interestingly enough, both journey and conceptual project remain connected to a new consciousness of time in connection to space, emphasizing locality within global flows. As the road tour shows, a sometimes willed, sometimes imposed slowing-down of movement – determined by road conditions and bikers' bodies – leads to slow forms of arrival and extended forms of encounter. In addition, the arrival on bike leads to public attention, which fosters the reclamation of public spaces for community politics and propogates places like plazas and beaches for public performances. Reminiscent of the avant-garde strategies of groups such as The Living Theater, The Ginger Ninjas' Pleasant Revolution Tour aims at bridging the gap between musicians and audience, art and life by getting the audience "on bike" as well and actually involving them in the process of energy production for the amplification of the band's instruments. Their musical live performance style affirms that "for many critics, fans, and musicians," according to Roy Shuker, "there is a perceived hierarchy of live performances, with a marked tendency to equate the audiences' physical proximity to the actual 'performance' and intimacy with the performer(s) with a more authentic and satisfying musical experience" (2012, 201). In the Ginger Ninjas' road tour this perception goes beyond aesthetics and turns into a true act of collaboration between musician(s) and audience.

In a detailed and highly personalized way, the band's journey from California to Mexico is captured in the 2012 documentary *Los Ginger Ninjas Rodando México* by Argentine director Sergio Morin.

Figure 1: Film poster *Los Ginger Ninjas Rodando México* (© Wilfried Raussert 2013).

The film celebrated its début during the Guadalajara Festival de Cine in March 2012. Together with a camera team, Sergio Morin accompanied The Ginger Ninjas on their 2004 bicycle adventure tour from the U.S. to Mexico to create a road and music documentary that chronicles the journey through mapping and road scenes interspersed with camera close-ups of the band members and clips from performances. The film narrates the intersection of private journey and political mission, sonically with voice-over song lyrics and visually with clips of conversations between band members. Interviews between director and individual band members and explicit commentaries on the band's song lyrics interact on a narrative level to reveal the human touch, joy, and suffering of the journey.

From physical exhaustion to emotional disappointment, personal anger to private lament over failed love, the film exposes the human undercurrents of the band's larger eco-political mission. While the film gives insights into individual shortcomings and the failures of group members, it shares the overall eco-political mission of The Ginger Ninjas by portraying their endeavor sympathetically. This becomes especially visible in scenes in which musicians and listeners join in the act of "pedalling bikes" to produce energy while at the same time sharing the aesthetic experience of the music performed. The basic concept is interaction and interdependence. Particularly at the moment of arrival in the towns and cities of Mexico, it becomes obvious that the "slow motion" arrival is crucial for establishing contact with the new and unfamiliar. As the documentary reveals, The Ginger Ninjas look for alternative forms of global connectedness outside cars, trains, and planes. In a fast-paced globalized world it is slowing down that makes true encounter and contact possible. Far from elitist notions of cosmopolitanism, The Pleasant Revolution Tour allows musicians and audience alike to temporarily experience "actually existing cosmopolitanisms," to borrow a term from Malcomson (1998, 240), and to accordingly rethink identity politics in such a way as to combine moral with cultural forms of worldliness by emphasizing the value of acknowledging difference. This applies to differences within the band, which range from aesthetic to emotional tensions, as well as to differences between the band and their changing audiences during the tour.

By promoting ciclismo – movement by bike – the musicians' transnational journey provides an alternative to Marshall McLuhan's utopian and technocratic conception of the global village. Indeed, another way to conceive of this new global interconnectedness is to acknowledge the ongoing devastation of the world. In this sense, David Held, one of the leading proponents of a cosmopolitan politics, speaks of "overlapping communities of fate" (2004, 168), asserting that environmental developments such as global warming, natural disasters, and diminishing resources render us a world community equally culpable, as well as responsible for protecting the earth. Clearly, The Pleasant Revolution Tour takes its motivation here, as it promotes old forms of mobility as new ways of saving the planet. Aesthetically, it is important to note that the music does not preach; the lyrics are sometimes political, sometimes personal, yet always lyrical. And aesthetic pleasure seems equally important to the band as well as to the audience. The overall concept behind The Ginger Ninjas' touring performance is based on a fusion of physical movement, aesthetic pleasure, and ecological global awareness. Moreover, its grassroots conceptualization is essential because it is music from the people, for the people. This is particularly visible when the band arrives in Mexico City and refuses to perform on an upper-level stage on the Zócalo. Ignoring the resistance of the security guards, the musicians step down with instruments and amplifiers to be symbolically and literally on one level with the audience.

Fandango Sin Fronteras

Another recent grassroots movement in the Americas of the New Millennium is the Fandango Sin Fronteras Project. Communal as well as musical in its orientation, it transports the idea of border crossings rhythmically as well as geopolitically. The movement links musical agents and performances in cities such as Veracruz, Los Angeles, Seattle, and Vancouver and demonstrates a continuous presence at the U.S.-Mexican border, overcoming the fence literally through music and dance. By creating new diaspora links it contributes to the makings of a transnational civil society. What we can frequently see and hear are people joining in a musical interaction on both sides of the fence, celebrating a transborder communal spirit, simultaneously protesting against and mocking U.S. border control agencies. Fandango events at the border remind us that, in the words of Martin Munro:

> Rhythm … plays a fundamental role in bonding societies and groups and in structuring the collective experience of time. […] A society's notion of time becomes 'second nature' to its people through collective, rhythmic interactions. People learn how to keep together in time through various forms of movement socialization, and these movements are mediated by rhythm. (2010, 5)

Munro's observation is important for understanding the essence of "sonic cosmopolitics from below." To clarify, I am not referring to high and low in terms of high culture and low culture, nor do I intend to place grassroots music in a subaltern context. I am referring here to a concept of music in the streets, music in public urban spaces, and music for people beyond the divide between performer and audience. The *Fandango sin Fronteras* shares exactly that with The Ginger Ninjas' conception of reclaiming public spaces, mobilizing communities, and creating alternative forms of mobility to cross boundaries. *Fandango sin Fronteras* does not necessarily seek festival grounds to perform. On the contrary, performances often take place within local communities and community centers as well as in public spaces directly south and north of the border. Precisely in these nationally demarcated spaces marked by fences, walls, and border control, the performances of *Fandango sin Fronteras* conquer public spaces for the performance of transborder communities. Professional music groups engage in these performances, with community building appearing to take precedence over market interests.

Figure 2: Border Fandango poster (© Wilfried Raussert 2010).

While the link between music, market, and politics in neoliberal capitalist society is generally undeniable, this grassroots musical movement is an attempt to open up new venues of distributing music and ideas of community. Fandango sin Fronteras contains this element of connecting the individual and the local with the transnational. Both, aesthetically and spatially, Fandango sin Fronteras locates itself in the border zone between ethnic, racial, and national identities. While the Fandango project and the musical activities of related groups such as Quetzal rebuild collective memory, it bears mentioning that their understanding of latinidad fuses Spanish, Indigenous, Arab, and African elements and opens a venue for new transnational identities, thus challenging a monolithic latinidad north and south of the Rio Grande. For the Fandango grassroots movement the son jarocho becomes an aesthetic means of expanding mexicanidad as well as latinidad, revealing native, Arab, African, and Spanish elements of rhythm and performance. In the words of Shannon Dudley and Quetzal lead singer Martha Gonzalez, influential figures of the Seattle Fandango project, the emergence of the project goes back to collaborations between musicians and communities on both sides of the border:

> To avoid creating a new orthodoxy of their own, professional groups in the grassroots movement, including *Mono Blanco*, *Son de Madera*, *Chuchumbé*, *Los Utrera*, *Los Cojolites*, *Estansuela*, *Relicario*, and *Los Negritos* continued to organize and participate in community fandangos, where they took part in a collective dialogue about the future of the tradition. This practice continues today, and many musicians in the movement contribute part of their earnings to the community centers that host free workshops and fandangos. This vibrant scene caught the attention of a new generation of community-oriented Chicano artists in Los Angeles who began making trips to Veracruz in the early 2000s. Chicanos shared their own experiences and techniques of community building through art. Back in Los Angeles they shared what they had learned about the fandango and brought up musicians from Veracruz. (Dudley and Gonzalez 2009, n. pag)

The Nuevo Movimiento Jaranero took shape through a process of research and reclamation, and the multiethnic roots of music in "Veracruz, as a Caribbean site" were reaffirmed (Gonzalez 2011, 66). This return to heritage, past, and cultural memory created a new interest in the living tradition of Son Jarocho, which most Chicanos had previously known through commercial recordings (or through Ritchie Valens's 1957 rock and roll remake of the traditional son jarocho song "La Bamba"). As Dudley and Gonzalez tell us:

> In 2002 *Fandango Sin Fronteras* was established as an informal musical dialogue between Chicanos and Jarochos. In 2004 members of Quetzal

> traveled to Mexico to help record and produce Son de Madera's CD, 'Las Orquestas del Dia'. In 2005, Son de Madera, one of the premier *son jarocho* ensembles from Veracruz, came to Los Angeles to perform with Quetzal at a fundraiser for the South Central Farm, an inner-city farm that the community had reclaimed from industrial wasteland, and from which the authorities were then trying to remove them. Through these and many other exchanges, Fandango Sin Fronteras has taken shape as a transnational musical dialogue rooted in the spirit of convivencia. (2009, n. pag.)

This music, Son Jarocho, is a style specific to the Veracruz region of Mexico, emerging from the mix of indigenous, Spanish, and African cultural influences on that society. The Mexican government canonized this music in the 1940s, moving it to the stage while taking out the culture and improvisation at the music's heart. It was reclaimed in the 1970s, representing a return to community values.

As Martha Gonzalez explains:

> As a participatory music and dance practice *fandango* conceptualizes community as a central aesthetic principle. Veracruzian communities utilize *convivencia* as a collective production of auditory identity, a culmination of memory through sound. Spanish, African, Arab and Indigenous legacies are present in the multiple dialogues and musical inflections. This musical dialogue is achieved through the expressions of *son jarocho's* multiple instruments, notably the heartbeat or pulse, of la *tarima. Bailadoras* (percussive dancers) are the drummers that produce the central pulse of the *fandango fiesta* through their footwork. In this sense they are percussionists. As percussionists these women dialogue with other instruments and singers in the *son jarocho* ensemble. (2011, 65–66)

Despite the overwhelming historical evidence of an African presence in colonial Mexico, its presence was not recorded in the nation-state's official history of Veracruzian cultural tradition. Caught up in an obsession with modernizing the nation in the early 1900s, the Mexican nation-state created a Veracruzian cultural identity that emphasized the Spanish influence and reduced the Indigenous and especially African elements. In the United States today, but also increasingly in Canada and Latin American countries, Son Jarocho and Fandango are performed in Chicana/o and Latin diaspora communities as a way for members to connect with one another. As its multidirectional and transversal flows illustrate, Fandango has gone transnational by building new diasporic links across the boundaries of nation-states.

3.4 Sonic cosmopolitics from within market circuits

According to the George Yúdice, the Black Civil Rights movement in the U.S. marked the beginning of a growing link between performativity and identity politics. For marginalized groups the political message included a "social imperative to perform" (2004, 40). Yúdice's principal claim is that "the role of culture has expanded in an unprecedented way into the political and economic at the same time that conventional notions of culture have been emptied out" (9). In his reading, culture no longer functions as a realm of legitimation, but, rather, must itself be legitimated on the basis of its political and economic utility.

Contemporary urban culture cherishes festival, spectacles, and a re-aestheticization of public space. At the same time, leftist and neo-Marxist intellectuals have been criticizing the spectacularization of urban spaces (Debord 1995; Zukin 1995). Yúdice's argument points toward the radical changes these social developments imply for our understanding of culture. The general critical direction asserts that the culture of spectacles commodifies all forms of social, cultural, and political life. Yet, critics like Goldstein and Gotham arrive at a more complex vision of spectacle culture. While recognizing commodity interests, they locate a potential of rebellion, resistance, and subversion in contemporary urban spectacles. Goldstein claims that "spectacles, like other public events, are systems for not only the performance but also the creation or transformation of social order" (16). With a nod to the New Orleans Mardi Gras, Gotham maintains that public spectacles have the potential to create "a radical critique" especially with respect to class and race inequalities" (235).

Spectacle certainly depicts well the conceptual framework of sonic politics in contemporary performance arts. Key actors of the popular music scene demonstrate that music may be commodified but not automatically lose its political potential. African American musicians like Alicia Keys, who performed at the Women's March in 2017; Kendrick Lamar, who delivered a provocative chain-gang performance in the 2016 Grammy Award ceremony; and Beyoncé, who inserted Black Panther choreography into the 2016 Super Bowl half-time show, use their privileged position as global pop icons to reach a worldwide audience with their performances of the political in the midst of popular spectacle. Their examples demonstrate that the channels of popular music can effectively serve to address social and political injustice, reinvent the social, and spread visions of political renewal. They also show that 'protest' sells well, especially in liberal and leftist intellectual circles. Hence, there seems a double strategy at work that enhances the individual economic success of the artist while pushing new political objectives at the same time. Even in the context of expanding neoliberal global markets, music continues to play a key role for both the entertainment business and political activism and continues to infiltrate new channels to reflect the social.

The early twenty-first century has witnessed a new rise of right-wing political and fundamentalist movements. The racial violence against people of African descent ranges from Brazil and the Caribbean to the U.S. and Canada. Music enters the discourse of all political directions, but in particular those such as the Black Lives Matter movement that challenge this new right wing turn. As Daphne Brooks puts it," this is a new age of injustice, one with a heightened awareness of state violence and a national reckoning with the state-sanctioned disposability of black lives, and so this moment clearly demands a new set of jams" (2016, n. pag.). She makes us aware that "with the rise of new technologies, the killings of unarmed black men as well as women – Trayvon Martin, Michael Brown, Tamir Rice, Freddie Gray, Rekia Boyd – are etched into our public consciousness" (2016, n. pag.).

This forceful resurfacing of racial violence and hatred has brought forth artistic responses. Local hip hop artists and other musicians are creating lyrics that spotlight the new intensity of a seemingly ever-present undercurrent of racism from the West to East, South to North, Brazil to Canada. It also seems that contemporary icons of popular music like Beyoncé and Kendrick Lamar have heard critical laments about artistic silence in the face of injustice. From within the circuits of music industry and from the pinnacle of artistic success in the world of popular music, they appear to have launched what Daphne Brooks calls a "new wave of black pop protest music" that "captures and grapples with racial catastrophe in the 21st century: the prison-industrial complex, globalized wealth inequality and the violent expenditure of women and children" (2016, n. pag.).

I argue that Kendrick Lamar is the quintessential example of the new sonic dissent that emerges from the very center of stardom within the pop music world. Minutes after Lamar received his fifth Grammy of the night for Best Rap Album in February 2016, he delivered a spectacle-like performance to raise historical consciousness and voice his rage about racial injustice. Performing a medley that included songs like "Alright" and "The Blacker the Berry," he approached the microphone chained to other black men in a makeshift prison block. Next to the musicians of the chain gang there were musicians performing from within a prison cage. The performance ended with the debut of an emphatic new verse about modern slavery, in memory of Trayvon Martin: "On February 26th I lost my life, too." A new call for solidarity and brotherhood was performed, televised, and spread through the new media instantaneously. His performance at the Grammy awards combined artistic craftsmanship, spectacle, and political action, with a gigantic fire behind the stage visually emphasizing his musical demand for awareness and justice (cf. Makarechi 2016).[1]

Figure 3: Kendrick Lamar Grammy award performance.

1 http://www.vanityfair.com/hollywood/2016/02/kendrick-lamar-2016-grammys-performance.

Kendrick Lamar's provocative performance creates a collage of historical time in which he relates the ball and chains of slavery with the current prison situation in the United States and racism on a global scale. He creates a powerful image of a threatening historical continuum that enslaves anew and prolongs colonial slavery into neocolonial practices of racist jurisdiction and police practice. Lamar's spectacular performance style also finds way into his video art. For instance, the choreography for the Alright video stages Lamar with a group of young African American males riding in a car carried by white police officers. The video juggles with spatial metaphors. Lamar moves above the city with a bird's-eye view of the world below. The spatially superior position is accompanied by rap dance movements underscoring the cherished physical freedom that contrasts sharply with the lyrics, which express critique, sadness, anger, and resistance. While floating above the city, Lamar transcends the ground pictures of white armed policemen pushing a young African American onto the pavement. His bold city flight eventually attracts the attention of a police officer, who pretends to fire a bullet at him through a finger gun. Lamar enacts his empowerment through the performative of urban song and dance. As Judith Butler puts it, "naming can operate in the service of a sovereign form of the performative" (2013, 137). "If we are always named by others" – a condition that Butler and Athanasiou highlight – "then the name signifies a certain dispossession from the start. If we seek to name ourselves, it is still within a language that we never made" (137). Performativity, however, provides a solution, according to Athanasiou: "Naming implies a performative which is necessarily interwoven in the fabric of appropriation that authorizes it, while at the same time it remains somehow capable of exposing and exceeding its prescribed limits" (138). Performativity's potential to challenge "ways in which the wrongs of oppression and dispossession are not audible within hegemonic discourses" (132) is doubly heightened when the performative emerges from within the very temples of cultural industry, as Lamar's performance and video underscore.

Despite the controversy about oversexualizing the black female body, Beyoncé's choreography referencing the Black Panther Movement at the 2016 Super Bowl halftime show illustrates the intergenerational vitality that spurs contemporary black protest performance. Backing dancers wearing Black Panther-style berets and black leather were also photographed after the performance posing publicly with raised fists, evoking the black power salute by Tommie Smith and John Carlos at the 1968 Olympic Games in Mexico City. The dancers backstage held up a poster with the slogan "Justice 4 Mario Woods," a young African American who was shot dead in December 2015 by police in San Francisco. The dancers' performance marked a powerful visual homage to the Black Panthers and commemorated the beginnings of their political movement in Oakland, California in 1966, 50 years before.

Figure 4: Beyoncé's Super Bowl Show 2016.

The new black protest music is a movement whose leadership, as Brooks maintains, reminds us that the art that accompanies it should be as capacious as 'blackness' itself. Thus, artists such as producer and musician Flying Lotus, with his old-school, new-school blend of gospel, R&B, hip hop, and Afro-futurist dance electronica, and queer black feminist Janelle Monáe, "the sci-fi Afropunk rebel-with-a-cause"– to name but a few – need to be recognized, alongside Beyoncé and Lamar, as creators of a new sonic fabric of black dissent for present-day crises (2016, n. pag.). Monaé's single "Hell You Talmbout" decries the violent death rate of African Americans by repetitively voicing victims' names. Originally a Target-exclusive bonus track on the deluxe edition of her 2013 album *The Electric Lady*, Monáe's 2015 rerecording transforms the song into a chant in which the listener, and, in live settings, the audience, is exhorted to say these names as well. Over a snare-based beat that suggests a military march, the song consists of Monáe and other artists from her Wondaland label chanting "Hell You Talmbout," stating the names, and calling, "say his name" or "say her name." While the vast majority of the names spoken during the song, from Walter Scott to Freddie Gray to Sandra Bland to Aiyana Jones and Eric Garner, connect the song directly to contemporary events, the inclusion of Emmett Till, Amadou Diallo, and others links contemporary racial violence with the history of white supremacist oppression in the United States. The song serves as a deliberate soundtrack to contemporary protest marches, in which Monáe participates regularly, and is frequently used in marches against injustice and discrimination outside the U.S., for instance in Brazil, South Africa, and England.

3.5 Conclusion

Contemporary music celebrities like Alicia Keys, Beyoncé, Janelle Monáe, and Kendrick Lamar can build their political mission on their firm positioning within global music markets, just as the Jazz Ambassador Program could build on jazz's popular global standing to turn the music into a strategic tool for spreading the U.S. American gospel of freedom and democracy. Likewise, the musicians who were invited – and sometimes more than obliged by forces of the music industry – to participate in the Jazz Ambassadors tours had reached stardom long before they toured. While many of jazz tunes presented had already hit the charts, the musicians' involvement in the tours certainly enhanced their record companies' sales. Music as cultural capital lent itself successfully to promoting U.S. cultural achievement. A synthesis of political impact and market success characterized the top-down program. We should not ignore, however, the tensions with respect to public relations between the jazz musicians as artists and as individual dissidents, and between the government officials and civil right mediators – all of which was exemplified by Louis Armstrong's critique that domestic racial policy was incompatible with the global gospel of freedom. The official political mission then was to achieve geo-cultural primacy by spreading "American" music conceived as a national or nationalistic expression. The Jazz

Ambassadors had to walk a tightrope between engaging in transcultural musical expression and serving as national ambassadors. Still, as Penny von Eschen points out, "the goodwill ambassadors' understanding of jazz as an international music complicates the characterization of jazz as 'America's music' – a label used by Willis Conover and others who have subscribed to the view that jazz won the Cold War" (2004, 250). It would be reductive to talk about jazz as the "soundtrack of American Empire" or "music of freedom" in a unilateral, one-directional way. Rather, as Penny von Eschen emphasizes:

> For these musicians, jazz was an international and hybrid music combining not just American and European forms, but forms that had developed out of an earlier mode of cultural exchange, through the circuitous routes of the Atlantic slave trade and the "overlapping diasporas" created by migrations throughout the Americas. And if the U.S. State Department had facilitated the music's transnational routes of innovation and improvisation, for many musicians there was a certain poetic justice in that. (250)

The psychological, cultural, and political forms of liberation that the *Jazz Ambassadors* helped spread are hard to sum up, but the program certainly helped free blackness from low culture, and it extricated jazz from the label 'American' by persistently spotlighting its African, Latin American, and European influences, and giving voice and sound to a sonic process of transcultural transformability within the Americas and beyond.

The critical performances of Beyoncé, Monáe, and Lamar show close alliances between the artist, the music industry, and curators of public space events. They disclose that creative production and the circuits of music industry are deeply immersed in matters of social and political life. With a nod to critics like Yúdice, it is safe to say that music, like culture in general, frequently legitimates itself on the grounds of its social, political, and economic utility.

Music from below – that is, the new transnational grassroots projects such as *Fandango sin Fronteras* and *The Pleasant Revolution Tour* by the California-based rock group The Ginger Ninjas – may be read as a movement to democratize cultural production, distribution, and reception. The non-state actor constellation is certainly more horizontal. Frequently, the musicians themselves are the distributors of their music, using new media accesses, and the double role of artist and public spokesperson is less conflicted since the musicians of *Fandango sin Fronteras* and *The Pleasant Revolution Tour* share a self-willed political mission and rhetoric of resistance. Not only do these grassroots projects open venues for composers and musicians to reach new audiences through new channels, locally, regionally, nationally, and transnationally; they also introduce changes to agency and power in the production of and control over 'culture' by emphasizing the notion of participatory culture. While their music has not hit the charts, it cherishes a good standing in translocally-connected communities. *Fandango sin Fronteras* and *The Pleasant Revolution Tour* represent "sonic cosmopolitics" from the people, for the people, and are vital parts of grassroots movements within the Americas that function multidirectionally and transversally, being thus different from the unilateral Jazz Ambassador approach. As the comparison reveals, global flows move in different directions, and global circuits are by no means ideologically unified in our globalized age.

Clearly, *Fandango sin Fronteras* and the *Pleasant Revolution Tour* attempt to create, respectively, transnational diasporic communities and transnational ecological communities from grassroots agendas, whereas musicians involved in *The Jazz Ambassadors* and *The Rhythm Road* never have lost touch with U.S. cultural diplomacy interests completely (even if the individual artists and musicians may hold dissident views themselves). The *Fandango sin Fronteras* movement goes beyond what is considered classical resistance in colonial and postcolonial discourse. While it feeds on the utopian spirit of the African American sound of freedom of earlier decades, its participants choose a distinct transnational diasporic paradigm of identity politics. A similar utopian spirit propels the enterprises of *The Ginger Ninjas*' ecological politics. Still, I do not want to fall into the trap of overtly idealizing the political power of music. I share Josh Kun's warning that we should not "romanticize popular music as a safe-house for revolution and resistance" (2005, 17), and I also agree with him that

> Popular music is one of our most valuable tools for understanding the impact of nationalism and citizenship on the formation of our individual identities. And second, it is also one of our most valuable sites for witnessing the performance of racial and ethnic difference against the grain

> of national citizenships that work to silence and erase those differences. (11)

Kun's explanation illustrates that music in the Americas has continuously given voice to difference, and that includes voices from above, below, and within the music circuits. Unlike the Jazz Ambassadors program, with its elitist approach of sending world-famous musicians abroad, the current Rhythm Road project, while directed by the State Department, clearly borrows from grassroots egalitarian approaches to mobilize music from the people, for the people. Accordingly, it does not select musicians and performers of star-cult status like Duke Ellington and Louis Armstrong, but rather younger musicians that need to apply and go through a selection process. The program annually sends ten bands (mainly jazz, some hip-hop, all of which audition for the gig) to approximately more than fifty countries. Also, the politics seem to have changed and become more moderate. Whether this is a sign of revised diplomacy and/or of a falling empire remains to be answered. The emphasis is now on dialogue; frequently musicians do not export music made in America but attempt to adapt to the musical cultures of the regions and nations visited. As an official report declares:

> Before the bass player Ari Roland went to Turkmenistan last year, he learned some Turkmen folk songs. His band played jazz improvisations of these songs with local musicians – the first time such mixing had been allowed – and a 15-minute news report about the concert ran on state television several times the next day. (Kaplan 2013, n. pag)

And who knows – such a dialogical approach might not only foster a participatory culture that supports local and global community-building; it might also eventually lead to market success. Martha Gonzalez, lead singer of Quetzal and spokeswoman for Fandango sin Fronteras, won a Grammy award (Best Latin Rock, Urban, or Alternative Album) with her band for their album *Imaginaries* in 2013.

Works cited

Anderson, Amanda. 1998. "Cosmopolitanism, Universalism, and the Divided Legacies of Modernity." In *Cosmopolitics: Thinking and Feeling beyond the Nation*, ed. Pheng Cheah and Bruce Robbins, 265–289. Minneapolis: University of Minnesota Press. Print.

Appadurai, Arjun. 1996. *Modernity at Large: Cultural Dimensions of Globalization.* Minneapolis: University of Minnesota Press. Print.

Appiah, Kwame Anthony. 2006. *Cosmopolitanism: Ethics in a World of Strangers*. New York: W. Norton. Print.

Archibugi, Daniele. 2016. "Cosmopolitan Democracy and its Critics: A Review." *European Journal of International Relations* 10.3: 437–473.

Avant-Mier, Roberto. 2010. *Rock the Nation. Latin/o Identities and the Latin Rock Diaspora.* New York: Continuum International. Print.

Batliwala, Srilatha. 2012. "Grassroots Movements as Transnational Actors: Implications for Global Civil Society." *Wiego* online edition, June.

Blau, Judith R. 2001. "Bringing in Codependence." In *The Blackwell Companion to Sociology*, ed. Judith R. Blau, 58–70. Malden, MA: Blackwell Publishing Ltd. Print.

Brooks, Daphne. 2016. "How #BlackLivesMatter started a musical revolution." *The Observer* online edition, March 13.

—. 2011. "Planet Earth(a): Sonic Cosmopolitanism and Black Feminist Theory." In *Cornbread and Cuchifritos: Ethnic Identity Politics, Transnationalization, and Transculturation in American Urban Popular Music*, ed. Wilfried Raussert and Michelle Habell-Pallán, 111–126. Trier: WVT, Tempe: Bilingual Press. Print.

Butler, Judith, and Athena Athanasiou. 2013. *Dispossession: The Performative in the Political.* Cambridge: Polity Press. Print.

Debord, Guy. 1995. *The Society of the Spectacle.* New York: Zone Books. Fainstein S. Print.

Dudley, Shannon, and Martha Gonzalez. 2009. "The Seattle Fandango Project." *Harmonic Dissidents Magazine. A Chronicle of Street Band Culture*, Issue 2, November.

Eschen, Penny von. 2004. *Satchmo Blows up the World: Jazz Ambassadors Play the Cold War.* Cambridge: Harvard University Press. Print.

García, David F. 2006. *Arsenio Rodríguez and the Transnational Flows of Latin Popular Music.* Philadelphia: Temple University Press. Print.

Goldstein, Daniel. 2004. *The Spectacular City: Violence and Performance in Urban Bolivia.* Durham: Duke University Press. Print.

Gonzalez, Martha. 2011. "Sonic (Trans)Migration of Son Jarocho 'Zapateado': Rhythmic Intention, Metamorphosis, and Manifestation in Fandango and Performance." In *Cornbread and Cuchifritos: Ethnic Identity Politics, Transnationalization, and Transculturation in American Urban Popular Music*, ed. Wilfried Raussert and Michelle Habell-Pallán, 59–72. Trier: WVT, Tempe: Bilingual Press. Print.

Gotham, Kevin Fox. "Theorizing Urban Spectacles: Festivals, Tourism, and the Transformation of Urban Space." *City* 9.2: 225–246. Print.

Held, David. *Global Convenant: The Social Democratic Alternative to the Washington Consensus.* Cambridge: Polity Press, 2004. Print.

Huntington, Samuel P. 2004. *Who Are We? The Challenges to America's National Identity.* New York: Simon and Schuster. Print.

Kaplan, Fred. 2013. "When Ambassadors Had Rhythm." *New York Times* online edition, June 29.

Krims, Adam. 2012. "Music, Space, and Place: The Geography of Music." In *The Cultural Study of Music. A Critical Introduction*, ed. Martin Clayton, Trevor Herbert, and Richard Middleton, 140–148. New York: Routledge. Print.

Kun, Josh. 2005. *Audiotopia. Music, Race and America.* Berkeley: University of California Press. Print.

Makarechi, Kia. 2016. "Watch Kendrick Lamar Escape Handcuffs in 2016 Grammys Performance." *Vanity Fair* online edition, February 15.

Malcomson, Scott L. 1998. "The Varieties of Cosmopolitan Experience." In *Cosmopolitics: Thinking and Feeling beyond the Nation*, ed. Pheng Cheah and Bruce Robbins, 233–245. Minneapolis: University of Minnesota Press. Print.

Miklitsch, Robert. 2006. *Roll Over Adorno: Critical Theory, Popular Culture, Audiovisual Media.* Albany: State University of New York Press. Print.

Morin, Sergio, dir. 2012. *Los Ginger Ninjas Rodando México.* Chubusco. Film.

Munro, Martin. 2010. *Different Drummers. Rhythm and Race in the Americas.* Berkeley: University of California Press. Print.

Raussert, Wilfried. 2011. "Introduction: Ethnic Identity Politics, Transnationalization, and Transculturation in American Urban Popular Music: Inter-American Perspectives." In *Cornbread and Cuchifritos: Ethnic Identity Politics, Transnationalization, and Transculturation in American Urban Popular Music*, ed. Wilfried Raussert and Michelle Habell-Pallán, 1–25. Trier: WVT, Tempe: Bilingual Press. Print.

Sandberg, Curtis. 2008. "Jam Session: America's Jazz Ambassadors Embrace the World." *Meridian International Center*, January 12. Web.

Shuker, Roy. 2012. *Popular Music Culture. Key Concepts.* New York: Routledge. Print.

Stein, Daniel. 2012. *Music is My Life: Louis Armstrong, Autobiography, and American Jazz.* Ann Arbor: The University of Michigan. Print.

Travis, Dempsey J. 1997. *The Louis Armstrong Odyssey: From Jane Alley to America's Jazz Ambassador.* Chicago: Urban Research Press. Print.

Wicke, Peter. 1990. *Rock Music: Culture, Aesthetics, and Sociology.* Cambridge: Cambridge University Press. Print.

Yúdice, George. 2004. *The Expediency of Culture: Uses of Culture in the Global Era (Post-Contemporary Interventions).* Durham: Duke University Press. Print.

Zukin, Sharon. 1995. *The Cultures of Cities.* Oxford: Blackwell. Print.

4 Tourism, Nostalgia, and the Fabrication of 'Authenticity': 'Sonic Urban' Identities

4.1 Tourism and local and global music circuits

Tourism is an industry in itself. Growth in cultural tourism bears witness to the emergence of different niches, such as "heritage tourism, arts tourism, gastronomic tourism, film tourism and creative tourism" (Richards 2018, 12). Music adds yet another dimension to the cultural tourist industry. In particular, it helps fabricate sonic imaginaries to promote cities on a global tourist market. In the context of tourism, music, with its multifaceted capacity for cultural promotion and commodification, oscillates between cultural heritage politics, consumption, and new creative outlets. Music itself becomes, at times, an agent conflicted between preserving its expressive artistic power and its role as provider for the various social, cultural, and economic functions within the tourist industry. An embrace of nostalgia and a fabrication of authenticity shape music's role in tourism. Tourism, in return, provides additional economic capital for preservation and new productivity in the music industry.

London welcomes its visitors with a series of walking tours circling around the world of music. "The Beatles Magical Mystery Tour," "The Beatles: In My Life Tour," and "The London Music Tour" celebrate the British capital as a site where rock 'n' roll reputations are made. The guided walking tours bring the visitor to places, apartments, and music studios that tell the histories of rock music cult figures such as The Rolling Stones, The Beatles, Jimi Hendrix, David Bowie, The Sex Pistols, Oasis, The Clash, and Blur, among others. While London presents itself as central contact zone for rock music celebrities, cities like Chicago, New Orleans, Rio de Janeiro, Buenos Aires, Havana, and Kingston prefer a genre-based approach to promote their cities as sonic attractions for visitors. Chicago celebrates its links to urban blues, New Orleans poses as a cradle of jazz, Rio de Janeiro selects a white-washed samba identity, Buenos Aires of course draws upon its tango history, Havana chooses the son, and Kingston adopts a reggae affiliation, attempting in each case to give the city a musical identity and popularity. Of course, nostalgia for past decades and styles dictates the choice of music genres for each location. Taking the visitor back into music history in the context of tourist entertainment and spectacle culture, the cultural tourist industry reinvents musical traditions. This involves, on the one hand, the necessity to create a sense of sonic authenticity that makes the experience credible and desirable. On the other hand, this provides potential new economic capital for musical creativity and diversity beyond the particular genre that is the focus of tourist industry nostalgia.

Urban sonic identity politics (as framed by tourist spectacles) and the entertainment industry rely on music's power to create a sense of place and a feeling of belonging. In times of heightened time-space compression (Harvey 1989), increased mobility and the accelerating speed of everyday life, this power of music appears most desirable for relocating the tourist in a simplified and nostalgically constructed space of authentic music experience. With a nod to thinkers who see in tourism the religious quest of humanity in the twenty-first century, one may argue that music represents the secular sound of the spiritual search within contemporary urban tourism. Festival cultures like those of the New Orleans Jazz Festival and the International Mariachi Festival in Guadalajara are hubs of cultural confirmation and commerce (Falassi 1987). "Etymologically the term festival goes back to festum, expressing public joy, merriment, revelry, and feria, meaning 'abstinence from work in honor of Gods'" (2). Feria eventually became the term for "market and exposition produce" (2). Festivals also function "as sites of self-identification and community-building" (de Valck and Loist 2009, 180). As we see cultures in rapid transition throughout the Americas (and on a global scale), music festivals serve as central markers of tourist politics and occupy new functions of bonding and orientation in time and space. In addition, music fills the cities with sound, and the stories behind the music that link soundscapes and cityscapes help create a simulacrum of a more intimate relationship between music, city, and the tourist, thus allowing for an intense cognitive, kinesthetic, and affective identification of the visitor with the tourist site (cf. Urry and Larsen 2011).

4.2 Reinventing the city, reinventing music

Urban identities and musical authenticity are both reinvented in the realm of tourist industries. It is notable that from Rio de Janeiro to New Orleans, Buenos Aires to Guadalajara, and Kingston to Miami urban sonic identity politics walk a tightrope between claiming authenticity in the form of cultural heritage and promising newness in the ways they bring forth new dance and music cultures. Thus they provide a cross-generational appeal that addresses older and younger people simultaneously. Music's capacity to rapidly produce ever-new forms of hybridization along sound and rhythm allows it to become culturally and economically integrated in new promotional tracks for urban tourism and to promote the city as site of past, present, and future music. Selling authenticity (frequently drenched in ethnic and nationalist narratives) involves the reinvention of musical traditions. This involves the blues tourism in Chicago, the samba tourism in Rio de Janeiro, and the tango tourism in Buenos Aires. For instance, historians consider the early twentieth century as the heyday of tango when the music moved from raw and improvised to sophisticated and classically trained performances. Buenos Aires served as the primary locus of enunciation from which the music and dance spread to the North and Europe. As a global musical expression it requires new local anchoring to become pivotal again for tourist politics at home. As Sarah Woods puts it, "the city remains awash with tango shows, milongas (events for social dancing), tango schools, tango themed cafés and hotels, tango tours and even dial a-tango-partner agencies …" (2017, 238). Bringing the global music back home, and with it large crowds of visitors, tango then gets reinvented in these new settings. This is further extended in a growing festival and spectacle-based cultural framework in which, among others, the World Tango Festival and the City Tango Championship embrace mass events while casual bars like Café Tortoni, El Faro, and El Querandi provide more intimate settings for an 'authentic' tango experience (240).

Miami is arguably America's new capital of diasporic fusion-music in the early twenty-first century. For certain, it is a most vibrant spot for knotting diverse – in particular Afro-Latin, South American, and Caribbean – sounds and rhythms into new patchworks of music from the Americas. As a point of arrival as well as transit, Miami is at the very intersection of flows of people, music, fashion, and ideoscapes (Appadurai 1996) from the South to the North. Little Havana and Little Haiti add a pulsating beat to Miami's urban scenery. If there is one musical nucleus in Miami, it is Calle Ocho, the home of Miami's annual street festival. Little Havana's signature street turns into carnival scenery every

March. "Thousands of hip-swaying salseros form a mile-long conga that snakes through sizzling arepa stalls to the drumming of timbales. Mournal ballads derived from the idioms of Cuban farmers mix claves, tumbao, cuica and cavaquinho with tuneful laments," Sarah Woods writes (2017, 185). Miami is home to a pedestrian mall culture that resonates with music bombarding its visitors with mariachi, cumbia, salsa, and bossa nova sounds that express Pan-American Afro Latin soundscapes. In this way, the visitor encounters Miami's sonic and cultural Latin American diasporas in the U.S. Such exposure can be found particularly in The Design District, located in Midtown and Wynwood, which hosts a vibrant street art and graffiti scene, as well as small music studios that provide an outlet for low-budget alternative music expressions from local bands and visiting musicians who draw from the pulsating minor music industry in Miami's most alternative cultural zone. The music that emerges here forms a sharp contrast to the big budget music productions along South Beach. A blossoming DJ culture forms the backdrop to the breeding ground of an ever-changing hip hop scene and a Miami hit factory for the U.S. charts.

While its music industry might still be less sophisticated than that of other U.S. music capitals (Woods 2017), Miami demonstrates that music in tourism is multi-faceted. It boosts pedestrian mall culture, it feeds new youth culture, it provides culture for consumption along the beach restaurants, and, yet, it propels new sonic expression. Musical celebrities like Beyoncé, Gloria Estefan, and Lauryn Hill shape the music scene as do local musicians who preferably record and perform their music in the Design District. Despite their class differences, all of these artists collectively generate a pulsating music culture rather than stifling it. Consumption and production fuse and collide in Miami's music scene that is at the very heart of tourism. Leisure culture and artistic creativity enter a fairly symbiotic relation that keep feeding each other. Culturally, music in Miami creates a pan Latin@ sound tapestry and helps promote the city as the new Caribbean and Latin@ cultural capital in the North. Tourism clearly helps push new music production by bringing musicians into the city, creating platforms for testing music's popular appeal, and providing the cash flow needed to sustain an accessible music industry for young, upcoming musicians, and bands. The tourist himself becomes an agent through preferences and choices, through active participation in karaoke and dance cultures and by supporting young and alternative DJs, songwriters, and performers within the local circuits of music culture.

4.3 Ethnicity in the context of global commodity culture

New package tourist tours draw on the recognition of cultural diversity within societies. Multiculturalism, in the aftermath of the turbulent 1960s, has become a highly contested concept in various spheres such as politics and academia. We witness a growing diversity in terms of communities along the lines of religion, class, ethnicity, gender, and sex (Banerjee, Birkle, and Raussert 2006, 311). Also new nationalisms have transformed not only the idea of cultural origin but redefined boundaries as well as affiliations within a multi-ethnic spectrum of cultures throughout the Americas. More recent debates circling around multiculturalism have shown that 'ethnicity' not only figures as a culturally and politically but also as an economically powerful signifier within processes of globalization. Critics like bell hooks point toward ethnicity's strategic role in cultural industry politics to create an exciting authentic other within mainstream culture (1992, 21). "Selling Ethnicity" is both frequent economic manifestation as well as powerful marketing strategy and both phenomena have emerged from the omnipresence of multiculturalism in discourses within contemporary urban society. Various discourses intersect when the increasing interest in postcolonial studies, the academic institutionalization of ethnic studies, the ever-growing expansion of the tourist industry as well as the consumers' interest in ethnic products in terms of food, fashion and culture meet, collide, and fuse in global economic and cultural exchange. The processes behind "selling ethnicity" are manifold as are the questions about agency revolving around the processes of commodifying self and other.

Music with its rapid assimilation and fusion of new styles and rhythm keeps the ethnic other and exotic alive and pulsating and offers a departure from everyday routines (Foster 1982, 22). Tourism is part of what Huggan calls a whole "cosmopolitan alterity industry" that depends on reinventing and selling myths within narratives of ethnic otherness, nationalist identity, and youth culture difference (2001, xiii). The products of the tourist industry tend to be designed for fast and easy consumption. Still, tourism and related processes of the commodification of nationalist myth, cultural difference, and youth resistance are seldom only one-sided. They fulfil communal and educational functions. While Huggan seems right that the tourist industry in its embrace of alterity as economic capital is mainly targeted toward the capitalist societies of the West (68), it also opens venues for local and alternative cultural productions especially in the realm of music performance and production.

4.4 Exploring the intersection of cultural and economic politics

"Selling ethnicity" then is one among numerous factors that highlight the mobility and fluidity of identity today. Processes of globalization and transnational networking help produce and distribute notions and marketable adaptations of fluid identities and mobile ethnicities in transactions of global trade, in their impact on how culture is constructed, perceived and distributed. The fact that ethnicity has been discovered by capitalist interest does not necessarily mean that ethnicity loses its potential to function as a site of resistance. Ethnicity and nationalism have become a contested terrain between mainstream and margin. Most obvious, as I argue, such a competition becomes visible in the context of tourism and the tourist's desire to consume authentic otherness. The growth of cultural tourism and the expansion of the heritage industry aim at satisfying a growing longing for the archaic and authentic in times of rapid global changes. Tourist sites, in this context, are likely to be contested spaces because they are located at the intersection of competing, economic, social, cultural, and political influences. Frequently, tourist attractions are developed in collaboration between national and international companies and institutions and often lie outside the control of local residents. The latter may try to gain access to the tourist industry in their neighborhood and they may also develop strategies of resistance. In both cases questions about agency emerge addressing issues such as who will gain access to the market and who will shape the development of heritage industry (Selwyn 1996; Tucker 1997; Low and Lawrence-Zúniga 2003).

4.5 Contemporary Chicago blues scene: politics of authenticity and Chicago as 'Home of the Blues' city

In cities like Chicago the blues is a vital part of contemporary commodity culture especially with regard to recent tourist marketing strategies presenting the city of Chicago as "Home of the Blues" (Raussert and Seeliger 2011). The blues represents a particularly interesting case study since as musical expression it spans a long history of changes encompassing a leading role as secular vernacular expression in the Harlem Renaissance, a role as continuous backbone for innovations in jazz throughout the twentieth century, a role as major influence on the evolution of rhythm & blues, rock n' roll, and rock music in the sixties and beyond, and as universalist language to express pain and catharsis; in addition, the blues plays a role as background music in commercials and as recent tourist attraction for those who seek "their" black American authenticity in the context of music entertainment. To explore the intersection of cultural and economic politics, it is important to address the relationship between marketing strategies and discourses of authenticity, between tourist and local conceptions of musical authenticity, and the local agency within global tourist industry.

The marketing of Chicago as a city of ethnic diversity and authenticity is a propelling force behind the process of turning blues heritage and music into a vital part of Chicago commodity culture. Recent studies to urban spaces have emphasized postmodern developments of turning cities into sites of illusion and consumption. Christine Boyer (1994) refers to the "city of illusion," Charles Ruthesier (1996) labels the city "a non-place urban realm," and Sharon Zukin (1995) writes about the "city of cultural consumption." Such conceptions of the city are based upon Fredric Jameson's (1991) notion of postmodern urban spaces as a product of late capitalism. Frequently, the marketing strategy of turning the city into a space of consumption is already visible at the gateways into the cities. Chicago Hare International Airport represents one such site at which the process of establishing Chicago as home of the blues lures the arriving traveler and tourist into visiting the various sites of blues heritage and culture as they have emerged in tourism and recent urban planning in Chicago. The walls of the hallway between arrival gates and immigration are decorated with enlarged photographs and paintings of musicians and performances, and tabloids with historical data about music create an immediate aura of blues as an inseparable core identity of the city of Chicago. As Marc Augé puts it, airports along with superstores and railway stations are non-places that "do not contain any organic society" (1995, 112). They are sites of coming and going and invite the traveler and tourist into a realm of "translocality": new conceptions of space, identity, and commodity can flow freely within. The Chicago Museum shop at one of the crossroad sections of Chicago Hare International Airport makes it possible to consume the already installed aura of the blues city in forms of books, CDs, DVDs, photographs, and postcards and invites the traveler and tourist to purchase the blues spirit captured in recordings by home-based artists such as Koko Taylor, Carl Weathersby, and Junior Wells (I bought various items in February 2010).

Figure 5: Chicago city image map.

A series of records released by 'Big Chicago' Records including collections such as *A Chicago Jazz Tour*, *A Chicago Blues Tour*, *Hidden Treasures: Irish Music in Chicago* and *The Chicago Music Scene* underscore the culture-commodity, ethnicity-commodity link infusing the city's self-positioning as tourist attraction. As the example of *The Chicago Music Scene* illustrates, the music scene is ethnically defined and divided into Latin Mambo, Irish Traditional, African American Blues, and Jazz as global blackness. In addition to a selection of representative artists for the various genres the CD booklet also provides a city map, aptly named "club locator map," pointing towards city sponsored music venues and helping the tourist to navigate his way through Chicago night life.

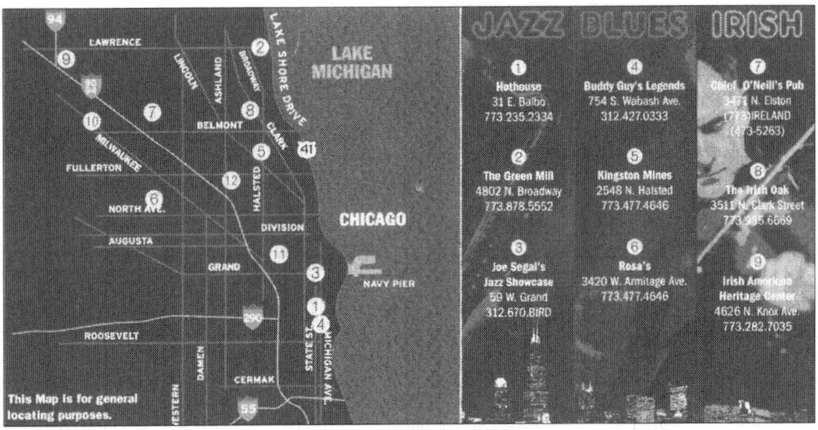

Figure 6: The Chicago music scene map.

Once the tourist has found his way into the heart of downtown Chicago, programs sponsored by the Chicago Office of Tourism and the Department of Cultural Affairs such as Chicago Neighborhood Tours (CNT) offer bus tours departing from the Chicago Cultural Center to numerous ethnic enclaves such as the Jewish commercial areas on Michigan Avenue, Puerto Rican neighborhoods in Humboldt Park and blues heritage sites of the South Side's Bronzeville District. As Grazian aptly puts it, "by capitalizing on exoticized notions of ethnicity, community, and urban space, these 'motorcoach excursions' transform local communities and their landscapes of everyday social interaction into commodified tourist attractions" (2003, 201).

Not surprisingly then the blues scene presented to tourists frequently differs from the contemporary local music clubs. The tourist agenda of Chicago Neighborhood Tours appears eager on accommodating the tourist's quest for black authenticity. When the Chicago blues tour bus hits selected blues joints, we often encounter all black performers on the band stand and their repertoire focuses on blues classics from "Hootchie Cootchie Man" to "Crossroad Blues" during special tourist nights. What is addressed, is the tourist's yearning for familiar sounds and well-established images embedded in a collective exotic blues imaginary. This imaginary is also fed with the unfortunate, yet persistent power of racially charged and essentialist ideas of black sexuality. Color of skin, run-down-juke joints and an ambiance of poverty frame the process of blackening of the tourist's experience of racial difference. If the same tourist may accidentally return to the club another night, outside a regular motorcoach excursion he would most likely encounter a different setting: a suburban, all white band performing recent local blues numbers emerging from current suburban experiences in Chicago.

4.6 Chicago's creation as "authentic blues city" and the transnational tourist

The Chicago blues tours guide the tourist toward a mix of venues that taken together help fabricate and propagate the image of a blues city (my personal experience dates back to the spring of 2013). Within such processes of fabricating we have to remember, as Richard A. Peterson claims, that the authentic is "a socially agreed upon construct in which the past is to a degree misremembered" (1997, 3). Not surprisingly, reconstructions of cultural memory and new creations overlap in building Chicago as blues city. In 1984, the first Chicago blues festival was launched and has become an annual attraction for blues fans, local and global. Naturally, the music festival is hailed as a milestone for preserving Chicago's African American heritage annually. While the clubs and pub venues focus on the performance of live music, institutes such as the Chicago Blues Archives as part of Chicago Public Library and the Chicago Blues Museum institutionalize the blues for the scholarly and public gaze. While the Blues Museum initially had its mobile home in a tent during the early Chicago Blues festivals, then had found a home in a 100-year-old former warehouse in an industrial park in Bridgeport featuring showcases with photos, memorabilia, music instruments, and live performance film footage of blues and jazz artists from the 1920s to the present (cf. Hanson 2007, 70–71). The displays are arranged in a multimedia manner so that the visitor is able to learn about the blues in its cultural and historical context. Next to the Blues Museum, there are stops at gravesites, at music studios such as Chess Studios and the Jazz Record Mart. Now, Chicago is waiting for the opening of its own downtown museum The Chicago Blues Experience whose opening is supposed to take place at 25 East Washington in the near future. With regard to blues clubs advertised, we frequently encounter an overemphasis on fetish to recreate a mythic rural Southern ambiance for the blues setting. The Voodoo Lounge at the Redfish, for instance, poses as black Southern through "Mardi Gras masks, voodoo dolls, cartoon alligators, and other faux swamp kitsch" (32). The Backporch Stage at the House of Blues presents itself as blues ambiance through Hoodoo candles, folk art painting, bas-relief portraits of blues legends from Charley Patton to B.B. King (9). Often these places look like pop-culture replica of real life. These clubs then combine multi-media in their decoration to create a nostalgia-based image of blues ambiance.

While it is true that the blues experienced earlier days of commodification in the heydays of the Harlem Renaissance with the success of Bessie Smith and Ma Rainey whose recordings with Race Records sold immensely and whose tours were propagated with great success not only in the South of the United States, the new phase of commodification is different. Whereas black consumers were mainly addressed and reached through Race Records in the 1920s, the blues bus tours of today and many of the blues clubs in Chicago aim at catching the attention of a transnational audience comprising Japanese, German, and French tourists. Certainly, one of the reasons for this shift is that blues music no longer holds the stronghold position among secular black musical forms as it did in the 1920s. Moreover contemporary conceptions of what blues is differ quite succinctly between black and white audiences. "The blues in the African American community often incorporates soul, funk, jazz, and R&B," as Karen Hanson reminds us (2007, 8). The blues is not only seen as one among many different musical idioms within the African American cultural heritage it is also seen as a developing and changing expression or part of what James A. Snead describes as a process of repetition with variation (1998, 73). What the "transnational tourist" (I am aware of the generalist reduction this expression may contain), as I call him, looks for in blues is an expression of African American authenticity which is based on racial as well as aesthetic expectations. Hence, the blues band the transnational tourist is expecting to find is all-black and, aesthetically, he longs to listen to blues classics such as "Hootchie Coot-chie Man" in a performance style that is generally described as raw, un-polished, and highly expressive. While the blues archive and the blues museum intend to preserve the memory of the origins and developments of blues in a historical perspective, the transnational tourist's exotic ex-pectations tend to confine the blues within a realm of static black musi-cal expression. In that way the transnational tourist is also different from the local listener in Chicago's suburban blues bars in which frequently all-white blues bands as well as ethnically mixed bands perform original song material for their local audiences and in which open jam sessions with audience participation are regular features of the performances.

4.7 Politics of authenticity: politicization and commodification of blues music/differences between African American and mainstream perceptions

The ways blues clubs are decorated in a pop culture replica fashion and the fact that frequently all-black bands are hired to perform on tourist nights raise questions: What is the role of authenticity in the blues tourist industry and how is authenticity fabricated in the commodification of blues music today? Walter Hill's film *Crossroads*, released by Columbia Pictures in 1986, illustrates an important aspect of politics of authentici-ty in the context of black music and debates about cultural proprietor-ship. The encounter between Eugene Martin, white student of classical guitar at the Juilliard School and the African American master of the blues harmonica Willie Brown in the prison hospital re-enacts a frequent call for a re-authentification of black music. At the same time their even-tual trip to the Mississippi Delta performs a tourist journey into the past. In a moody and sardonic way, Willie Brown initially dismisses Eugene Martin's enthusiasm for blues and his search for the one lost song by blues legend Robert Johnson. He mocks him as a want-to-be bluesman from Long Island ridiculing his privileged social condition as a white college boy. He also doubts his musical talent to play the blues – "you are lacking mileage, what you are playing sounds like 'bird-shit'" – and accuses him of art piracy – "you just want to be another one of those white musicians ripping off our musical heritage" (Hill 1986, 18:40–19:10). In his critique of Martin, Willie Brown at the same time fabricates a blues authenticity based upon race, place, and class.

Figure 7: *Crossroads* film scene. Eugene Martin playing the blues for Willie Brown (Hill 1986, 18:30).

Authenticity itself, as David Grazian reminds us, "is never an objective quality inherent in things, but simply a shared set of beliefs about the nature of things we value in the world" (2003, 12). As Grazian explains,

> authenticity […] is always manufactured: like life itself, it is a grand performance, and while some performances may be more convincing than others, its status as a contrivance hardly changes as a result.[…] Like other kinds of stereotypes, images of authenticity are idealized representations of reality, and are therefore little more than collectively produced fictions. (11–12)

When Willie Brown signifies upon the conception of the ideal bluesman, he draws upon collective memory that embraces myths about the origin of blues as well as the legend of Robert Johnson's encounter with the devil at the crossroads. While Willie Brown's narrative highlights that authenticity is fabricated, it also reveals that authenticity is always created for certain purposes and that its fabrication is driven by desire. For Willie Brown, this serves the protection of cultural heritage. In his reclaiming of the blues for black musicians, authenticity becomes an expression of proprietorship, with membership determined not just by musical ability but also by race, class, and geographical belonging. Authenticity therefore becomes a means of asserting the self and claiming one's place in the cultural spectrum of the United States. Thus, Willie Brown's narrative also riffs on at times radical forms of black self-assertion during the black nationalist period of the 1960s, when critics and poets such as Amiri Baraka created the image of African Americans as "blues people" (cf. Baraka 1963) and excluded whites from both the process of participation in and reception of African American art forms. In his narrative about geographical origin, Willie Brown fabricates blues authenticity. He claims the blues as African American property and locates its cradle in the Mississippi Delta, symbolically protecting it from white intrusion when he refuses to reveal his knowledge about the lost Robert Johnson song to Eugene Martin. At the same time the story shows his awareness of the synergistic relationship between culture and commerce, because a recording of the one lost Robert Johnson song would turn it immediately into a part of commodity culture.

The narratives describing the symbols of authenticity in the context of tourism and contemporary local blues clubs differ only slightly from Willie Brown's in that they favor lower class all-black bands and ramshackle juke joints. Regarding the local blues club in the collective public imagination, David Grazian comments sardonically that clubs are considered genuine only if

> [t]hey hire authentic looking blues musicians, who are generally uneducated American black men afflicted by blindness, or else they walk on a wooden leg or with a secondhand crutch; as they are defiantly poor, they drive beat-up Fords and old Chevy trucks, and usually cannot read or write their own name. Their audiences are usually black as well, with the occasional white customer surfacing only if they are sufficiently old, poor, drunk, or blind. (2003, 13)

Why in the first place does the tourist from Japan, Germany, or Russia crave an authentic blues setting? The fact that he does is obvious, as is the fact that the tourist market responds to such desire and offers music tours accordingly. A number of factors coincide, and, as I argue, a fast-paced, increasingly globalized world that imposes changes on local as well as global communities perpetually intensify the longing for so-called "authenticity." Authenticity, in this context, signifies relic and a longing for origin as well as a longing for the real in what Baudrillard labels "simulacrum," a world that constantly fabricates copies and prefers the virtual to the real. Within a culture industry that favors reproduction, reproducibility and repetition for the purpose of selling, what Walter Benjamin has called the work's "aura" seems long gone. But, more importantly, I argue, the strongly felt loss of stability and continuity in times of globalization and transnational migration in places that were once called home in a static sense, has created an ever-increasing urge to find the authentic someplace else. Especially in context of performances, not only the content of the performance seems to play a role for the perceived authenticity, but also, crucially, the identity of the performer. As Timothy Brennan remarks, 'exoticism' is more and more used "in both does and is" (1997, 115) – the touristic demand thereby overlaps interestingly with the culturally radical position of e.g. Willie Brown in the example above. However, the apparent demand for authenticity might not just be an indication for touristic naivety, but could also be seen as a willing acceptation of the deceit, or a willing suspension of disbelief. As Graham Huggan points out it is "paradoxically [...] the very falseness of nostalgia that makes it all the more appealing" (2001, 179), as the "inauthenticity of nostalgia is its own motivating force" (Huggan and Holland 1998, 20).

While authenticity, to cultural critics such as Matthew Arnold, signals culture as juxtaposed to and superior to manufacture, thus becoming an essential quality standard for and within the overall perfection of society, authenticity, in the mind of the contemporary tourist, has turned into a quest for the static and the nostalgic. And when it comes to ethnicity this search is often accompanied by idealized and exoticized visions of unchanged and still functioning communities.

4.8 New agency in the process of commodification: black cultural politics in Chicago

One of the driving forces behind the creation of the Chicago Blues Festival in 1984 was the election of Harold Washington as Chicago's first African American mayor in April 1983. Just one day after his election, on April 30th, the famous blues composer and guitarist Muddy Waters passed away. The dynamics of celebration and mourning within the African American Chicago community helped spur a call for paying tribute to blues music as major manifestation of black cultural expression within the United States and as a signifier for Chicago's urban identity as cultural hub. A growing black political agency due to Washington's election and a steadily increasing presence of black culture within the public spheres of the United States coalesced in this early process of institutionalizing the blues as both cultural heritage and tourist attraction. "The one-stage festival was scheduled for June 8, 9, and 10 and was dedicated to the memory of Muddy Waters. To open the festival Mayor Washington signed an official proclamation extolling the blues as 'the heart and soul of the Chicago experience'" (Hanson 2007, 55). More than thirty years later, the heart and soul of the Chicago experience has turned into a blues industry comprising blues clubs, blues archives, a blues museum, and blues tourist bus tours. Hence, one can distinguish a process of institutionalization but with a clear shift in agency. African American cultural politics, to a large extent, are responsible for institutionalizing and preserving African American cultural heritage. Special blues sessions offered for parents and children illustrate that educational purposes are also part of the process of institutionalization and show that blues has moved from cultural marginalization into the center of American Cultural education. While the blues tours play with the desire for the exotic and do not necessarily support the neighborhood policies necessary to rebuild structures for communal living, the process of commercialization has offered both black and white blues musicians the chance to participate not only in propagating and selling, but also in transforming blues traditions into something new. While the tourist blues clubs may thrive primarily on nostalgia and present the blues as a static and authentic expression of the past, it is in the suburbs of Chicago where local blues clubs and their musicians profit from Chicago's self-created image of a home-of-the-blues city. And while blues may no longer be explicitly "black," it prospers as a developing and changing musical form that gives new creative expression to contemporary urban experience among white and/or multiethnic communities.

In a self-reflective and critical way, we as scholars, too, may have to give up a certain nostalgia for the authentic and stop chasing an abstract aesthetic ideal that does not reflect socio-economic reality. Otherwise, we limit the critical endeavor to understand the changes of musical forms such as the blues as part of an ongoing process of shifting ethnic markers, of changing political and economic agency, and as part of the migration of sounds that has taken on new speed in times of global tourism and transnationalization. The blues has gone white, Asian, and, one might say, global. But selling, as I insist, does not necessarily mean selling out. And while the process of commodification always also signifies an immersion in liberalist-capitalist marketing strategies, it allows for shifts in agency and thus opens venues for self-representation and self-affirmation. While the new Chicago Blues may be white, many of the institutional forces preserving and propagating the blues as an African American art form in Chicago have shifted from white to black. The Chicago Blues Experience museum bound to be opened soon will further strengthen Chicago's old and new sonic identity.

4.9 Reggae tourism in Jamaica

On November 29, 2018, reggae was added to the World Heritage list as an intangible cultural heritage of humanity. UNESCO, the UN's Educational, Scientific, and Cultural Organization, described the Jamaican music genre as "at once cerebral, socio-political, sensual and spiritual" and recognized its "contribution to international discourse on issues of injustice, resistance, love and humanity."[1] While this distinction might push reggae tourism in Jamaica into new dimensions and directions, it was already Bob Marley's global success, posthumously honored with the Grammy Lifetime Achievement Award in 2001 and again in 2012, that

1 "Jamaica's Reggae Music Inscribed on Unesco's World Heritage List." https://www.euronews.com/2018/11/29/jamaica-s-reggae-music-inscribed-on-unesco-s-world-heritage-list.

launched early waves of reggae tourism in Jamaica. Reggae tourism, particularly up until 2016, almost exclusively evolved around Bob Marley as the most iconic figure of reggae music and politics. One-icon tourist policies centered the tourist industry and its Jamaican musical maps on the arguably most important Jamaican artist.

Marley's presence in a global cultural industry that produces records, shirts, caps, cups, and other paraphernalia propels new imaginaries that conflate image, music, and body. A rather homogenizing cultural industry has emerged that explicitly links reggae and Jamaica to the face and body of Marley. Image and sound become equally important for promoting Jamaican music tourism. Popular Marley museum tours take the visitor to various sites in and near Kingston that had personal and professional importance during his lifetime. Part of the tour is a visit to his former house, kept in his original state and staged as the Bob Marley Museum. The tours also include a visit to his various homes and recording studios; the Nine Mile tour includes a visit to Mount Zion where Marley often meditated and composed music. Nine Mile, a small town in the Saint Parish hills, is the musician's birthplace and site of Marley's grave. Hence, individual biography and music history get somehow conflated and simplified. Rastafari indigenous village tours complement the program, showing the contemporary practice of Rastafarian religion and culture in in the hills of the Montego River Gardens. The tour provides access to guiding principles of the Rastafari religion – based on Marley's classic "one love, one heart," – and to a deeper understanding of Rastafari culture.[2]

The dominant presence of Marley as symbol of artistic, political, and spiritual achievement is lucrative for a cultural heritage politics geared toward international tourism. Reggae tourism in Jamaica builds on the star cult hype within popular culture and feeds on a musical authenticity created by fetishizing a one-icon music history. The narrative camouflages the more complex history and diversity of reggae music in Jamaica, however. Reggae represents an amalgam of numerous musical influences, including earlier Jamaican forms as well as Caribbean, North American, and Latin strains. In time, Neo-African styles, soul, and rhythm

2 "Bob Marley Reggae Tours in Jamaica." https://www.viator.com/Jamaica-tourism/Bob-Marley-Reggae-Tours-in-Jamaica/d34-t21621.

and blues from North America were incorporated into the music, gradually transforming ska into rock steady and then into reggae.[3] Initially, a voice of the marginalized, reggae continues to carry important social and spiritual functions in local and global reggae communities. More recently, reggae festivals and concerts such as Reggae Sumfest and Reggae Salute depart from Marley's historical achievement and expand the music's narrative, providing an annual outlet for young contemporary artists. The reggae tourist narrative may further change with the most recently opened Peter Tosh museum, which opened its doors in October 2016 in Jamaica.

Marley's outstanding achievement as a reggae musician still tends to overshadow the rich and diverse history of reggae music in Kingston and on the island. While Marley's music propels local and global cultural industries, the Jamaican reggae tourist industry's central narrative of his artistic achievements functions as a cathartic redemption of Trench Town's history, which is one of poverty, violence, and struggle in everyday social life. Historically, West Kingston and Trench Town in particular became unsafe and conflicted from the early 1970s onwards. The high concentration of mostly impoverished homes made the general area a prime target for the two rival Jamaican political parties – the People's National Party (PNP) and the Jamaica Labour Party (JLP). Already in the mid-1960s, new housing units were built to accommodate growing numbers of political supporters of whichever party was in power. These tendencies soon led to politically motivated violence between supporters of the two rivaling parties beginning in the mid-1970s. Continuing into the late twentieth century, the violence claimed the lives of hundreds of inner-city youth residing in the highly impoverished neighborhoods of West Kingston – including communities like Trench Town. These violent urban politics formed the backdrop of reggae's emergence as a form of musical expression (Rhiney and Cruse 2012, 3). With the advent of reggae, Jamaican music gained unprecedented international fame and recognition. By the end of the 1960s, reggae artists like Bob Marley, Jimmy Cliff, Marcia Griffiths, and Desmond Dekker and the Aces maintained a continuous presence in the British pop charts. International record companies producing reggae albums conquered the US and Euro-

3 "Reggae Music of Jamaica." https://ich.unesco.org/en/RL/reggae-music-of-jamaica-01398.

pean markets, and with the making of The Wailers' album *Catch a Fire* in 1972, reggae established itself as a global musical success in pop history (Stolzoff 2000).

Music history has accredited Trench Town for its significance in the creation of reggae as a distinct and widespread popular musical art form. As the career of Peter Tosh demonstrates, Trench Town has produced several local and world-renowned reggae musicians in addition to Marley and the Wailers. For many people in this poor quarter of Kingston, music provided one of the few avenues for members to create a sense of self and to advance economically. The inner city of Kingston developed a local music scene that shaped Jamaican culture and became an internationally successful entertainment culture. A "subculture of entertainment" emerged that would become the major engine for Jamaican cultural tourism (Rhiney and Cruse 2012, 4). Reggae, no doubt, plays a pivotal role in promoting Kingston and its surroundings as a site of cultural heritage and cultural consumption. The strategy of local agents has been principally to create the Kingston urban imaginary around Jamaica's musical identity (6–7). From murals in the streets to the yard part of the museum, from the home of Marley as a museum to the tour stop at his burial ground, reggae represents the source of the sonic narratives in and around Kingston. The inclusion of Marley in many murals in strategic locations establishes him as an absent/present tour guide for all visitors coming to Kingston. Clearly, Marley's connection to Trench Town was intense. Songs like "Trench Town," "Trench Town Rock," "No Woman No Cry," and "Concrete Jungle" are either located in Trench Town or inspired by its history. Cherishing a one-man narrative leaves out many successful and important local musicians such as reggae pioneer Joe Higgs, Delroy Wilson, Leroy Sibbles, Bongho Hermon, Alton Ellis, Jimmy Cliff, Ken Booth, and Dean Fraser and the I-Threes, as well as vocal groups like the Heptones and the Abyssinians. Tourism keeps the reggae heritage alive, but the cultural heritage politics involved preserve a reductive music history in Kingston, Jamaica. Marley's success story is uplifting for Trench Town as a tourist location but also tends to distort the difficult economic conditions and urban violence that keep haunting this culturally rich section of the Jamaican capital. Reggae's sonic narratives continue to give voice to both phenomena in contemporary music festivals.

4.10 Brazil's rock at home and samba tourism

Festival Culture is at the very base of music's role as an agent in tourism in Brazil. Music festivals in general are potential sites for self-examination, self-realization, the announcement of new policies, the launch of new artistic expressions, challenges to traditions, and the promotion of new music cultures. In the context of the tourist industry, festivals are designed to reflect local tradition and promote and preserve local history and culture (De Bres and Davis 2001). While a festival may contribute to the development of local culture, it also has the potential to connect local and global networks of music production, consumption, and appreciation. McClinchey (2008) explores politics and image, identity and representation, cultural authenticity, and neighborhood differentiation as fundamental concerns for festival promotion and place marketing. Large festivals particularly run the risk of becoming placeless because of increased globalization and commodification of culture. Yet, at the same time, they can turn into fertile cultural and economic spaces for promoting music cultures and traditions, and enhancing their presence in the cultural industry. It seems fair to say that for cities of any size, festivals are signs of development potential and viability. Festivals can contribute to the development of urban identities through performing sonic stories that reconnect citizens, migrants, and tourists to place, culture, and urban life.

While Rio de Janeiro holds many attractions for urban dwellers and visitors, it is its expanding festival culture that decisively shapes music's presence and role for community building and tourist promotion. In the eyes of many beholders, Brazil is the embodiment of music. Brazilian popular culture is increasingly playing an important role in the development of contemporary expressions of mass culture. As Röhrig reminds us, "samba, axé-music and other styles of Brazilian Popular Music (MPB), as well as the martial art capoeira, are not only widely consumed on a global scale, but young people all over the world also dance, play and perform them" (Röhrig Assunção 2003, 159). Brazil's national musical repertoire embraces a unique blend of Native American sound, African rhythms, European harmony, and Latino beats. Brazil's music increasingly goes global and thus also attracts visitors from abroad. Music tourism in Brazil, as advertised by travel agencies outside Brazil, is at first glance primarily samba tourism. Samba is the driving force behind Brazil's carnival. And samba is arguably Brazil's most powerful global player in music. However, samba is also a profoundly and distinctly black cultural expression within the diverse spectrum of Brazilian culture.

An engine of tourism, samba's colonial history as an Afro-descendent musical form often goes unmentioned in tourist promotion for Samba City tours – the genre's black origins forgotten, hidden in the background, or consciously camouflaged. For the alert observer it is evident that samba's central role for carnival is repeatedly downplayed in a continuous process of whitening the carnival spectacle in Rio that annually captures global attention. Black consciousness movements in Brazil have reacted and criticized Brazilian nationalism for underplaying the cultural contribution of African slaves. According to them, "samba and capoeira are, above all, cultural expressions of Africans in the Diaspora, and therefore represent African 'extensions' rather than genuinely Brazilian 'inventions'" (Röhrig Assunção 2003, 159). They call for an extended acknowledgement and recognition of black cultures as vital parts of a hybrid Brazilian cultural panorama.

The effort to revitalize downtown Rio in the context of tourism and heritage politics began in 2009, and as it continues, various black history sites are being exposed and introduced to a country that only relatively recently has begun to esteem its black history. Without a doubt, black cultural and political movements have succeeded in providing more visibility to black cultural heritage in Brazil, the museum on Afro-Brazilian History and Culture in Rio being a most significant marker of a new historical consciousness on a national scale. Encouraged by Brazil's contemporary black movement, Brazil passed a law in 2003 rendering the teaching of Afro-Brazilian and African history and culture compulsory in public and private schools, and current actions aim to upgrade black history teaching materials for schools and universities. Still, black cultures in Brazil struggle to regain full recognition even in the samba-based carnival spectacles, and tourist cultural practices continue colonial politics of mimicry and exclusion (Whitefield 2014, n. pag.). A striking example is the conflicted presence of blackface that continues in Carnival today. As Martha Abreu highlights, historically "the songs of slaves became spectacles at social and religious events organized by the slave-owners, and throughout the nineteenth century they came to be sung and represented, in a stereotyped and derogatory manner, by Blackface performers in the United States and Cuba, and in theatrical reviews in Brazil" (2015, 2). With reference to the music industry she claims that "slave songs, in the form of cakewalks or *lundus* often appeared in the potentially lucrative market of musical scores, in music halls, in theaters and even in the nascent music industry – but not necessarily the black protagonists that those songs depicted" (2).

Abreu's historical example bears relevance even for today. The participation of a blackface group in the 2018 parade in Rio ironically exposes the continuous attempts to whitewash carnival cultures. While black Samba performers are frequently excluded from the parade, Brazil's tradition of blackface resurfaces regularly during Brazil's most visible celebration of national identity and pride. With a nod to the 2018 parade, Kiratiana Freelon points out that "Brazil has its own version of blackface, and it is most often on display during Carnival, when some revelers sometimes dress up as "Nega Maluca," translated as "crazy black woman" in Portuguese" (2018, n. pag.). During the 2018 Carnival in Brazil, blackface also made an appearance in the parades of three samba schools: "Mangueira, Salgueiro and Beija Flor" (n. pag). Contemporary carnival practices extend colonial practices of exclusion and appropriation.

To a large extent, the tourist promotion of the samba experience in Rio de Janeiro separates the music's history from the spectacle culture. As concerns the latter, Rio favela tours take visitors to the poor quarters of Rio largely populated by Afro-Brazilians. These quarters, however, are also the urban sites where most of samba styles emerged and developed, a fact that is largely ignored by the "dark tourism" packages. It seems that music tourism in Brazil pays homage to the Brazilian creation myth – the country's version of Canada's "cultural mosaic" or the U.S. "melting pot." As the dominant national imaginary maintains, Brazil represents a racial democracy. This imaginary emerged from the belief that from the day slavery ended, Brazilians of all colors and ethnic origins were equal. After all, the national political discourse did not enforce either segregation or apartheid; nor did it pass Jim Crow laws. By ignoring huge disparities between free whites and recently freed Afro-Brazilians slaves, Brazilian elites dared to spread an image of a post-racial Brazilian nation. Thus, while it is a cornerstone of national identity that Brazil is racially mixed, the national imaginary is based upon cultural homogeneity. Similarly, Brazilian official music history seems to favor post-racial and post-ethnic narratives to commemorate and promote its sonic cultural heritage and production.

While the annual carnival is certainly the best known example, tourism in Rio de Janeiro develops around a diverse and manifold festival and spectacle culture. As tourist flyers and package tours reveal, samba schools have turned into cultural industries within and beyond carnival culture. A visit to Samba City, now located in warehouses on the earlier trading grounds for newly arriving slaves, gives insight into samba's enlacement with the carnival culture, in particular the Sambodrome parade. In Samba City tourists can take guided tours in which they are introduced to the various instruments of Samba, allowed to preview the sewing of costumes, witness the construction of the floats involved, and given the opportunity to take short samba lessons. Music is presented as entwined in a growing cultural industry geared toward mass entertainment that looks for close connectedness to Western global music flows, such as rock music.

Brazil, therefore, now includes rock music as part of its capital's sonic identity. It was already in 1985, as Brazil turned from dictatorship toward democracy, that Rock in Rio was born (Woods 2017, 230). A ten-day music festival bringing international rock icons such as Queen, AC/DC, Ozzy Osbourne, and Brazilian stars like Gilberto Gil and Rita Lee, this was the first music festival of such size in South America, and it launched an annual festival culture that has established Rio as a rock music tourist destination. This is arguably Brazil's most effective contemporary post-racial, post-ethnic sonic identity that both contrasts and complements the samba imaginary and celebrates Rio de Janeiro as a hub of Western rock music. To date, headlining music icons such as Bruce Springsteen, Bon Jovi, Carlos Santana, Elton John, Neil Young, and Rihanna have given Rio's rock festival global fame. After the first festival in the purpose-built City of Rock, the festival moved to the largest soccer stadium on the globe, the Maracana, and then to Olympic Park, eventually branching out to Portugal and Spain as well. The case of Rio shows that music shapes a dual discourse in Brazilian tourism. In its deracialized dimension, samba shapes an integrationist homogenizing nationalist myth and narrative; Rock in Rio, by placing the South American metropolis in the center of Global North cultural industries, promotes a Brazilian exceptionalism within South America. A diversity of musical sounds and rhythms framed by an expanding festival and spectacle culture creates Rio's fluid urban identity in the twenty-first century. Its sonic identities can be linked equally to local place and global space, depending on the context and commercial, cultural, and political needs involved.

Works cited

Abreu, Martha. 2015. "The Legacy of Slave Songs in the United States and Brazil: Musical Dialogues in the Post-Emancipation Period." *Revista Brasileira de História*. São Paulo 35.69 (June): 1–28. http://www.scielo.br/scielo.php?pid=S0102-01882015000100177&script=sci_arttext&tlng=en.

Appadurai, Arjun. 1996. *Modernity at Large: Cultural Dimensions of Globalization*. Minneapolis: University of Minneapolis Press. Print.

Augé, Marc. 1995. *Non-Places: Introduction to an Anthropology of Supermodernity*. London: Verso. Print.

Banerjee, Mita, Carmen Birkle, and Wilfried Raussert. 2006. "Introduction." *Amerikastudien/American Studies* 51.3: 311–321.

Baraka, Amiri. 1963. *Blues People: Negro Music in White America*. New York: W. Morrow. Print.

Boyer, Christine. 1994. *The City of Collective Memory*. Cambridge: MIT Press. Print.

Brennan, Timothy. 1997. *At Home in the World: Cosmopolitanism Now*. Cambridge: Harvard University Press. Print.

De Bres, Karen, and James Davis. 2001. "Celebrating Group and Place Identity: A Case Study of a New Regional Festival." *Tourism Geographies* 3 (3): 326–337. Print.

De Valck, Marijke, and Skadi Loist. 2009. "Film Festival Studies: An Overview of a Burgeoning Field." In *Film Festival Yearbook 1: The*

Festival Circuit, ed. Dina Iordanova and Ragan Rhyne, 179–215. Glasgow: St. Andrews Film Studies. Print.

Falassi, Alessandro. 1987. "Festival, Definition and Morphology." In *Time Out of Time: Essays on Festival*, ed. Alessandro Falassi, 1–10. Albuquerque: University of New Mexico Press. Print.

Fluck, Winfried. 2007. "Theories of American Culture and the Transnational Turn in American Studies." *REAL Yearbook of Research in English and American Literature* 23, ed. Winfried Fluck and Thomas Claviez, 59–77. Tübingen: Narr Francke Attempto. Print.

Foster, Stephen. 1982. "Exoticism as a Symbolic System." *Dialectical Anthropology* 7: 21–30. Print.

Freelon, Kiratiana, 2018. "Samba and Misogynoir: Will 2018 Be the Last Year of Blackface in Brazil's Carnival?" *The Glow Up*, February 14. https://theglowup.theroot.com/samba-misogynoir-will-2018-be-the-last-year-of-black-1822964862.

Grazian, David. 2003. *Blue Chicago. The Search for Authenticity in Urban Blues Clubs.* Chicago: University of Chicago Press. Print.

Hanson, Karen. 2007. *Today's Chicago Blues*. Chicago: Lake Claremont Press. Print.

Harvey. David. 1989. *The Condition of Postmodernity: An Inquiry into the Origins of Cultural Change.* Hoboken: Blackwell Publishers. Print.

Hill, Walter. 1986. *Crossroads*. Los Angeles: Columbia Pictures. Film.

hooks, bell. 1992. *Black Looks: Race and Representation*. Boston: South End Press. Print.

Huggan, Graham. 2001. *The Postcolonial Exotic. Marketing the Margins*. London: Routledge. Print.

—, and Patrick Holland. 1998. *Tourists with Typewriters.* Ann Arbor: University of Michigan Press. Print.

Jameson, Fredric. 1991. *Postmodernism, or the Cultural Logic of Late Capitalism*. New York: Verso. Print.

Low, Setha M., and Denise Lawrence-Zúniga, ed. 2003. *The Anthropology of Space and Place*. Oxford: Blackwell Publishing. Print.

McClinchey, K. 2008. "Urban Ethnic Festivals, Neighborhoods, and the Multiple Realities of Marketing Place." *Journal of Travel & Tourism Marketing* 25.3/4: 251– 264. Print.

Peterson, Richard A. 1997. *Creating Country Music. Fabricating Authenticity*. Chicago: University of Chicago Press. Print.

Raussert, Wilfried, and Christina Seeliger. 2011. "'What Did I Do to Be so Global and Blue?' Blues as Commodity: Tourism, Politics of Authenticity, and Blues Clubs in Chicago Today." In *Selling EthniCity: Urban Cultural Politics in the Americas*, ed. Olaf Kaltmeier, 41–54. Farnham: Ashgate. Print.

Rhiney, Kevin, and Romain Cruse. 2012. "'Trench Town Rock': Reggae Music, Landscape Inscription, and the Making of Place in Kingston, Jamaica." *Urban Studies Research* 2012: 1–12. Print.

Richards, Greg. 2018. "Cultural Tourism: a research in recent trends and research." *Journal of Hospitality and Tourism Management* 36 (September): 12–21. Print.

Röhrig Assunção, Matthias. 2003. "From Slave to Popular Culture: The Formation of Afro-Brazilian Art Forms in Nineteenth-Century Bahia and Rio de Janeiro." *Iberamericana Nueva época* 3.12 (December): 159–176. Print.

Ruthesier, Charles. 1996. *Imagineering Atlanta: Making Place in the Non-Place Urban Realm*. New York: Verso. Print.

Selwyn, Tom. 1996. *The Tourist Image: Myths and Myth Making in Tourism*. Chichester: John Wiley. Print.

Snead, James A. 1998. "Repetition as a Figure of Black Culture." *The Jazz Cadence of American Culture*, ed. Robert O'Meally, 62–81. New York: Columbia University Press. Print.

Stolzoff, Norman C. 2000. *Wake the Town and Tell the People, Dancehall Culture in Jamaica.* Durham: Duke University Press. Print.

Tucker, Hazel. 1997. "The Ideal Village: Interactions through Tourism." In *Tourists and Tourism: Identifying People and Places*, ed. Simone Abrams, Don Macleod, and Jackie D. Waldren, 91–106. Oxford: Berg. Print.

Urry, John, and Jonas Larsen. 2011. *The Tourist Gaze 3.0.* Los Angeles: Sage. Print.

Weber, Max. 1978 [1909]. *Economy and Society: An Outline of Interpretive Sociology* 1. Berkeley: University of California Press. Print.

Whitefield, Mimi. 2014. "Recovering Rio de Janeiro's Black History." *Miami Herald*, June 22. https://www.miamiherald.com/news/nation-world/world/americas/article1967611.html.

Woods, Sarah. 2017. *Greatest Musical Places of the World.* London: Icon Books. Print.

Zukin, Sharon. 1995. *The Cultures of Cities*. Oxford: Blackwell. Print.

Web

https://ich.unesco.org/en/RL/reggae-music-of-jamaica-01398.

https://www.euronews.com/2018/11/29/jamaica-s-reggae-music-inscribed-on-unesco-s-world-heritage-list.

https://www.viator.com/Jamaica-tourism/Bob-Marley-Reggae-Tours-in-Jamaica/d34-t21621.

5 Music Goes Museum: Cultural Heritage Politics and Museums of Popular Music in Brazil, Jamaica, and the U.S. Deep South

The name of this tune is Mississippi Goddam
And I mean every word of it;
Alabama's gotten me so upset
Tennessee made me lose my rest
And everybody knows about Mississippi
Goddam;
Alabama's gotten me so upset
Tennessee made me lose my rest
And everybody knows about Mississippi
Goddam.
(Nina Simone)

Some call it tamjee
Some call it the weed
Some call it marijuana
Some of them call it ganja.
Never mind, got to legalize it
And don't criticize it
Legalize it, yeah yeah
And I will advertise it
(Peter Tosh)

Negro, acorda, é hora de acordar/
Não negue a raça/Torne toda manhã dia de graça"
[Negro,wake up/don't deny your race/
make every morning a day of grace]
(Candeia)

Former First Lady Michelle Obama is no doubt one of the most distinguished admirers of the Delta Blues Museum in Clarksdale, Mississippi. She presented the 2013 National Medal for Museum and Library Service to the Delta Blues Museum in the East Wing of the White House. A year later, she awarded the National Arts and Humanities Youth Program Award to the Delta Blues Museum and the Delta Blues Museum Band during a televised White House ceremony. Her husband and former U.S. President Barack Obama remains one of the most distinguished visitors of the Bob Marley Museum in Kingston, Jamaica, having visited the museum in 2015 as part of his official visit to the Caribbean island. A large group of political leaders such as Jamaican Prime Minister Andrew Holness, Minister of Culture, Gender, Entertainment, and Sport Olivia 'Babsy' Grange, and officials like William Mahfood, Josef Bogdanovich, Dimitris Kosvogiannis, Omar Davies, Lisa Hanna, Wykeham McNeil were present at the inauguration of the Peter Tosh Museum in Jamaica in 2016; the Jamaican capital Kingston had been declared a Creative City of Music by Unesco a year before. Kátia Bogéa, Director of Brazil's Institute of National Historic and Artistic Heritage, and numerous other high-ranking Brazilian politicians, participated in the opening of the Museo do Samba in Rio de Janeiro, Brazil, celebrating Brazilian samba's 100-year anniversary in 2016. In all three cases, heritage politics and state and regional politics shook hands with popular music culture.

The museum in Rio positions itself as the "safeguard of samba," with a mission statement to "valorize and stimulate samba as culture" ("Rio's Museum of Samba" 2017). Having changed from Centro Cultural Cartola to the Museo do Samba upon receiving UNESCO recognition, the museum receives support from private sponsors, Rio's municipal government, the Ford Foundation, and the Institute for Brazilian Geography and Statistics.

The new wave of music museums shows that afro-descendent music from the Americas has not only achieved global popular success but also gained cultural and political recognition in the late twentieth and early twenty-first century (Taylor 1994; Fluck 2014). The origins of blues, reggae, and samba as musical expressions are geographically distant, but they all emerged from hybrid black cultures in the Americas. The three musical expressions went through years of struggle to achieve cultural, economic, and political recognition. The blues had to liberate itself from its denigration as low-class 'primitivist' folk music and Voodoo-inspired devil's music even within the African American community in the U.S. Reggae had to overcome obstacles of racial and drug discrimination and stigmatization in a Jamaica burdened with class and racial violence as lingering colonial baggage. The history of samba is one of racial and cultural discrimination and persecution in Brazil, especially during the early decades of the twentieth century. Recent shifts in cultural politics and new alliances between heritage politics, tourism, and cultural industries opened new venues for innovative yet conflictive forms of recognition of black music in the Americas. Like music history, the relation between music and the social is narrated anew in the above museums of popular music. While different in content and style, the museums of blues, reggae, and samba reinvent music historiography and the respective social contexts in multi-media museum narratives.

As Sharon Macdonald asserts, "museum studies has come of age" (2006, 1) and "museums have become popular subjects of academic study and critique" (Philipps 2011, 17). Museum studies, however, have paid little attention to museums of popular music. This is all the more surprising given that the flourishing of music museums in recent years shows how much they have gained cultural, educational, and economic relevance. To put popular music into a museum may, at first glimpse, seem like trapping a songbird in a cage. How to combine textuality, performativity, and visual and sonic texts to create a coherent narrative? A central objective of this chapter is to find out which types of narratives emerge in blues, reggae, and samba museums. How do they narrate music and how do they account for the music's historical context(s)? Referring to contemporary memory practice, Rosemarie Beier-de Haan mentions that "we can see changes in the ways in which history is staged, and in how societies (nations or smaller collectivities) remember the past" (2006, 186). For a state like Mississippi and a region like the Delta, with their loaded history, but also for Jamaica and Brazil and their remnants of colonial thinking, this remembrance seems all the more precarious. History always represents both past and present, and "must be understood as being about the present, and as embedded in a continuing cultural practice, as much as about the past" (186). Whereas the study of history is generally dominated by textuality, "museums are shaped by a fundamentally different presentational mode" (191).

This chapter departs from the premise that multimedia narratives are the basis of exhibits in music museums, and with a cultural studies approach, looks at music museums as multimedia narrative sites embedded in heritage and tourist politics. Museums are often devoted to topics and events that appeal to a particular audience. "While open to all, and usually keen to attract a wide section of society, these museums serve communities of interest who share specialist knowledge" (Watson 2007,

3). The visitors to the blues, reggae, and samba museums include scholars of music and cultural studies, nostalgic music fans, tourists on a Highway 61 package or on reggae and samba tours, global travelers, exotic gazers, and kids who take advantage of educational programs to learn how to play the blues, reggae, or samba. The range is as rich as the diversity of blues, reggae, and samba musicians. The expectations and the level of acquired knowledge differ from visitor to visitor and, in general, a museum visit turns site into experience, since "the museum is more than a place. It is a network of relationships between objects and people" (Henning 2005, 11).

In this context, multimedia narratives serve a double purpose: they allow for the coexistence of orality, textuality, performativity, and interactivity. In addition, they provide a rich spectrum of different narrative modes to appeal to diverse groups of visitors. The multimedia concept enhances the narrative options, establishing flexibility and mobility as key concepts for contemporary museum culture. Danielle Rice reminds us that "museums are dynamic, complex social institutions that are constantly reinventing themselves in response to self-scrutiny and external stimulus" (2003, 79).

In my reading of multimedia narratives in selected museums of popular music, I will bear in mind that "most effective studies of museums are those that are informed by history *and* theory *and* practice" (Philipps 2011, 17). As a scholar of African American culture and music, I visited a series of museums in March 2017 and March 2018, traveled various music trails, put myself in the shoes of the museum visitors, searched archives, and talked to visitors and staff in the museums. Research results affirmed that music heritage today is closely linked to cultural tourism, which includes both "tangible and intangible elements" (Soper 2007, 96) from historic sites to sites of worship, folklore, and myth. Blues, reggae, and samba museums, like all sites of popular music heritage, walk a tightrope between the music as performance, entertainment, cultural heritage, political expression, educational tool, and a cultural industry. It is important to note that the strategies chosen depend to a large extent on the economic and cultural conditions in which the selected museums are able to operate.

5.1 The Museo do Samba in Rio de Janeiro

Let me turn to Brazil and the *Museo do Samba* first. The museum delineates a collective history of selected modes of samba music by commemorating different generations of musicians. As its mission statement expresses, the museum positions itself as the "safeguard of samba," with a mission statement to "valorize and stimulate samba as culture" (cf. Grand 2017).

The museum's opening represents a further step in samba's recognition as a national heritage.[1] Overall, samba has been declared by critics and musicologists as a national symbol, the summary of the contribution of the three races that have shaped Brazil, a legacy of the racial democracy that, according to the national myth, has ruled the country since the 1930s. In 1970, the Afro-Brazilian composer Candeia (1935–1978) from Rio de Janeiro released the samba song *Dia de graça* (Gonçalo 2012, n. pag). The song's lyrics contained the above cited symbolic words: "*Negro, acorda, é hora de acordar/Não negue a raça/Torne toda manhã dia de graça*" [Negro, wake up/don't deny your race/make every morning a day of grace]. As an explicit call to action, the composition enlisted samba in the expanding Black Power movement throughout the Americas, a movement that cherished black pride and challenged Brazil's conception of national culture. The song awakened public consciousness to the black roots of samba and the neglected presence of Afro-Brazilian culture. Decades later, the *Museo do Samba* appears on a mission of reconciliation between Afro-Brazilian heritage and Brazil's imaginary of national culture. The *Museo do Samba* celebrates samba's origins and its development over the twentieth century. It draws particular attention to *samba de terreiro*, the meeting spaces for samba, as well as samba music's distinctive composition and beats, known as *partido-alto*, and the development of the *samba-enredo* – the plot used to tell a story by samba schools during parade competitions. As Natasha Pravaz explains, "the discourse on *mestiçagem* is the basis for dominant narratives of national identity and celebrates samba and other Afro-Brazilian cultural forms as

1 "Rio's Museum of Samba Earns National Cultural Recognition." https://riotimesonline.com/brazil-news/rio-entertainment/rios-museum-of-samba-receives-national-cultural-recognition/.

symbols of Brazilianness and racial democracy" (2008, n. pag.). Such political use of culture was initiated by President Vargas's appropriation of subaltern performance genres in his populist project of modernity. At the same time, as expressions of Afro-Brazilian culture, samba, and carnival are contested performances; many celebrate the "racially democratic" character of samba spaces "as a core domain of Afro-Brazilian sociability" (n. pag). In multi-media narrative style the *Museo do Samba* narrates the music's history (histories) anew.

Including a short historical background in its mission statement that addresses the racial urban politics and displacement of the black population, the museum's narrative highlights the black musical heritage's intrinsic connectedness to the slums and, now, *favelas* in Rio de Janeiro at the fin de siècle and the beginning of the twentieth century. The visitor is reminded that descendants of African slaves and Brazilian migrants occupied the inhospitable mountains of the city after being evicted from the city center. With their removal, the early traces of samba music moved from the slums of 1900s central Rio, the houses of *Tias Baianas* [Aunties from Bahia], *Pedra do Sal* [Salt Stones], and *Praça Onze* [Place Eleven] to the *morros* [mountains] and the emerging *favelas*. In the *favelas*, Afro-Brazilian communities celebrating their African heritage gave voice to black musical expression, and samba began to flourish outside the city center. Initially rejected for its black roots, samba returned to the city center of Rio de Janeiro with the carnival parades in 1932.

Overall, the museum's narrative follows a historical line from past to present and emphasizes a strong time-space correlation by reconstructing and reenacting the locations and performances of samba. The museum space creates simulacra of the environment and atmosphere of the *Tias Baianas Pedra do Sal*, and *Praça Onze*. While carnival, strongly shaped by the various expressions of samba, has become a central marker of Brazilian national identity and global promotion of Brazilian culture, samba in Rio de Janeiro continues to face urban exclusion and marginalization. Inspite of the numerous samba schools and tourism in the samba city area, the music remains rooted in the *favelas* and marginalized even in the carnival shows.

With its location right on the edge of the Mangueira community, one of Rio's oldest *favelas* and home to over 50,000 people, the *Museo do Samba* provides a space of recollection and recognition that by means of multi-media narratives addresses the visitor on a textual, visual, sonic, and kinesthetic level, especially when the museum space becomes a site of performance. The visitor encounters a mix of historicity, spectacle, and education. Personifying the history of samba, the museum entrance greets the visitor with a larger-than-life- a sculpture of Cartola, Afro-Brazilian composer and performer of samba who grew up in a favela in Rio de Janeiro and shaped samba in the late 1920s and 1930s. Visualizing the different historical epochs and various modes of samba, exhibit rooms in the museum turn into memorial walls showcasing important samba composers and performers from different generations in archival photographs, concert posters, and aestheticized visual representations. Reinscribing samba into the carnival tradition of Rio de Janeiro, the museum showcases spectacular carnival costumes that invite the visitor to imagine him- or herself as a samba practitioner. Decorated to recall the houses of *Tias Baianas*, "*the house of Tia Ciata*, *Pedra do Sal*, *Plaza Onze*, [and] some neighborhoods such as *Saúde*, *Gamboa*, *Estácio*, *Vila Isabel*, *Pavuna*, among others" (Lopes da Cunha 2018, 6), the museum area provides the link between past and present samba practice by serving as a space for contemporary samba classes and performances. The museum ties samba's history to major urban contexts and changes. While the city of Rio de Janeiro changed radically from the 1920s to the 1940s, "with new technologies, avenues and spaces of leisure and entertainment … samba was also modifying until arriving at its maximum sophistication regarding timbre with the *sambas-exaltação*" (5). Several modalities developed within the genre such as *samba-canção*, *samba-choro*, and *samba-enredo*, but "only three were chosen to become official records as the main arrays of samba in Rio as intangible heritage: *partidoalto samba*, *samba de terreiro*, and *samba-enredo*" (5). The museum's multimedia mix creates storylines that are eclectic and selective in retelling the music's history with the city. Torn between cultural preservation, national heritage politics, and tourist promotion, the narratives in forms of photographs, costumes, and sculptures visualize the black cultural elements of samba without explicitly addressing the racial politics in Brazil of whitening or deracializing both carnival and samba as national cultural identity markers. By emphasizing the close link between the different spaces in which samba emerged and the city of Rio de Janeiro, the dominant narrative is one of urban and national identity not one of racial difference and exclusion. By using the museum space as rehearsal and practice area for contemporary samba groups, the institution puts emphasis on linking past, present, and future. At the same time, the museum embraces an interactive and performative approach to commemorating. The mission includes the wish to turn memory into actual practice of performing and composing samba for future generations. Nostalgia propels the desire to keep samba as 'musicality'alive in a recent and current music scene driven among others by a robust *funk carioca* music industry with DJs and sound systems in the lead; '*Tecnobrega*,' from Belém do Pará, combines Afro-Brazilian rhythms from the State of Pará, such as carimbó and lundu, with popular genres like Caribbean calypso, on electronic drum machines. *Tecnobrega* is an electronic form of popular music and 'Champeta' an electronic urban dance music that blend Caribbean (rap-raggareggae, zouk, soca, calypso) and African (soukous, highlife, mbquanga, juju) rhythms with Afro-Colombian-Indigenous hybrid sounds (bullerengue, mapalé, zambapalo and chalupa); both are played by DJs in elaborate sound systems.

5.2 The Bob Marley Museum in Kingston, Jamaica

The house of the Bob Marley Museum at 56 Old Hope Road, Kingston, Jamaica, was built during the 1800s in the British colonial style of the time. It is located in downtown Kingston in the musicians's former residence that he acquired in 1975 from the Island Record owner Chris Blackwell. The building served as the musician's work place and home until 1981. During his lifetime the home housed Tuff Gong studios, in which Marley recorded regularly. The home was also the site of an infamous attempt on Marley's life in 1976 and thus provides a rich historical and narrative spectrum for museum culture. His wife, Rita Marley, converted the house into a museum space in 1987. The museum space represents an eclectic mix of colonial architecture and flashy pop cultural design, and with the additional theatre, shop, and café-restaurant space provides all requisites for a culturally and economically oriented site of heritage – a prototypical example of contemporary museum culture. The Marley Foundation manages the business matters and creates links between heritage preservation and new cultural industries.

The museum provides insight into the personal history and private treasures of Bob Marley and stylizes his look, appearance, clothing, hairstyle, instruments, and award records in such a fashion that the Marley-in-the-museum turns from a historical figure into full blown reggae legend and icon of contemporary pop music culture. In spite of the mix-media design behind the Bob Marley museum, the narrative never loses its focus on Marley himself. Hence, the narrative is channeled toward building up and conserving Bob Marley's pivotal role for Jamaican and global music culture, as well as his promotion of rastafarianism. The photo gallery, memorabilia, framed records and awards, and showcase with Marley's guitar work with repetition-variation patterns and create a density of visual effect. All narrative threads circle around Marley's iconization in various forms of visual representation. The Bob Marley Museum stands for a highly individualized narrative of cultural heritage. The conceptualization of the overall museum estate ties in with urban cultural and tourist politics in Kingston and also resorts to a variation-repetition pattern outside the museum that strongly visualizes Bob Marley's presence in Trench Town, Jamaican culture, reggae and rastafarianism. From the muraled courtyard to the gallery inside, the museum recreates Marley's presence and cultural impact through a series of images. As iterations of postmodern, serial style pop art, many visualizations of Marley have become so iconic that the image alone appears sufficient to serve as a catalyst for the preservation of Jamaican cultural heritage. The museum's narrative visualizes and reenacts the constant presence of Trench Town's musical flagship, as well as a timeless uplift and musical success story for a society still burdened with coloniality, class differences, political divide, and racial struggle.

The museum space also serves as last resort in Kingston for promoting and selling Marley's contribution to the Jamaican reggae world. Marley gets "only token play nowadays on the local radio and his message appears 'increasingly' lost on today's Jamaican youth" (Foster 2011, n. pag.). The main exhibit of the museum finds further extension in a well-equipped eighty-seat theatre for video, film, and musical performances; and commercial sections that include a gift shop with T-shirts, caps, and mugs, a record shop with a large selection of Marley's and other reggae albums, and the bistro-style restaurant One Love Café. The museum is clearly geared toward international tourism, and its one-icon narrative overshadows the rich diversity of Jamaican reggae and musical tradition. In sum, the museum creates an aura of authenticity by inviting the spectator into the historical rooms in which Marley lived and worked. In addition, the museum unfolds a multi-media narrative in a pop-cultural style that is geared less toward a historical narrative of reggae and more toward iconic celebration and consumption. Commemorating the arguably most iconic figure of reggae music, the museum draws on pop-art serial-style repetition that turns the museum exhibits into a warm-up for consuming culture in the gift and record shop awaiting the visitor. The Marley museum has long lifted the torch for museums around the globe capitalizing on musical nostalgia, giving people a chance to revisit and celebrate music that defined generations.

5.3 The Peter Tosh Museum in Kingston, Jamaica

Compared to the spatially generous Bob Marley Museum in the two-story-house and added exterior spaces, the Peter Tosh Museum occupies a tiny space. It is a one-room exhibit concept. Also, low budget in comparison to the Marley estate, the museum opened its doors on October 19, 2016 to honor the life and work of Peter Tosh, another one of Jamaica's global music legends and founding member with Bob Marley of the critically acclaimed reggae group, The Wailers (Meschino 2016). However, Peter Tosh is a challenging test case for Jamaican heritage culture politics. More rigid in his political attitudes and more radical in his expression of resistance than Bob Marley, he sang "If you wanna live" in Jamaica's National Stadium, "treat me good." While Bob Marley performed reconciliation rituals during the famous 1978 "peace" concert in Kingston, Tosh, also nicknamed "Stepping Razor," publicly confronted socialist Prime Minister Michael Manley and right-wing opposition leader Edward Seaga and a large contingent of well-armed police, voicing bitter social and political truths. His open and direct campaigning to legalize ganja was a long-standing crusade, and his support for the ganja farmers brought class and race issues to the foreground. Tosh experienced prison and torture in Jamaica. It is not surprising that it took Jamaican officials decades to acknowledge his important contribution to Jamaican musical and political culture. The museum honoring him is located at the Pulse Centre on Trafalgar Road in New Kingston, a joint collaboration between The Peter Tosh Estate, Pulse Investments, Ltd., and Andrea Marlene Brown. The museum marks another important stepping stone to embed Jamaican musical culture into larger social, cultural, and economic structures. For instance, local and transnational actors cooperate to link Peter Tosh's musical and political legacy with new directions in the medical use of marijuana. On May 3, 2018 the *GlobeNewswire* in Toronto announced that Jamaica-based cannabis sponsor Marigold Projects Jamaica Ltd. "is set to establish its first medicinal cannabis dispensary and herb house at the Peter Tosh Square, home of the Peter Tosh Museum at the Pulse Centre in New Kingston" (*GlobeNewswire* 2018, n. pag.). The museum narrates Tosh's significant contribution to Jamaica's music and cultural history, but also his social justice advocacy and his position on equal rights, apartheid, and the legalization of marijuana that still resonates around the world. The recently installed Peter Tosh Square is a site for contemporary musical performances and offers to link the museum's heritage with contemporary cultural practice. While not completely linear in its one-room design, the multi-media narrative remains close to Tosh's life line and even addresses his unfortunate murder in a sensitive way. The story starts the roots of the early Wailers and marks a difference to the one-icon narrative of the Marley museum. Tinier in space, the exhibit appears richer in text and condenses information onto plaques. Artifacts like Tosh's custom-made M16 gun and his well-known unicycle, photographs, and audio-visual music examples create a mixed-media narrative that links the personal life story with the community's history and related political struggles. The storyline emphasizes Tosh's posthumous reconciliation with Jamaican culture.

The museum's contents are tastefully presented, covering a surprising amount of ground. As you enter, there is an overview of Tosh's turbulent youth, his involvement with The Wailers, his subsequent gravitation to the Rastafari faith, and the life-changing car accident that resulted in the death of his girlfriend in 1973. His solo years are explored at length, including memorabilia like the golden microphones he got as a gift from friend and Rolling Stones frontman Mick Jagger. Tosh's coveted Grammy, received for his final studio album *No Nuclear War*, is given a prominent place (it was reportedly retrieved from a Massachusetts pawn shop following its unauthorized sale), and the fabled M16 machine gun-shaped guitar that Tosh turned into a musical weapon during his performances on stage. The final section, which covers Tosh's senseless murder in 1987, relays the information of the tragedy sensitively, without sensationalist rhetoric (O'Brien 2016). The museum also holds a little museum shop. While the connection between heritage, tourism, and commodity is evident, Niambe McIntosh, daughter of the Grammy winner and administrator of the Peter Tosh Estate, gives us a political reading: "This is an important turning point in the preservation and advancement of my father's legacy, and the museum will allow my father's message of equal rights and justice to be heard by generations, both young and old" (qtd. in Hill 2016, n. pag.). As her comment highlights, the museum pursues a clear political message within and beyond cultural heritage and marketing policies.

5.4 The blues museums in the Mississippi Delta

The next part of this chapter takes us to the Deep South of the United States, namely to Mississippi, arguably the poorest state but the richest in terms of popular music museums, and leads us back to Nina Simone's song cited in the prologue. "Mississippi Goddam," a song written and performed by one of the most influential African American jazz singers and pianists, captures all too well the national imaginary of the state of Mississippi as a racist backwater. Written in 1964, one of the most turbulent periods in U.S. history, the song was released on her album *Nina Simone in Concert*, a compilation of three performances she gave at Carnegie Hall the same year. The song is Simone's response to the racial violence in the 1960s, in particular the murder of African American Medgar Evers in Mississippi, and the 16th street Baptist Church bombing that killed four black children. Released as a single, the song became an anthem of the Civil Rights movement. Today, the state of Mississippi invests cultural capital to improve its image and reputation. It welcomes visitors with the sign "Welcome to the Home of America's Music." Formerly known as the Magnolia State, Mississippi now officially boasts its reputation as the home of American national music.

Paul Simon's song "Graceland" wistfully anticipated the newly courted imagery. With the lines "the Mississippi Delta is shining like a national guitar," the song helped push an alternative imaginary of the Deep South (*Graceland* 1986). As legend and history has it, the Mississippi region provided the cradle for an African American musical success story from blues and jazz to rock, soul, and hip hop around the globe. Cleveland, Mississippi is now home to the second Grammy Museum in the U.S., after Los Angeles. The state of Mississippi's new welcome sign underscores the fact that the local, regional, and national cultural industries have joined forces to promote perhaps the most tropicalized and demonized state in the nation as an attractive tourist site, home of American cultural heritage, and cherished part of the nation. Music museums, blues trails, and new juke joints have recently emerged to celebrate a new renaissance of the blues. Educational programs, cultural heritage foundations, recording industry, and music festivals join hands to keep the blues legacy of the Mississippi Delta alive.

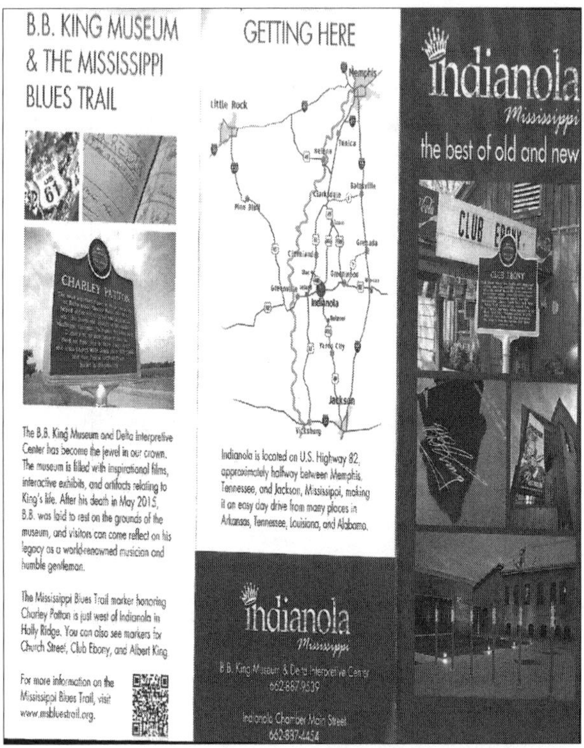

Figure 8: Official flyer of Indianola tourism.

Beginning in the mid-1990s, official tourist companies began to incorporate blues heritage tours into their marketing strategies for the state of Mississippi. In close collaboration with the Memphis Convention and Visitor's Bureau and the Mississippi Division of Tourism, the initiative America's Blues Alley has emerged to draw national and international tourists to Beale Street and music spots in Mississippi. As Stephen A. King describes it, "[s]ince 2000, local and state organizations have emerged to begin the slow and tedious process of coordinating the state's blues tourism industry" (King 2011, 71). The U.S. Senate's designation of the year 2003 as the "Year of the Blues" further boosted the new blues culture in the American South, and King calls this year "the latest major blues revival" (3). With Martin Scorsese's documentary series *The Blues* (2003), which included the work of seven internationally acclaimed film directors and the support of a national education program for schools, the blues gained new prominence on public broadcasting. Mississippi founded its own state Blues Commission, with the objective of creating blues maps and blues trail markers along the highways and major roads, helping "travelers in locating blues-related sites" (King 2011, 68).

Figure 9: Mississippi Welcome Sign (© Wilfried Raussert 2017).

The first blues museum opened its doors in Clarksdale in 1979, founded by local library director Sid Graves. In 1999, the Delta Blues Museum was bought by the City of Clarksdale and became a "stand-alone" museum in the former freight depot of the Illinois Central Railroad. A small budget museum, the Delta Blues Museum emerged from a grassroots interest to commemorate the blues heritage of the Delta. More endeavors by institutions and private citizens have emerged in recent years. Many museums have been added to the musical map of Mississippi, including the Rock 'n' Roll and Blues Heritage Museum in Clarksdale, the Highway 61 Blues Museum in Leland, the River City Blues Museum in Vicksburg, the Greenwood Blues Heritage Museum and Gallery in Greenwood, and the elaborate $15 million high-tech B.B. King Museum in Indianola, King's hometown (cf. King 2011, 17).

Stephen A. King writes that in most of the museums in Mississippi, the blues is hardly remembered as a political medium of struggle and protest: "The social conditions that gave rise to the development of the blues, and the harsh realities experienced by many Mississippi blues musicians, are conspicuously absent" (2011, 140; cf. Duffett 2015). The focus is on entertainment and escapism. However, Paige A. McGinley argues that such a view misses the mark:

> It may seem as though the front-porch-styled stage at Beale on Broadway, like the stages at the well-known chain House of Blues, represents something of a Disneyfication of blues – late capitalist fiction that bears no resemblance to the 'real thing.' But such a claim only holds water if we neglect the intensely intertwined histories of blues performance and the popular theater – histories that throw into question the premise that the 'real thing' ever was. Far from descending from authenticity into theatricality, black vernacular blues have moved in tune and in time with theatrical conventions since the moments of their earliest emergence. (2014, 4)

While King emphasizes the importance of historical context, McKinley's comment recalls the close link between the blues, showbiz, and performativity throughout the history of the blues. The truth lies somewhere in between. One could argue that the blues looks back on a long trajectory of interpretations and reinventions: Ralph Ellison defined the blues as catharsis (Raussert 2017, 96). Thinkers like Amiri Baraka interpreted the blues as weaponry for resistance and political struggle. Musicians from the Rolling Stones to U2 claimed the blues as foundation of youth and rock culture. B.B. King considered the blues the very soul of America. These are metaphysical, political, and cultural enhancements of the blues beyond its sheer musicality. With respect to blues heritage cultures, it comes as no surprise, according to Jennifer Craik, that cultural tourism involves marketing "cultural sites, events, attractions, and/or experiences" (1997, 113). The blues museums in the Delta are no exception.

The history of tourism may have begun with the works of Alan Lomax. When he visited Clarksdale in the early 1940s, he described the town as "the cotton capital of the nation, locus of the biggest cotton plantation in the South" (1993, 28). People called the largely African American business area "the bustling 'New World'" and Clarksdale "the social and amusement center for all the plantation workers from 30 miles around" (28). The current visitor to Mississippi faces a rich map and network of music museums, music sites, and blues trails that fill the former cultural gap between the cities of New Orleans, Louisiana and Memphis, Tennessee. Whereas New Orleans – the Crescent City and mythic cradle of jazz – has held a high place in American tourism before and after Hurricane Katrina, and Memphis lures visitors with sites such as Elvis Presley's Graceland and the famous Beale Street, Mississippi had been absent from the musical map of the cultural tourist industry for a long time. However, Mississippi has gained new momentum by being part of the Highway 61 Blues Trail, which has become part of package tours.

As King argues,

> as a subset of a larger international tourism industry, blues tourism encompasses a complex series of often interrelated and multidimensional public- and private-sector organizations, from blues museums to chambers of commerce to local entrepreneurs which attempt to draw tourists to specific areas […] (e.g. Chicago, Memphis, the Mississippi Delta) to experience the culture or heritage of the blues. (2011, 3)

In his analysis, blues tourism has become a pivotal example of cultural tourism. Indeed, "the growth of cultural tourism and the expansion of the heritage industry aim at satisfying a growing longing for the archaic and authentic in times of rapid global changes" (Raussert and Seeliger 2011, 43).

In its analytical part, the following section selectively explores two mixed-media narratives of the blues by looking at the Delta Blues Museum in Clarksdale, Mississippi and the B.B. King Museum in Indianola, Mississippi. Both museums form part of "transmedia storytelling" (Jenkins 2006, 17–19) which is the creation of a narrative through multiple documents belonging to various media. These storyworlds are channeled through narrative progression. Bharat Dave reminds us that "[h]eritage as a heterogeneous terrain is simultaneously framed by and frames the perspectives through which it is viewed. Some vehicles through which heritage are sustained include the preservation of material culture, emulation, preservation through surrogates and copies, documentation, simulation and rituals" (Dave 2007, 41). The storyworlds in a given music museum also include various sites like exhibit rooms, film sections, music auditoriums, a music bar and/or coffee corner, and, not to forget, the museum shop.

The narrative progressions in these blues museums show different ways of guiding the visitor through the exhibition spaces. Both museums share an agenda that writes a new history of the blues as quintessentially American music and creates an image of the South as a unity of land, music, and people. Both draw upon multimedia narration combining acoustic, visual, performative, and interactive material. Nonetheless, they differ decisively in their narrative progression.

5.5 The Delta Blues Museum in Clarksdale, Mississippi

As William Ferris put it, "if there is a musical navel or crossroads for Mississippi Delta Blues, it must be on the streets of Clarksdale, a city that lies in the heart of the region known for the blues" (2009, 143). From his own field work, he gathers that "generations of young black musicians fled surrounding plantations and moved to Clarksdale, where department stores, restaurants, barbershops, and WROX radio station provided hope and excitement" (143). The Delta Blues Museum invites the sojourner on an imaginary journey into the blues world of the Delta, presenting a multimedia and non-chronological narrative that introduces him or her to the many blues trails, markers, and sites that mark the effervescent and ephemeral history of blues. The Delta, with its unpopulated, open, and raw landscape, makes it difficult to provide solid touchstones to remember. Conversely, it provides the ideal setting for mythmaking. The blues trail is an invitation to track the roots and routes of blues events, sites, and performers. It accepts the gaps and holes in the blues map and allows multiple gravesites, myths, and storylines to exist side by side. The basic structure of the Delta Blues Museum shows the same conceptual approach to history and memory: it is fundamentally interactive. Through the exhibited props and costumes of performers, the museum becomes a dressing room for the sojourner to slip into their blues' persona. The exhibition strips the blues of a definitive history. Each tourist becomes a performer in their own right to revisit the Delta's musical contributions to the world of blues.

Figure 10: Entry of the Delta Blues Museum, Clarksdale, Mississippi (© Wilfried Raussert 2017).

The Delta Blues Museum throws the visitor into an open museum space with multiple directions to choose from. As Hillier and Tzortzi point out, reflecting on spatial politics in museums, "[one] alternative is to design space in such a way that sequences are more localized, and interconnected so as to allow visitors to choose different paths and construct their own pattern of experience" (299). This also aptly describes the open choreography of the exhibits. Not surprisingly, the Delta Blues Museum marks the starting point of the blues trails and tours in the Delta. Its open structure invites the visitor to engage with the history of the blues imaginatively and creatively. In its seemingly arbitrary arrangement of instruments, paraphernalia, festival posters, photographs, and blues art work, the museum provides more simulacra than "the real thing." The costumes, T-shirts, and props create a theater setting in which visitors can imagine themselves in the clothes of a blues musician or blues festival participant. The visitor's performative acts are part of the exhibit's strategy to fill the absence of "the real thing." Upon entering the exhibit space, the visitor encounters a sign attesting to the unity of music, land, and people in a new imaginary of Mississippi. The opening walk leads the visitor through a sequence of showcases on the left that display musical instruments from Africa. On the right, the visitor is faced with a series of festival posters displaying the recent blues festival history in Clarksdale (Sunflower Festival, Juke Joint Festival) in the twenty-first century. Past and present appear simultaneously to the viewer. Similar to the spatially open structure, the timeline follows no chronological sequence. The viewer's imagination wanders between African past and American present. With the juxtaposition of ancient African instruments and contemporary festival posters, the museum exhibits tradition and variation side-by-side (reminiscent of the Bantu sense of time, which is essentially a place-time). As visitors enter deeper into the exhibit space, they can decide which direction to turn to next. Photographs, posters, paraphernalia, and instruments point to a male-dominated blues history (female blues musicians are conspicuously absent) and introduce the visitor to renowned blues musicians like Robert Johnson, John Lee Hooker, Charly Patton, and Muddy Waters in abstract fashion. A firm material grounding of the blues occurs in the extended section of the museum, which is now home to the remnants of Muddy Waters's cabin. Opposite the cabin, there is a long glass window gallery with a series of portrait busts of blues musicians in the newly extended part of the museum, directing the visitor's gaze outward. Looking through the window, the viewer faces a Robert Johnson mural in contemporary street-art-style. This view demonstrates that the Delta Blues Museum is primarily designed to attract the visitor to the city of Clarksdale, the Delta region, and its related blues trails. Like the Muddy Waters sculpture whose gaze looks out on the urban surroundings, the extended window front marks another substitute of "the real thing." It points to the reinvention of the blues in the streets of Clarksdale. A street-art painted Cadillac with Delta motifs and a mural of perhaps the most mythologized Delta blues musician, Robert Johnson, illustrates the new mobility of blues tropes.

Figure 11: Robert Johnson Mural in Clarksdale, Mississippi (© Wilfried Raussert 2017).

Starting at the car, the viewer's gaze drifts to the porch, sign, and walls of the Ground Zero Blues Club, a site plastered with posters of recent and up-coming blues events. The Ground Zero blues club complements the museum with a performative space for regular local gigs and concerts during the the Juke Joint Festival and the Sunflower blues festival. One of the owners of the recently created juke joint is the African American actor Morgan Freeman. The blues club carries a name with heavy symbolical reference: In the context of the new Mississippi Delta music culture it suggests that this is the location of a new beginning, showing visitors that they are in Clarksdale just at very beginning of their journey into blues history.

Figure 12: Ground Zero Blues Club in Clarksdale, Mississippi (© Wilfried Raussert 2017).

The gift shop at the Delta Blues Museum provides a map for the visitors containing shops, galleries, other museum spaces, gig locations, hotels, and bars in Clarksdale that are intended to intensify the new blues experience. Memorial walls holding the names of local and regional blues performers and site markers throughout Clarksdale provide further information to fill the absence of a lost blues culture. A clear homage to the blues as the backbone of modern and contemporary popular music culture, the new blues in Clarksdale is more geared toward cultural production than cultural heritage. The objective is to culturally and economically create a new blues culture that cherishes its heroes in artistic production like blues painting, sculptures, and blues literature. This creates a new blues imaginary geared to uplift the region from its image of racist backwater and attract new business into Clarksdale and the surrounding region. The deserted Paramount Theatre, with one letter suggestively missing in its marquee, hints, however, that "authentic blues" still remains a myth. Creating a new cultural industry and integrating it into the community appears to be a slow process.

Figure 13: Paramount Theater, Clarksdale, Mississippi (© Wilfried Raussert 2017).

As McGinley points out, "the Delta is filled with sites that multiply the grounds upon which blues tourism stakes its claims of priority. These multiple birthplaces, multiple crossroads, and multiple headstones establish blues' historical sites as transitive or processual, rather than substantive or positivist" (2014, 199). The visitor to the Delta becomes a surrogate: "The irreducible profusion of transitive sites of blues tourism in the Mississippi Delta sets authenticity in motion, constructing it as always mobile and multiple" (199).

Authenticity itself, David Grazian reminds us, "is never an objective quality inherent in things, but simply a shared set of beliefs about the nature of things we value in the world" (2005, 12). As he explains, "authenticity [...] is always manufactured: like life itself, it is a grand performance, and while some performances may be more convincing than others, its status as a contrivance hardly changes as a result. [...] Like other kinds of stereotypes, images of authenticity are idealized representations of reality, and are therefore little more than collectively produced fictions" (11–12).

5.6 The B.B. King Museum in Indianola, Mississippi

The B.B. King Museum, however, is a different story. While the Delta Blues Museum and the Delta blues heritage trails lack a cohesive center, the B.B. King Museum has established itself as the arguably most frequented tourist attraction in the Delta. The museum opened its doors in September 2008 and "reflects, in part, the vision of the B.B. King Museum Foundation and Board, a heterogeneous group made up of whites and African Americans who wanted to develop a 'critical tourist designation in a struggling region'" (King 2011, 17). Economically, the B.B. King Museum project raised $15 million to install its multimedia, high-tech version of a blues museum. Its narrative concept provides a mix of a chronological and circular narration that aims for unity and cohesion. The museum is the result of an active engagement of B.B. King to commemorate and celebrate the blues as an African American cultural achievement. Throughout his music career, King artistically and economically supported academic programs and cultural heritage endeavors to collect and preserve blues material. His collaboration with William Ferris helped build the Blues archive at the Center for the Study of Southern Culture at the University of Mississippi. King eventually donated his blues record collection, thus providing the base for the largest blues collection in the world today and "an academic home of the blues" (Ferris 2009, xi). He also worked with Ferris during Ferris's appointment as chairman of the Endowment of the Humanities in the 1990s and helped bridge the scholarly world and the world of music. The B.B. King Museum, in part, draws on collections of texts, music, and paraphernalia from King's own collection. The floating signifiers that characterize much of the exhibition in the Delta Blues Museum find solid ground in the life story of B.B. King and his mission to preserve his community's oral culture.

Figure 14: The B.B. King Museum, Indianola, Mississippi
(© Wilfried Raussert 2017).

The museum's narrative also pays tribute to the well-intentioned but ambiguous overall state policy of reconciliation. While the history of the often state-sanctioned racial divide and racial violence in Mississippi before the Civil Rights movement is absent from the Delta Blues Museum and most trail markers, the B.B. King Museum does integrate pointed references to racial segregation. In B.B. King's memories in the "Jim Crow on the Road" section of the exhibit, the years of rigid segregation remain alive.

Figure 15: "Jim Crow on the Road Showcase," B.B. King Museum (© Wilfried Raussert 2017).

The museum's overall narrative, however, emphasizes the blues as a national music and promotes racial reconciliation by emphasizing an essential unity between land, music, and people. The narrative of the B.B. King Museum seeks closure; it does so through the incorporation of King's graveside into the terrain and through a circular structure that frames King's life as a success story of the blues. The museum's narrative emerges from the privileged position of the protagonist. It provides historical material such as citations, photographs, and material objects from King's guitars to tour bus fragments. In addition, King's last tour bus now serves as a vehicle for blues tours in the Delta and is parked outside the museum. Whereas the narrative in the Delta Blues Museum needs to compensate for the lack of material available to document the music and life story of Robert Johnson, the B.B. King Museum can select which pieces to show and in which narrative sequence. The B.B. King Museum thus occupies a unique role in the network of blues trails and sites in the Delta region: it represents the ultimate success story of the Delta blues on a global scale.

Figure 16: Guitar 'Lucille' and B.B. King tour bus
(© Wilfried Raussert 2017).

The B.B. King Museum invites the visitor on a circular tour. The first room of the exhibit is a small movie theater that plays a documentary about King's return to Indianola, Mississippi and his personal and musical links to the Delta. After watching the film, the visitor enters a room that travels back in time to King's childhood and the Delta region's cotton industry. The structural concept is a circular and chronological narrative. The narrative voice – spoken and written – is King's. Information boards spread throughout the exhibit rooms contain citations from King that allow a first-person autobiographical narrative to guide the visitor on his tour. The personal narrative is carefully linked to the history of the land and music. King's musical progression from the Delta through Memphis to Las Vegas and around the globe is embedded in a success story of the blues as the musical backbone to the development of rock. Each section is self-contained as part of a chronological life narrative, welcoming the viewer with a particular design. If the visitor moves from room 1 to room 2, the optics signal a move from a rural to an urban setting. The visitor encounters a fragmented model of a tour bus which indicates the long years on the road. A replica of an early B.B. King recording studio links the archaic blues world to the recording, production, and the music market.

The showcase holding King's Grammys marks a final point of recognition and fame. After leaving the section with two interactive stations that allow viewers to practice their own guitar skills alongside B.B. King, visitors enter a second small movie theater. The final film highlights King's recognition by the white music world, showing concert gigs with U2 and Eric Clapton. The museum's films construct a narrative of King's trajectory from local recognition to worldwide fame. They connect his global success story with his rural beginnings and create a story of interrelated roots and routes.

One could say that the B.B. King story gives a positive answer to the open questions and uncertainties along the blues trail through the Mississippi Delta. The B.B. King Museum depicts a bluesman finally coming home, telling his own story, and creating his own house of the blues. King's narration in the opening film is a conscious performance of (re)integration. It links the protagonist with his Mississippi birthplace and the Mississippi region with the nation at large. It presents him as a master of performance in musical and verbal skills. He gives his voice to an oral reenactment of the music's history in the Delta. The thrill is gone – to borrow from one of his late blues titles – but the music's history continues to shape cultural, economic, and racial politics. B.B. King always favored a dialogical and relational approach to the white world. The narration in the autobiographical style speaks through King, and his reconciliatory voice is surely welcomed by the state policy of reconciliation.

5.7 Heritage in local and global commodity culture

As Dallen Timothy and Gyan Nyaupane emphasize, "Being inherently about power and control, heritage is often utilized intentionally by governments [and other institutions, *addition mine*] to achieve some measured ends and to demonstrate their authority over people and places" (2009, 44). The blues museums are part of a larger strategic use of music heritage to inject new economic and cultural life into the region and are bound in networks of different social actors. These networks also dictate to differing degrees the narrative and spatial politics within the museums. The tourist industry is a major factor in the process of promotion and conceptual orientation. It is also important to consider that "cultural commodification frequently results in the loss of control over cultural resources as outside agents begin to capitalize on cultural elements that belong to others" (62). Like most contemporary museums, the blues museums in the Delta include museum shops. For sale are CDs and scholarly books, but primarily musical paraphernalia, decorated cups and plates, as well as T-shirts and posters picturing blues musicians and festivals. The racial exotic is sold neither in the B.B. King Museum nor in the Delta Blues Museum. In tune with the overall conceptualization of the Mississippi blues map and trails, there is a tendency to sell merchandize – objects, texts, images – that reinforce the mystique about the holy trinity of land, music, and people, enigmas of the life of Robert Johnson, and the like. Certainly, Mississippi blues tourism, with its multiple gravesites, also taps into what Philipp Stone describes as a "dark tourism" that "may be referred to as the act of travel to sites associated with death, suffering and the seemingly macabre" (146).

It is common knowledge that 'selling ethnicity' and 'selling the exotic' are both frequent economic manifestations as well as powerful marketing strategies. Both phenomena have emerged from a strong multiculturalism and pluralist cultural orientation in discourses within contemporary urban society. Various discourses intersect when postcolonial studies, the academic institutionalization of ethnic studies, the ever-expanding tourist industry, and consumer interest in ethnic products (food, fashion, and culture) meet, collide, and fuse in global economic and cultural exchange. The processes behind 'selling ethnicity' are manifold, as are the questions about agency revolving around the processes of commodifying self and other. As black feminist scholar bell hooks argues, "[t]he commodification of otherness has been so successful because it is offered as a new delight, more intense, more satisfying than normal ways of doing and feeling" (1992, 21). The person who buys a ticket to a blues tour is probably drawn by a mix of nostalgia and curiosity, and yearns for a rural black culture as the other to modern society. "Within commodity culture," as hooks has it, "ethnicity becomes spice, seasoning that can live up the dull dish that is mainstream white culture" (21). Although a racial dimension is conspicuously absent from the museum narratives, we can assume that for the majority of visitors on the blues tours, it is a given that the roots of blues are black music and experience.

A mix of heritage as invention, a new blues cultural industry, free-floating markers, and mysterious stories multiplied by speculative gravesites describe the Delta blues world as exotic. Foster reminds us that fully domesticating the exotic would limit its potential to create surprising effects, thereby assimilating it "into the humdrum of everyday routines" (1982, 21–22). Thus, while the exotic may be used to assimilate and neutralize cultural differences, it also signifies a comprehension of difference and diversity that is inevitably distorted and always uncontrollable. Hence, assimilation is necessarily limited and, as Huggan points out, "as a system, then exoticism functions along predictable lines but with unpredictable content; and its political dimensions are similarly unstable …" (2001, 14). Moreover, it is necessary to take into consideration that political as well as economic changes bring about shifts in agency that influence who, where, when, and how 'the exotic' is sold and for what purpose beyond simply gaining profit. In this context, Huggan speaks of a whole "cosmopolitan alterity industry" that relies heavily on selling not only ethnicity, but "exotic myths" (xiii). While the products of this industry are mainly geared for easy consumption, Huggan points out that the commodification of cultural difference is seldom one-sided because it also, at least partly, aims to fulfil an educational function. But even though the alterity industry offers a space of agency to Huggan's "postcolonial exotic," its target groups are nevertheless "mostly, if not exclusively, […] the capitalist societies of the West" (68). In the B.B. King Museum and juke joints like Ground Zero in Clarksdale, we encounter sites of multiple agencies involving black and white actors. A common interest is certainly the economic push for the region combined with a sincere appreciation of the blues as cultural expression. It is true that "the simultaneous invocation and erasure of black suffering is as central to blues tourism as it was to the [blues] revival, as is a post-civil rights-era desire for racial reunion and reconciliation" (McKinley 2014, 185). This tightrope walk is a risky one. McKinley may be right in warning us that "the constant minimizing of the state sponsored history of violence toward its black residents" may ultimately undermine "the goal of racial reconciliation that many in Mississippi seek to achieve" (185).

Mississippi's music museums encompass a complex set of politics. The museums are sites of heritage, nostalgia, education, and worship. Backed by museum awards and financial investment, they embody an overdue recognition of African American cultural achievements in the Mississippi Delta. The Delta Blues Museum, despite its low budget, has gained national recognition by winning numerous awards in recent years. In 2009, the museum's website was awarded a 'gold' certification in the Corporate Design, Small Budget, Multimedia category, by the Southeastern Museums Conference.[2] As the current director Shelly Ritter proudly shares, in 2013 the museum "was honored by the Institute of Museum and Library services with a National Medal for Museum and Library Service, the nation's highest honor for museums" (qtd. in "Delta Blues Press Release" 2017). As mentioned earlier, in November 2014, Michelle Obama presented the National Arts and Humanities Youth Program Award (NAHYP) to the Delta Blues Museum and the Delta Blues Museum Band in a White House ceremony ("Delta Blues Museum Acceptance" 2014). The B.B. King Museum and The Delta Interpretative Center received further economic endowments with a grant from the Mississippi Art Commission in 2011 and 2012.[3] These awards highlight that the blues museums in the Delta look not only to the past, but also decisively to the future. The multimedia narrative designs provide storyworlds that integrate the blues museums into a larger network of local and global music tourism. But beyond this, the museums are projections into the future on the level of educational training for the younger generations and as catalysts for a growing entertainment and cultural industry intent on reinventing the blues one more time. The multimedia narratives draw on diversity, and at the same time, they open doors to think, paint, write, and perform the blues anew. After all, the blues, since its beginnings, has always been performative in both its musical and its political dimensions.

---

2 http://www.deltabluesmuseum.org/about.asp.

3 "B.B. King Museum and Delta Interpretive Center Receives Mississippi Arts Commission Grant." https://myemail.constantcontact.com/B-B--King-Museum-Receives-Mississippi-Arts-Commission-Grant.html?soid=1102037602779&aid=nQIFWJqDLV0.

5.8 Coda

Popular music in the museum transcends the sonic and propels a new cultural industry closely tied to tourism, heritage culture, educational programs, merchandise, serial art, and design production. Samba, reggae, and blues turn into ways of remembering and ways of living, deeply entrenched in nostalgia for music that once shaped the identities and identity politics of generations. As musical expressions, samba, reggae, and blues can celebrate long deserved cultural and political recognition. By historicizing the music, museums of popular music tend to narrate eclectic success stories and downplay the harsh social, cultural, and economic conditions in which these musical forms once emerged, however. This move is by design, to create museums with high popular appeal. While these cultural heritage strategies also aim to reconcile cultural and racial divides and foster new regional and national consensus, the new chauvinist and racist rhetoric voiced and tolerated by the current political leaders in the U.S. and Brazil shows that a stronger presence of context and history in these museums of popular music may be a much needed corrective to the current mixed-media success stories in which samba, reggae, and blues get deservedly enshrined in the realm of global popular music.

Works cited

Beier-de Haan, Rosemarie. 2006. "Re-Staging Histories and Identities." In *A Companion to Museum Studies*, ed. Sharon Macdonald, 186–197. Malden: Blackwell Publishing. Print.

Craik, Jennifer. 1997. "The Culture of Tourism." In *Touring Cultures: Transformations of Travel and Theory*, ed. Chris Rojek and John Urry, 113–136. London: Routledge. Print.

Dave, Bharat. 2007. "Virtual Heritage: Mediating Space, Time and Perspectives." In *New Heritage: New Media and Cultural Heritage*, ed. Yehuda E. Kalay, Thomas Kuan, and Janice Affleck, 40–52. New York: Routledge. Print.

"Delta Blues Museum Acceptance of National Arts and Humanities Youth Program Award (NAHYP) in White House Ceremony." 2014. Delta Blues Museum online edition, November 10. https://www.deltabluesmuseum.org/nahyp-award-acceptance-2014.asp#.

"Delta Blues Press Release." 2017. Delta Blues Museum online edition, May 15. https://www.deltabluesmuseum.org/newsletter/pressrelease-May-2017.asp.

Duffett, Mark. 2015. "Why I didn't Go Down to the Delta: The Cultural Politics of Blues Tourism." In *Sites of Popular Music Heritage. Memories, Histories, Places*, ed. Sara Cohen, Robert Knifton, Marion Leonard, and Les Roberts, 239–256. London: Routledge. Print.

Ferris, William. 2009. *Give My Poor Heart Ease. Voices of the Mississippi Blues*. Chapel Hill: The University of North Carolina Press. Print.

Fluck, Winfried. 2014. "The Concept of Recogniton and American Cultural Studies." In *American Studies Today: New Research Agendas,* ed. Winfried Fluck, Erik Redling, Sabine Sielke, and Hubert Zapf. Heidelberg: Winter. Print.

Foster, Anthony. 2011. "Bob Marley: The legacy wanes but the cult is going strong." *Times Malta* online edition, May 11. https://www.timesofmalta.com/articles/view/20110511/world/Bob-Marley-The-legacy-wanes-but-the-cult-is-going-strong.364722.

GlobeNewswire. 2018. "Scythian Announces Marigold's Exclusive Agreement with Jamaica's Peter Tosh Museum," May 3. https://www.globenewswire.com/news-release/2018/05/03/1495958/0/en/Scythian-Announces-Marigold-s-Exclusive-Agreement-with-Jamaica-s-Peter-Tosh-Museum.html.

Gonçalo, Júnior. 2012. "The Politics that result in samba music." *Pesquisa: Sounds and Ideologies* Vol. 192. https://revistapesquisa.fapesp.br/en/2012/02/27/a-política-que-acaba-em-samba/.

Grand Junior, João. 2017. "Culture and Development Connection: The Case of *Rede Carioca de Rodas de Samba*." http://portal-assets.

icnetworks.org/uploads/attachment/file/99719/02_ARTIGO-JOAO-JUNIOR_EN_AF.pdf.

Grazian, David. 2005. *Blue Chicago: The Search for Authenticity in Urban Blues Clubs*. Chicago: University of Chicago Press. Print.

Henning, Michelle. 2005. *Museums, Media, and Cultural Theory*. Berkshire: Open University Press. Print.

Hill, Maralyn D. 2016. "Reggae Legend Peter Tosh to be Honored With Opening of New Museum in Kingston, Jamaica This October." *The Epicurean Explorer* online edition, August 16. http://theepicurean explorer.com/2016/08/reggae-legend-peter-tosh-honored-opening-new-museum-kingston-jamaica-october.html.

Hillier, Bill, and Kali Tzortzi. 2006. "Space Syntax: The Language of Museum Space." In *A Companion to Museum Studies*, ed. Sharon Macdonald, 282–301. Malden: Blackwell Publishing. Print.

hooks, bell. 1992. *Black Looks: Race and Representation*. Boston: Southend Press. Print.

Jenkins, Henry. 2006. *Convergence-Culture: Where the Old and New Media Collide*. New York: New York University Press. Print.

King, Stephen A. 2011. *I'm Feeling the Blues RIGHT NOW: Blues Tourism and the Mississippi Delta*. Jackson: University of Mississippi Press. Print.

Leonard, Marion, and Robert Knifton. 2015. "Engaging Nostalgia: Popular Music and Memory in Museums." In *Sites of Popular Music Heritage. Memories, Histories, Places*, ed. Sara Cohen, Robert Knifton, Marion Leonard, and Les Roberts, 160–173. London: Routledge. Print.

Lomax, Alan. 1993. *The Land Where the Blues Began*. New York: Pantheon Books. Print.

Lopes da Cunha, Fabiana. 2018. "Samba locations: An Analysis on the Carioca Samba, Identies, and Intangible Heritage." In *Latin Ameri-*

can Heritage: Interdisciplinary Dialogues on Brazilian and Argentinian Case Studies, ed. Fabiana Lopes da Cunha, Marilene dos Santos and Jorge Rabassa, 3–20. Cham: Springer International Publishings.

Macdonald, Sharon. 2006. "Introduction." In *A Companion to Museum Studies*, ed. Sharon Macdonald, 1–12. Malden: Blackwell Publishing. Print.

McGinley, Paige A. 2014. *Staging the Blues. From Tent Shows to Tourism*. Durham: Duke University Press. Print.

Meschino, Patricia. 2016. "Peter Tosh Museum Opens Today in Reggae Icon's Hometown: 'We Have Barely Scratched the Surface.'" *Billboard* (1st January): n. pag. https://www.billboard.com/articles/news/7564564/peter-tosh-museum-reggae-icon-kingston-jamaica-photos.

O'Brien, Andrew. 2016. "A New Peter Tosh Museum Has Just Opened In Jamaica." (7th November): n. pag. https://liveforlivemusic.com/news/new-peter-tosh-museum-opens-in-kingston-jamaica/.

Phillips, Ruth B. 2011. *Museum Pieces: Toward the Indigenization of Canadian Museums*. Montreal: McGill-Queen's University Press. Print.

Pravaz, Natasha. 2008. "Hybridity Brazilian Style: Samba, Carnaval, and the Myth of 'Racial Democracy' in Rio de Janeiro." *Identities: Global Studies in Culture and Power* 15.1: 80–102. https://www.tandfonline.com/doi/abs/10.1080/10702890701801841.

Raussert, Wilfried. 2017. *Diferentes conceptos de tiempo en diálogo: el blues, el jazz y la novela afroamericana*. Translation By María Luisa Arias. Guadalajara: Universidad de Guadalajara. Print.

—, and Christina Seeliger. 2011. "'What Did I Do to Be so Global and Blue?' Blues as Commodity: Tourism, Politics of Authenticity and Blues Clubs in Chicago Today." In *Selling EthniCity: Urban Cultural Politics in the Americas*, ed. Olaf Kaltmeier, 41–53. Farnham: Ashgate. Print.

Rice, Danielle. 2003. "Museums: Theory, Practice, and Illusion." In *Art and Its Publics: Museum Studies at the Millenium*, ed. Andrew McClellan, 77–96. Malden: Blackwell Publishing. Print.

"Rio's Museum of Samba Earns National Cultural Recognition." 2017. *The Rio Times* online edition, 18 January. https://riotimesonline.com/brazil-news/rio-entertainment/rios-museum-of-samba-receives-national-cultural-recognition/.

Soper, Anne K. 2007. "Developing Mauritianness: National Identity, Cultural Heritage Values, and Tourism." *Journal of Heritage Tourism* 2.2: 96. Print.

Stone, Philip R. 2006. "A dark tourism spectrum: Towards a typology of death and macabre related tourist sites, attractions and exhibitions." *Review* 54.2: 145–160. Print.

Taylor, Charles. 1994. "The Politics of Recognition." In *Examining the Politics of Recognition*, ed. Amy Gutman, 25–73. Princeton: Princeton University Press. Print.

Timothy, Dallen J., and Gyan P. Nyaupane. 2009. "The Politics of Heritage." In *Cultural Heritage and Tourism in the Developing World. A Regional Perspective*, ed. Timothy Dallen J. and Gyan P. Nyaupane, 42–54. London: Routledge. Print.

Watson, Sheila. 2007. "Museums and Their Communities." In *Museums and Their Communities*, ed. Sheila Watson, 1–24. New York: Routledge. Print.

Websites

http://www.deltabluesmuseum.org/about.asp.

https://www.deltabluesmuseum.org/.

https://www.deltabluesmuseum.org/nahyp-award-acceptance-2014.asp.

https://myemail.constantcontact.com/B-B--King-Museum-Receives-Mississippi-Arts-Commission-Grant.html?soid=1102037602779&aid=nQIFWJqDLV0.

6 Music in Literature and the Arts: Black Historiographies

Music shapes expressions of cultural production in the Americas that are far beyond the domain of sound. Outside of pleasure and entertainment, music serves as a sonic medium for rethinking time and space. Rhythmically, it triggers cognitive processes, evokes memory, and inspires vision. Hence, it appears natural that it also functions as a matrix, template, or source of inspiration for writers and artists to rethink the social, helping them challenge concepts of linear time, reinvent temporality as a social force, and place individual and collective identities in relation to process and change (Bauman 2000; Ferris 2009; Raussert 2017).

Blues, calypso, jazz, reggae, samba, soul, and hip hop are exemplary music genres that emerged in the Americas from different loci of enunciation like Brazil, the Caribbean, and the U.S., infusing cultures around the globe with adaptable polyrhythmic "models of time." Black cultures from Africa to African diasporas in the Americas in particular have kept music at the center of performing "alternative histories" and "utopian futures" (Chaar-Pérez 2013, 29). With its global presence and formative influence on music styles and cultures, black music has established itself as a central reference point for endurance, creativity, and agency within cultural production.

African American music seems to be not only one of the most ubiquitous art forms today, but also among the most propelling media in the way it boundaries aesthetically, geographically, politically, and ideologically. And African American music continues to feed the literary and historical imagination of African American writers in the twenty-first century. As recent books like Hooper, Sanchez, and Simanga's *44 on 44. Forty-Four African American Writers on the Election of Barack Obama 44th President of the United States* show, the dialogues between music and literature, music and politics, and music and history thrive in contemporary times. The book presents poetic, literary, philosophical, and journalistic reactions by contemporary black writers to Barack Obama's election as the first African American President of the United States of America.

In "First President and First Lady," Michael Simanga wistfully comments on the dancing couple Michelle and Barack Obama: "we watched them dance/deep inside a sweet soul music trance/her head on his shoulder/his hand on her back/movin/to a promise/to love/each other/ and us" (2011, 139). Sharan Strange, in her poem "Inaugural," continues analogies between blues, vision, and writing by relating change and vision to expressions of blues rhythm:

> How to capture the sagacity of a swagger announcing change/like the tremolo of a new Blues … /How to croon … the rhythm's shift-slight enough, though enough/that we might dare to breathe, loosen, lean toward/one another, cultivate a human wealth?/My breath quickened by that historic exchange, that wealth. (2011, 94)

Antoinette Brim links past and future to the singing voices of people watching the inauguration of Barack Obama in "We Winter Still": "Consider the changing sky. Today is the prayer, every prayer sung in a field, juke joint, church or jail. Schoolhouse, roadhouse" (2011, 96). She concludes: "Every wail of every whip now joins the chorus of mothers and the swell of our ancestors to sing: Ooh child, things are gonna get easier" (96). And in "The Day the Earth Stood Still," E. Ethelbert Miller connects jazz and sacred music with the idea of historical change and triumph: "Many of us. Maybe millions went down/to the Mall to hear Obama./I stood behind Duke Ellington and Billy Strayhorn. Duke was composing on the spot" (2011, 103). He concludes expressing renewal and supreme feeling: "Sacred music was in the air. I wanted to lift every voice and sing/I wanted to hear the thunder and watch the first drops of a new American rain" (103). The above poems respond to a threshold moment in Black American history, and they all reflect the event's social and political significance through musical tropes.

How music inspires the historical imagination in literature and the arts, how it shapes representations of temporality, and how it thus also challenges the grand narratives of coloniality and modernity (Mignolo 2011) in the cultural productions of African American, African Canadian, and Caribbean artists and writers is at the core of this chapter. Exploring music's central role for remembering history and envisioning new historiography in other art forms, these writers draw upon the long trajectory of oral cultures performing history in black cultural contexts.

Writers like Ishmael Reed, Ntozake Shange, Afua Cooper, and Lillian Allen, and visual artists like Aaron Douglas and Adrian Hayles adopt musical techniques, themes, and strategies to create transcultural visions of history in literature and the arts. Musically inspired literary historiographies have also been penned by writers such as Nicolás Guillén, Langston Hughes, Zora Neale Hurston, Miguel Covarrubias, Alejo Carpentier, Mário de Andrade, Toni Morrison, and Julio Cortázar, to mention but a few. These examples suggest a continuous and expanding trans-American influence of music on other areas of cultural creation.

6.1 Black modernism and music-inspired historiography

Already in the early decades of the twentieth century, poems, manifestoes, and novels by writers like Zora Neale Hurston, Langston Hughes, Nicolás Guillén, and Mário de Andrade reflected the significance of music for rethinking culture, the social, and the nation. For instance, in *Motivos de Son* Guillén uses the rhythm of black Cuban street vernacular to express images and imaginaries of popular culture and expose the Africanness of Cuban culture and history. In his poems, Guillén (1988) creates explicit links between the Cuban present and the African past, juxtaposing and superimposing various temporalities. The flow and sound of *son* music becomes a tool for reflecting Cuban identity as a fundamentally mulatto identity. In her work as anthropologist and novelist, Hurston embraces music as an expression of endurance and life celebration. In *Mules and Men* and *Their Eyes Were Watching God* she builds on oral tradition and music to write black womanist history and rewrite modernism through the lenses of folklore and music. For Andrade, Brazilian culture translates the polyrhythmic simultaneity of black music into a "cannibalistic" matrix that is all-embracing, eclectic, and prone to creating new cultural expressions by creolization and syncretism.

Visual artists like Aaron Douglas, Romare Bearden, and Miguel Covarrubias likewise turned to music – blues and jazz tropes in particular – to express newly emerging black cultures and identities in a transcultural fashion. For many writers and artists music became a reference point to rethink black cultures and histories in the American hemisphere. Slavery, free trade, human migration, and cultural flows have had a tremendous impact on shaping cultures in the Americas from Brazil to the Caribbean, from the Gulf cultures of Veracruz, Mexico, to the Georgia islands, from the Deep South of the United States to African Canadian communities in Toronto. Throughout the Americas mobilities have brought forth displacement, relocation, and transversal movement. Within these flows music from colonial times onward has functioned as a means of orientation in time. It has continuously reinvented itself to express the sense of rupture caused by frequent dislocation and oppression. In response it has fostered imaginaries of cultural and temporal connectedness, rootedness, and belonging.

Music's relation to and expression of temporality is naturally foremost rhythmical. Afro-descendent musical forms like blues, jazz, reggae, son, samba, calypso, and hip hop bear close relation to African rhythms and African time concepts. African cultures generally view time from a holistic perspective. Accordingly, past, present, and future coexist simultaneously. Historically, Egyptian culture did not even provide an abstract term for time. An understanding of time has always been directly related to specific events or actions and likewise to a specific place in which they occurred (cf. Baker 1972). As the strong presence of rhythmic improvisation in black musical expression underscores, intensity and simultaneity characterize the experience of happening and place. Time, overall, remains neutral until an incident marks its significance. Likewise, the notion of an abstract temporal sequence is absent from African thinking (cf. Achtner, Kunz, and Walter 1998). Thus, black dance helps extend our understanding of temporal differences between African and Western rhythms. Rhythmic elements in African music are multidimensional in space and time. Unlike European dances, which signify bodily movement in space, African rhythms call forth a dance movement that is bound to a certain place.

Kinetic energy in African dances expresses a polycentric movement on the spot. African American jazz dance and other Afro-descendent dance patterns in the Americas fuse polycentric movements with spatial movements. For instance, in jazz dance, motion, and locomotion are differentiated. While the first category refers to the polycentric movement of the body-head, shoulders, chest, arms, legs, and pelvis form independent centers of motion, the second category – jazz walks, for instance – express a movement from one point to another (Rosenberg 1995).

Rhythm in general reflects the way in which music is organized within a spatio-temporal dimension and signifies a sequence of unaccented and accented beats and their relation to one another.

Music of Afro-descendent origin embraces cross-rhythms, offbeat-phrasing, and polymetric progression. Musicians of blues, calypso, and jazz frequently play around the beat. These changes of the pulse open up numerous possibilities for individual improvisations. And these changes also put musicians in the position to express the experience of time and place rhythmically (cf. Raussert 2017, 6–8). This superb proximity to the experience and expression of time makes polyrhythmic music a good reflector of multiple uneven temporalities, synchronicity, and temporal ruptures in literature and the arts. While many writers and artists directly collaborate with musicians, others use music as intertextual reference and medium for reflecting temporality. Black music in the Americas, as it has developed in multiple music genres, is profoundly polyrhythmic and a result of multiple transculturation (Lenz 2002, 2011; Raussert and Isensee 2008). As music continuously interacts in context, music's mobilization of the social and historical affects various cultural expressions. Its mobilization regularly takes place in boundary-crossing processes between media and cultures, turning contact zones into productive sites for the creation and performance of temporality and historiography. It seems safe to claim that since the Jazz Age black musical forms have had an increasing impact on the developments of the written and visual artistic expressions in the Americas and on how they reflect history and historical entanglements.

6.2 Black modernism: Music in Aaron Douglas's and Langston Hughes's rendering of temporality and history

At the turn of the twentieth century, a call for a gathering of intellectuals in London to explore the conditions of peoples of African ancestry living in Africa, North and Latin America, the Caribbean, and on the African homelands, captured the attention of black activists, artists, and intellectuals. Along with the hope for overcoming allegations of "Negro inferiority" in scientific circles, a Pan-African movement emerged to confront global issues of colonial discrimination against peoples of African descent. Involved thinkers from different peoples of African ancestry shared the belief that historical experience, cultural values, social anxieties, and hopes united many black cultures around the globe. London's Pan-African conference echoed the impact of the "American Negro Exhibit" that had taken place a few months prior at the *Rue des Nations* in Paris. This exhibit combined books, visual art, photography, industrial, and fine arts products to celebrate black cultural and industrial production of post-slavery U.S. The common theme among black intellectuals was the celebration of black equality and productivity "once the veil of slavery had been lifted" (Powell 2002, 24). Pan-African ideas gained momentum and encountered a new exotic fascination with the black continent and its diasporic offspring in the so-called "African craze." An ambiguous embrace and clichéd representation of African cultural expression pushed artistic expression in music, cabaret, visual arts, and literature to new horizons. U.S. America found itself in the middle of reinventing modernity, nourished by the desire for a truly "American" aesthetic and vernacular. The Harlem Renaissance, also called the New Negro Movement, formed an important black contribution to this new American aesthetic. Blues and jazz music, with the emergence of "race records," became central expressions of a modernist way of living. The "New Negro" seemed the perfect metaphor for a society and culture at a moment of intense rupture, change, and transition. While the Harlem Renaissance cherished many artistic collaborations between poets, painters, photographers, and musicians, for many, the 'New Negro' entity was first of all a "mood, or a sentiment" in which black cultural workers were acknowledged as equal partners in the world of cultural production (42).

The emergence of "The New Negro" as a powerful metaphor was also the result of comparisons in intellectual, political, and artistic circles of the time. The metaphorically constituted other, "The Old Negro" provided the backdrop against which "blackness" entered into dialogue and was renegotiated. As metaphorical constructions, both "The Old Negro" and "The New Negro" held the potential for multiple significations and were exposed to different performative, theatrical, artistic, and literary interpretations during the early decades of the twentieth century, particularly in the manifold cultural productions of the Harlem Renaissance. On various levels, "The Old Negro" signified what Athanasiou and Butler refer to as "the dispossessed" (2013) while, in different ways, "The New Negro" suggested agency and empowerment. "The Old Negro" stood for political conservatism and social accommodationism, while "The New Negro" represented renewal and change (Bernard 2011, 273). The basic metaphorical constitution of these *comparata* signals the complexity of a new synthesis of "blackness" (tertium). Comparisons between the "The Old Negro" and "The New Negro" inevitably involved questions of tradition and innovation. The debates entailed drawing comparisons between imaginaries of African, African American, and Euro American cultures and histories, a move that challenged long-standing paradigms of difference and hierarchy.

The painter Aaron Douglas was arguably the most prolific African American painter during the Harlem Renaissance who addressed temporality, history, and historical entanglements in modern visual arts. He was also one of the first black painters to use masks and develop "masking" strategies as a counterpoint to white hegemonic visions of blackness. And black musical motifs became central tropes for Douglas's historical imagination. "The New Negro" in Douglas's work came in hybrid African and African American attire. Douglas's artistic inclinations included experimental modernist forms like Braque's and Picasso's cubism, Winold Reiss's modernization of folk painting, and African art (Mehring 2016). In many of Douglas's paintings, faces are modelled on masks of the Dan people of Liberia, and strong bodies are depicted abstractly, in silhouette. By concealing individuality, he unfolded a painterly vision of collective narrative and history. Inspired by the use of masks in Cubism, he employed masks to look beyond Eurocentric visions of modernity and compare contemporary U.S. black culture with African cultures, particularly Egyptian. Commercially, the cubist mask opened a path into the American art world; he was commissioned to paint murals for the New York Public Library.

The murals demonstrated that Douglas saw himself as equally capable of adapting African art as the European masters of cubism, Picasso and Braque, were at the time. Yet, Douglas, inspired by new Mexican nationalism in muralist painting, was not primarily paying homage to Western modernist art. He used the mask in cubist style to celebrate black art and history from ancient Egypt to contemporary Harlem. His figures of African and African-American art and folk art merge in mask and silhouette-like presentations of blackness. His painterly practices of comparison built on the *comparata* Egypt and Black America(s), not on the *comparata* Black America(s) and Europe. Douglas created a complex vision of "The New Negro," presented in *Aspects of Negro Life*, a series of four murals sponsored by the federal Works Progress Administration (WPA). *Song of the Towers* (1934)[1] is arguably the most modern of the four. The murals collectively outline black history from its African roots through the Great Migration; *Song of the Towers* tells a story of the conflicted black struggle with modernity. Complex and multilayered, *Song* of *the Towers* relies on graphic designs as well as patterns of geometric shapes, and thus speaks through the practices of cubist painting. People and things appear in abstracted fashion. Dominating the mural's center are concentric circles, framed by jutting rectangular prisms. Through this careful improvisation of various forms, he unfolds a narrative that catapults the black figures into the whirlwind of modern, urban machinery. In a comparative, yet, relational way, cubist abstraction shows the dispossessed and the rising, the human and the machine, the left behind "Old Negro" and the arising "New Negro" in the center. In setting his black figures in a mix of Cubist-inspired dynamic forms, Douglas reflects the black origins of modernist art. The black figures, however, are still struggling to claim their position in the setting of modern metropolis. *Song of the Towers* wistfully celebrates the triumph of black artistic expression in the Harlem Renaissance: Douglas shows himself mastering Cubist modernism; the black musician in the center alludes to the musical blackening of Harlem and America during the heydays of race records in the 1920s. As the title of the mural series makes clear, music is a central inspiration for Douglas's work. The image of the saxophone player represents a moment of ascent. Music is portrayed as an act of empowerment. Held high, the saxophone forms an extension of the human body and links the body and architecture as towering forces. Douglas makes cubist geometrical forms "swing," and like the polyrhythmic nature of jazz, his mural captures the simultaneity of different temporalities within modernity.

Nevertheless, amid the struggle against history, the wheel of modernization, and the towering presence of metropolitan architecture, the upward-gazing central black figure suggests that a complete black arrival is still "a dream deferred" (Hughes). This interpretation is further

---

1 https://www.wikiart.org/en/aaron-douglas/song-of-the-towers-1934.

supported by the contours of the Statue of Liberty, which appears far in the distance. The mural intricately compares dream and reality, myth and history; the result is abstraction and ambiguity. Douglas displays mastery of form working in African, African American, and European traditions. Like other literary figures of the Harlem Renaissance, he used the master form to unfold a self-reflexive discourse on blackness, noting that all murals manifest diversity within blackness and relate different shades of blackness to a long trajectory of African diaspora history. The mastery of form gives Douglas the authority to speak for the modernist community, yet raises a racial critique of modernity. In the state-commissioned mural *Song of the Towers*, Douglas cannily inserted a critical yet self-empowering black modernist vision. By comparing and relating different figures and stages of African-American history with the emergence of the jazz-age modern metropolis, he reveals the cracks within modernist American utopian design, while pushing a concept of "the New Negro" that lies outside of Euro-American practices of comparing white versus black. His black figures demonstrate a difference within blackness in terms of history and identity. Africa and the African diaspora in the Americas serve as *comparata* reference points, and the visualization of rhythmic links becomes Douglas's technique for the creation of black historical entanglements.

Douglas consciously promoted a new vision of the social and cultural through black difference. Resulting from an editorial board meeting of the Harlem magazine *Fire!!*, he penned the following artistic statement in 1925 (cf. 2002):

> We are group conscious. We are primarily and intensely devoted to art. We believe that the Negro is fundamentally, essentially different from their Nordic neighbors. We are proud of that difference. We believe these differences to be greater spiritual endowment, greater sensitivity, greater power for artistic expression and appreciation. (qtd. in Kirschke 1999, 122)

Reflexivity characterizes Douglas's manifesto. The gaze is clearly inward. It is a reflection on the black self, the black collective, and their relatedness. His comparison between black and white cultures is based on gradual difference, and he concludes in an affirmation of black superiority. Douglas's emphatic message signals a difference along the lines of emotion, spirituality, and aesthetics, while presenting a radical reversal of white supremacist paradigms. The above quote from Douglas also shows that the emphasis on black differences as an essentialist strategy helped to challenge normative practices of comparison that order the world.

Figure 17: The Song of Tower Mural by Aaron Douglas (© Douglas Foundation).

While "masking" strategies meant an appropriation of white master models, the performativity within it allowed for in-group reflectivity, a multitude of affirmative "New Negroes," and a chance for new comparative models within black cultures. The primary models for performativity in the Harlem Renaissance were blues and jazz, their multi-layered call-and-response patterns providing a matrix for comparison and dialogue. Musical cross-overs created an understanding of deep and complex entanglements between black cultures beyond colonial histories and their racial baggage, and produced black modernist temporalities in cultural productions in the Americas.

Musically-inspired literary historiography also characterizes the poetics and work of Langston Hughes. He was arguably the most powerful poetic voice of the Harlem Renaissance and a pioneer in creating transcultural visions of black identity and historiography for the Americas. His poem "I Too" was first published in 1926. Similar to Douglas, Hughes also chose a masking strategy to challenge the white modernist discourse of Anglo-Saxon America. Practices of comparison work on the level of authorship and citizenship in the poem and are embedded in a reflective mode. Hughes already refers in the title to Du Bois's notion of twoness and double consciousness. Declaring himself the darker brother, the black poetic voice claims blood ties, citizenship, and communal belonging. As the short poem unfolds, Hughes describes a scene of ubiquitous domestic racism, against which he sets the initial comparison. In free verse form the black poetic voice, apparently that of a domestic servant, addresses his master's household. The comparison expressed through "darker brother" is simple and powerful. "The New Negro" is conceived in communal, political, and aesthetic terms: "How beautiful I am" (1926, 257). Hughes moves a step further from the familial/social/aesthetic to comparisons on the level of authorship. Writing through the mask of Whitmanesque self-celebratory expression and adopting the latter's free verse style for African American poetry, Hughes compares himself as poet and citizen to Walt Whitman, the canonically acclaimed founding father of modern poetry. The domestic servant's poetic voice not only claims black equality; it celebrates the beauty of blackness in Whitman's style of self-embrace.

The Whitmanesque mask provides an authorial space for bold cultural and social claims. Hughes uses it to refer to the blackening of America through music from slavery to the Jazz Age. The lines "I, too, sing America" claim black authorship for modern American artistic expression. At first glimpse simply an intertextual reference to the famous opening of Whitman's "Song of Myself," the verb, within the context of the Harlem Renaissance, expresses a celebration of African American oral and musical culture. Hughes's textual practice of comparison lifts African American folk culture into the realm of modernist American literature and culture. His singing voice is as biblical as Whitman's, but his sources are the spiritual, blues, and jazz. Underneath the surface of the Whitmanesque modern American utopia, Hughes inserts dissidence (laughter) and expands utopian ideals with his strong belief in social change based on and expressed through musical performativity.

> I, too, sing America.
> I am the darker brother.
> They send me to eat in the kitchen Music in Literature and the Arts
> When company comes,
> But I laugh,
> And eat well,
> And grow strong. … (1926, 257)

In "The Negro Speaks of Rivers" (1920, 259), Langston Hughes reflects on a long trajectory of black "high" culture by linking African and Black American cultures. "I heard the singing of the Mississippi when Abe Lincoln went down to New Orleans" is emblematic for Hughes's reference to music as a source of alternative black historiography. The oral and sonic bases of black cultures provide the foundation for comparing, challenging and reinventing culture and history. In a self-reflexive way, Hughes contemplates the freedom of the black writer and compares him to the vanguard, experimental, and ground-breaking group of artists and writers in his black vanguard manifesto "The Negro Artist and the Racial Mountain" (1926). "We younger Negro artists who create now intend to express our individual dark-skinned selves without fear or shame … . We build our temples for tomorrow, strong as we know how, and we stand on top of the mountain, free within ourselves" (91–95).

Hughes's reference to the "top of the mountain" has biblical and secular connotations. It compares the black artist to the prophet Moses on the mountain and to John Winthrop and his futurist model of a city upon a hill. Yet, Hughes's poetry breaks out of linear temporalities; his poetic translations of polyrhythmic jazz incorporate alternative temporalities, insisting on entangled yet distinctly black imaginaries of history. As the examples from Hughes and Douglas show, music and its strong cultural presence in society presented a superb medium in the Harlem Renaissance for rethinking modernity and its understanding of time by making reflexivity on blackness and its historical trajectory a public concern.

6.3 Revisiting music and history in black literary postmodernism: Ishmael Reed and Ntozake Shange

As critics commonly agree, postmodernist thought rejects grand narratives. This includes hegemonic narratives of coloniality and modernity. Postmodernism instead favors an anti-authoritarian attitude when analyzing the world and its cultural products. Put differently, postmodernism is frequently presented as distrustful of any entity or agency that tries to regulate what people can or cannot do, and postmodernist thinkers and artists share a deep distrust of any agent or element that attempts to fix the meaning that something might possess (Raussert, Lantz, and Michael 2020). Because of history, many African American, Afro-Latin, African Canadian, and African Caribbean writers naturally share particular distrust of narratives dictated by the colonizing and ruling classes. While postmodernity is perceived as the age of relativity, fragmentation, and uncertainty, many black thinkers in the Americas consider these things inherent to a human condition shaped by power division, racist discrimination, and psychological as well as physical violence, from the slave trade to today's politically sanctioned racism.

Postmodernism appears to share a belief system in which metaphysical, ethical, and epistemological relativism reign. For black writers working in the postmodernist mode like Ishmael Reed and Ntozake Shange, such a metaphysical condition represents threat as well as chance. A relativist thought system may open doors for further racist demarcation at the same time that it provides venues for challenging established narratives in creative and experimental ways. While postmodernism is often understood as questioning modernist beliefs in renewal and futurity (or apocalypse), writers like Reed and Shange created experimental literary work at a time when the Black Power movement and radical ideas of black agency and affirmation crisscrossed the Americas. Sun Ra provided cosmic visions for an Afro-futurism, and soul provided a sonic model for black identity across national boundaries (Van Deburg 1992). Free jazz in the style of Ornette Coleman and John Coltrane became a demonstration of black musical and intellectual power to transcend by radical experimentation and voice a political message. Strangely enough, the turbulent times of the 1960s and 1970s witnessed a rise of black confidence, agency, and authority that in its literary and artistic expressions drew on postmodernist devices, yet at the same time subverted postmodernity's sheer playfulness and relativism by linking experiment with ethics, fiction with history, and poetry with the social.

Looking at the impact of funk and soul on black liberation, and the dialogues and commonalities it brought forth in Afro-diasporic communities throughout the Americas, it becomes evident that black cultural production works within and against the postmodern grain of relativization, fragmentation, and individualization of cultures. Postmodern literature is commonly perceived as a form of literary expression which is marked, both stylistically and ideologically, by a reliance on such literary conventions as fragmentation, paradox, unreliable narrators, often unrealistic and downright impossible plots, games, parody, dark humor, and authorial self-reference. If the prospect of a break with the past does not come true, then time does not move forward, profound changes do not occur, and true novelty will not emerge. For that reason, artistic expression tends towards playfully relating and referring to what has been done in the past, subverting and inverting it (Raussert, Lantz, and Michael 2020). Postmodern practices of rewriting also blur the boundaries between "high" and "low" forms of art and literature, as well as the distinctions between different genres and forms of writing and storytelling.

Reed and Shange in particular provide groundbreaking work in postmodern fiction writing, but work with an ethic, political, and social mission to revisit black history in the Americas as transculturally and hemispherically interconnected, and with a need to be told through black authorial voices. For both writers, trickster tropes from Afro-descendant folklore are archetypal black figures that precede postmodernist parody. These figures are transculturally rooted in African and black diasporic cultures and serve well to reinvent history and affirm black agency. In Reed's and Shange's fictions, black music mobilizes these archetypes and turns literary expression into a performance of the social, far beyond postmodernist playfulness. Black music provides polyrhythm, solo, call-and-response, and chorus – structural elements which these writers translate into literary renditions of history. To revisit the social and the historical, their experimental literary expression plunges deep into oral and musical tradition to shape polyvocal modes of storytelling that enable more inclusive narratives of blackness.

Poet, essayist, and novelist, Reed demonstrates an explicit affiliation with blues and jazz in his writings and collaborations with musicians. Together with vanguard musician Kip Hanrahan, he produced two albums titled *Conjure*. The first album, released in 1983, presented poems by Reed arranged to blues and jazz pieces. Blues musician Taj Mahal and jazz virtuosos Lester Bowie and David Murray contributed to the production of the album. As a critic and commentator on the African American music scene, Reed has been active throughout his writing career as an intellectual voice reflecting the social through music. Most of his essays are devoted to jazz and jazz musicians. "The Old Music," "Music: Black, White and Blue," and "Remembering Josephine Baker" are but a few examples gathered in his essayistic autobiography *Shrovetide in Old New Orleans* (Reed 1978). In blues and jazz especially, Reed detects dialogical art forms subverting dualistic systems. In his hands they turn into cultural modes of expression that defy the signs and metaphors of controlling systems. Drawing on these musical modes, he reshapes time conceptions and their meaning for concepts of race and culture (Raussert 2017, 105).

Bebop, arguably the most important musical reference point in Reed's writing, represents jazz at an extremely individualistic end of the improvisation-communal dialectic. Embracing bebop's individualism and reflecting various black cultural movements from the 1920s to the 1960s, Reed distances himself from the sharp doctrines of the Black Aesthetic Movement in the 1960s. His view of history is also quite different from that of African American fictions of the socio-realist tradition. He embraces Black Power as an inspirational trope and draws from the Harlem Renaissance's legacy of sonic black politics to express experimental visions of black history.

Jazz informs his historical imagination particularly in his postmodern detective novel *Mumbo Jumbo* (Reed 1972). The novel's syncretic text borrows from various cultures and progresses in eclectic fashion, featuring ruptures and sudden turns in narrative progression. Reed performs a mode of "transmedia storytelling" that incorporates photography, newspaper clippings, dictionary citations, and other forms of documents (Jenkins 2006, 17–19). Conventions of the detective novel get interspersed with African American folklore and African myth. By embracing diversity and multiplicity in the aesthetic realm, Reed also acknowledges the fluidity of the social (Bauman 2000) as a basic constituent of existence. He thus makes the point that the social needs a polyglot language to be mediated and expressed. In addition to Standard English, Elizabethan English, and Black English stand side by side in the novel. Time and language cross cultural boundaries in Reed's literary rendering of history. Likewise, different culturally-coded conceptions of time interact in *Mumbo Jumbo*. African, African American, and Western senses of time collide, overlap, and fuse. The polyrhythmic simultaneity of bebop and free jazz in particular serves as an artistic model for Reed to capture temporal complexity. His imagination shows that black temporalities and black diasporic histories add a complicating level of temporal understanding to the progressive model of modernity. The here-and-now, circular, and repetitive temporal movements interact with a basic steady progression of time. Like black struggles for liberation, history seems to move ahead and then fall back again. From the Haitian revolution to the emancipation of enslaved people, from the New Negro movement to the Black Arts movement, progression and backlash mark history in Reed's literary imagination.

For Reed, the greatest alternative power to tell history lies in performing it in and through music. As a writer he needs to translate music's capacities into written discourse. The potential of music to cross boundaries guides Reed's translation of Bakhtin's assumption that "the new cultural and creative consciousness lives in an actively polyglot world" (Bakhtin 1994, 12; Raussert 2017, 125). In contrast to linear and teleological concepts of history, Reed develops a syncretic and synchronic view of history built upon musical time; for jazz thematically and rhythmically transforms syncretism into an art form, always adding, changing, and improvising. Synchronicity characterizes the structure of the novel. He achieves this temporal effect by introducing multiple events that take place simultaneously. Although they appear disconnected at first, they become meshed as the novel progresses. What results is a dense image of entangled black histories including ancient Egypt, independent Haiti, and swinging African American culture in the Jazz Age. By exposing inter-American as well as transatlantic connections at the level of time and place, Reed invites the reader to take a globalized look at black history.

The complexities of black geographies – shaped by histories of colonialism, transatlantic enslavement, contemporary practices of racism, and resistances – fuel a plot line in *Mumbo Jumbo* that moves between memory and visionary projection and certainly denies closure. Raymond Williams's scholarship highlights that there are always residual aspects of previous cultural stages within the so-called dominant culture as well as emergent aspects of a future culture (1977, 25–45). Reed shares these assumptions and follows in the footsteps of those postmodern writers who "are most adept at dramatizing the residual or emergent cultures within the dominant one" (Winders 1993, 28–29).

Mumbo Jumbo is set in the 1920s, the time of the Harlem Renaissance and the emergence of the "New Negro." The plots and subplots of the novel revolve around the culture war between the white Atonist path and the Mu'tafikah, a militant wing of the Jes Grew movement. The main story of the novel dramatizes the conflict between these opposed groups. The conflict is both cultural and religious, since the Atonist Wallflower Order stands for the Judaeo-Christian tradition, whereas the Jes Grew movement represents African and Afro-diasporic traditions in the Americas. A music and dance epidemic, Jes Grew is spreading all over the Americas and threatens the white hegemonic order. White America is horrified: "If this Jes Grew becomes pandemic it will mean the end of Civilization As We Know It" (Reed 1972, 7). The quest for the sacred book propels the actions in the novel and equals the search for a true black history. In order to stop the epidemic the Wallflower Order tries to get a hold of Jes Grew's sacred text. The ancient HooDoo detective LaBas attempts to save the text to safeguard Jes Grew's survival. Yet, the text is never found and rumor has it that Abdul Hamid, a radical black nationalist, has burnt it.

That the text is never found expresses Reed's postmodern sensibility according to which a recognition of multiple temporal possibilities in history writing is overdue. Winders reminds us that "taking other cultures (including pop culture) seriously will mean taking seriously the sometimes radically different notions and experiences of time their cultures have to offer" (1978, 43). Reed juggles black history between high culture and pop culture. Jazz music is seen as a major agent of cultural change. While being a principal expression of 1920s popular culture, jazz has moved from clubs to concert halls, from so-called "low" to so-called "high" culture. Reed locates in jazz and his epidemic protagonist "Jes Grew" a musical power to evoke the past and envision the future. The novel reads as a playful reflection on dynamics and tensions within black movements from different epochs. Reed thus compares different historical moments in the course of the novel. For instance, the battles and conflicts between the competing groups in *Mumbo Jumbo* reflect the Harlem Renaissance's obsession with creating a new imaginary of blackness. In Reed's superimposition of time levels, the setting of the Harlem Renaissance becomes the matrix for a critical reflection on the Black movements of the 1960s. The novel's ideological battles appear too similar to those between the Black Nationalist, Black Panther, and African American Civil Rights movement for one to miss the connection. Hence, Reed compares different historical moments with the applied black rhetoric in the black emancipatory struggle in order to come to a better understanding of the intergenerational and intertextual relationships of black history. To give the novel a still larger historical range, the novel returns to the Haitian Revolution, the first Black Republic in the modern world, and to the mysteries of ancient Egypt, arguably the first Black High culture.

Mumbo Jumbo challenges Western historiography. As a longstanding trope for black resistance, Haiti remains a constant reference point in the novel: "But little Haiti resists. It becomes a world-wide symbol for religious and aesthetic freedom" (Reed 1972, 72). Toussaint's successful slave rebellion against the French in 1796, his prevention of Spanish and British invasions, and Haiti's resistance against the U.S. American invasion in 1915 serve Reed well as a black stronghold within entangled histories of conquest and colonization. As HooDoo detective LaBas comments in the novel: "Jes Grew has no end and no beginning. … We will miss it for a while but it will come back, and when it returns we will see it never left (233). Metaphorically, Reed evokes the continuous stronghold of black music for writing, living, and making history in black cultures from ancient to colonial and postcolonial times. And black music, with its syncretic flexibility, is the cultural force to carry the torch of alternative history and historiography into the contemporary period. LaBas, accordingly, concludes: "We will make our own future Text. A future generation of young artists will accomplish this" (233).

Ntozake Shange's first novel *Sassafrass, Cypress & Indigo* (1982) narrates postmodern fragmentation and its possible transcendence through the history of the Effania family. Drawing upon her versatility as an accomplished poet and playwright, Shange unfolds polygeneric stories that depict the individual development of the three female protagonists, the Effania daughters: Sassafrass, Cypress, and Indigo. Shange mixes recipes, cartographies, poems, and dramatic dialogue with prose passages to relate each daughter's life story to family history and to the history of black cultures at large. The individual stories of the sisters Sassafrass, Cypress, and Indigo are set against the historical background of the tumultuous 1960s and early 1970s, when the Civil Rights and Black Power movements not only shook the foundations of white supremacy in the United States but advanced anticolonial black struggles throughout the Americas and other parts of the globe. While the Effania mother's home in Charleston, Carolina remains a constant reference point for both narrative and character progression, the individual storylines take the characters on literal and imaginary journeys within the United States and beyond: Charleston, the Gullah islands, San Francisco, Baton Rouge, Mexico, and Brazil to name a few. The characters transverse rural and urban zones, continental and island cultures, the U.S. South and the Caribbean, U.S. American, and Latin American locations on their search for self and belonging. Whereas the history of the Black Atlantic is evoked in Cypress's story and her entanglement with dance and music culture from Europe, the stories of Sassafrass and Indigo express inter-American entanglements, telling histories of extended African America in hemispheric ways.

We encounter a complex musical cartography for rethinking history in this novel, a book that incorporates the author's expertise as poet, playwright, and performance artist. Drawing on a Pan-American vision of black musical flows and influences, Shange brings in blues, R&B, jazz, calypso, funk, and soul to create a black diasporic temporality in which private and public time consistently interact. What Abrahams suggests is that music has helped disseminate a larger black imaginary in market circles beyond the boundaries of nation-states in the Americas. As he states, "These musics, and the peoples identifying themselves through them, knit together the entire region, even as they advertise local cultural invention to worldwide popular audiences" (2001, 100). What emerges is a vision of black Americas far beyond the U.S. South: "It is a region which not only includes the Caribbean and the U.S. South, but many coastal outposts in South America on both the north, east, and west coasts, and many areas of the latifundium of Central America, including Mexico, Belize, and Costa Rica" (100). Shange recalls this musical geopolitical vision by creating a vision of the social through music. Musical influence shows in the diction that often mimics the sound of musical voices and instruments, the structure that follows call-and-response-patterns, and the themes of the novel that are embedded within references to black music. Black women's empowerment occurs in and through music. The ways in which the daughters of the Effania family define their repertoire as musicians, poets and dancers – "Lilah James, Eleo Pomare, Rod Rodgers, Royal Brown … . All gonna be in this special gala for that grand lady of black dance, Sevilla Forte" (Shange 1982, 162) – reveal a transcultural historical consciousness. Shange opens the reader's eyes to a panoramic view of black cultures that have developed multiple sonic and rhythmic traditions within the Americas beyond the colonial Old World-New World axis.

Music infiltrates all spheres of the social in Shange's novel. She reminds us that many black cultures continue African traditions of linking music with the social sphere. As Roach maintains, "Well versed in songs for every occasion, African tribes had used music as practical art which reflected all facets of everyday living" (1985, 17). Working as a midwife, Indigo soothes the women in labor through song (221). Similarly, music turns into a commentary on and expression of social relations, be they generation, race, class, or gender based. It is through her protagonist's identification with music that Shange unfolds a long *durée* trajectory of women's agency in telling and making history. Music is the medium to converse with the past – "the fiddle be callin' our Gods" (1982, 26). Music is a way to resist. Sassafrass's secret conversations with Miss Brown Blues empower her to fight back against male hegemonic storytelling and history-making (89). And music is the medium for envisioning the future when Cypress joins the "Soil and Soul" dance company which supports the Civil Rights Movements (158). Music therefore takes center stage as an empowering creative medium for expressing unheard, forgotten, and silenced histories.

Besides African *griot* traditions, the blues, based on African and African American sound patterns, serves Shange as a cultural force for tapping the historical heritage of black women and expressing a black feminist future vision that embraces African, Caribbean, Afro-Latina as well as African American communities. The blues looms large in Indigo's verbal and musical exchange with Uncle John, for whom the blues signifies a way of "talkin' wit the unreal" (1982, 27). Signifying on a long trajectory of black music, the novel lets the reader traverse various genres and epochs of black musical expression. By adapting elements of bop, hard bop, and free jazz on the level of idiosyncratic diction, rhythmic syntax, and scat-like improvisation on words, Shange's narrative voices sing history and make history literally audible. "It is music, bebop, jazz that inform much of Shange's writing," as Sandi Russell explains, discussing the oral idiosyncracy of Shange's prose and diction (1990, 181; Raussert 2017, 132). Polyphony via the three sister's distinct voices and polyrhythm in the shifts of tempo, rhythmic phrasing, and references to different temporalities in black musical performance are all borrowings from the rich musical spectrum of black music. They create a dialogic and global vision of a black social seen through women's eyes. Shange builds on tradition since, historically, women have occupied a much more dominant role in the history of black music than their counterparts of Western descent. Music serves not only as cultural heritage but also as feminist futurist vision. Already in the 1920s, blues women like Bessie Smith and Ma Rainey rocked the music circuits; at the same time, they advocated gender and race pride. Singers like Nina Simone, Billie Holiday, Miriam Makeba, and Celia Cruz continued to carry the torch. Today, artists like Beyoncé, Rihanna, and Las Krudas reflect the social through black female chant from the center and the margins of contemporary pop music.

Shange rewrites black histories through the lens of optional forms of knowledge (Mignolo) such as recipes, medical advices, and healing songs produced over centuries within the domestic sphere. She lets these forms of knowledge travel in a black diasporic time-space compression, back in time and forward toward the future. The novel traces the lives of Hilda Effania's three daughters, situating them in the complex history of African diaspora in the Americas. "Like the slaves who were ourselves" (Shange 1982, 27), Sassafrass, Cypress, and Indigo confront their individual lives with a historical consciousness "grown deep like rivers," to borrow a term from Langston Hughes. Structurally, the vision of entangled black history and a shared social is expressed through a blues-derived call-and-response pattern that Shange establishes in the form of letters, conversation, and singing between mother and daughters. The women's cultural practices mediate tradition and innovation, past and present, the global black South and the Northern American hemisphere.

The lives of the three Effania daughters revolve around black music of the 1960s and 1970s and its dialectics of cultural heritage and renewal. Indigo improvises blues, soul, and funk tunes on the fiddle, Sassafrass absorbs the female blues tradition as a poet, and Cypress pursues black dance as career. The imaginary flights of these women point the reader to oral and musical traditions beyond the U.S. and throughout the Americas. In the images of the Charleston port, of bars and juke joints, and in the figures of colored sailors, the interconnectedness between the American South and the larger Caribbean crystalizes:

> Sassafrass stayed by the wharf whenever she cd/… there were drums & special dances the Bermudans & Trinidadian sailors played in the evenin/showd sassafrass what they called the "jump-up"/or the mambo/… she wd write it all down so other children wdnt feel lost … . (Shange 1982, 108–109)

The wharf at the port of Charleston becomes a site of sonic migrations from all over the Americas, and the sounds and rhythms from the port for Sassafrass turn into modes of remembering and constructing the social anew. Her musically inspired storytelling mobilizes black history at the intersection of race, gender, and the geopolitics of knowledge; it explicitly embraces the extended Caribbean as well as Africa and creates literary soundscapes echoing centuries of black song, endurance, and spirituality.

6.4 Contemporary dub poetry and diasporic historiographies: Afua Cooper and Lillian Allen

Dub poetry's beginnings date back to the 1970s in Jamaica, where it rapidly became a powerful expression of popular culture and political resistance. Within the Americas and beyond it quickly spread, in particular, to the Jamaican diaspora in Toronto and London. As concerns Caribbean beginnings, artists like Oku Onuora, Mutaburuka, and Michael Smith established dub poetry in Kingston, Jamaica. In London, poetically speaking to a continuing anti-colonial struggle, Linton Kwesi Johnson and Jean Binta Breeze wrote and performed dub poetry, creating an artistic scene that reached out to other Jamaican communities in England. Lillian Allen, Afua Cooper, and Clifton Joseph, among others, created a diasporic dub poetry scene in Canada, with Toronto as its center (Carr 1998, 10–12). Dub poetry stands for an Afro-Caribbean rhythmic mode of telling diasporic histories. Through musical and rhythmical elements dub poetry performs envisioned and lived bridges between uneven temporalities, distant, yet entangled hemispheres on various continents. Allen's and Cooper's poetry resorts to music as a rhythmic structure, content, and performance in order to mediate temporalities from the colonial past with the promised land of a better future. Both poets express historical transculturations (Raussert and Isensee 2008) in terms of language through a mix of Standard English and Jamaican Creole/Patois, and through a mix of oral and printed poetry. The blending of distinct linguistic rhythms of Jamaican Creole/Patois with musical beats from reggae creates a strong rhythmical expression of lived and remembered temporality (Habekost 1993). In sum, dub poetry in the style of Cooper and Allen is oral history. And its memory work is self-reflexive, including mnemonic patterns that support memorization in contemporary cultural work.

Born in Jamaica, Cooper moved to Canada in 1980. She literally makes history tangible and audible in her writing and performances. She embeds her writing within a conception of the social as changeable. History does not remain an abstract thing. History is felt, lived, expressed, and reflected in the work of this poet, who at the same time is a historian. As a founder of Toronto's Dub Poets Collective and a vibrant performer, with several recordings to her credit including *Love and Revolution* (2009), Cooper makes history come alive through a voice whose rhythm and accentuation is shaped by the soundings of reggae and other musical expressions. As Lisa Tomlinson puts it, Cooper's dub poetry and her literary historical work "reposition the path of the Black Atlantic" to include "the unique feature of cultural exchange between Canada, her native Jamaica, and the wider Caribbean" (2012, 107). Indeed,

Cooper puts black history and black literature on the cultural map of Canada. "Canada is the place where Black literature is happening," she insists, referring to contemporary writers such as Dionne Brand, Olive Senior, and Esi Edugyan (110).

Strongly influenced by Oku Onoura's dub poems from Jamaica, Cooper locates in reggae and its rhythms major possibilities for shaping "sound, rhythm, voice, and music" in her poetry" (qtd. in Tomlinson 2012, 112). In her diasporic historiographies she synthesizes the oral and the "page poet" (113). Like dub poetry overall, Cooper's poetry is frequently chanted and performed to reggae rhythms. It also borrows from and mixes together American rhythm & blues, calypso, jazz, Afro-Latin rhythms, and rap, and draws on African and Caribbean oral traditions while adding diasporic variations dependent on the performance setting. Her poetic historiographies spiritually resort to the Rastafarian movement (cf. Knopf 2005, 254) and reveal that her vision of the social embraces the rational as well as the spiritual. Her work fuses the factual with the affectionate, and archival memory with imagination.

Cooper is emblematic of a dub poetry scene in Canada characterized by dynamic compositions and performances, as well as mixed media borrowings from theatre, video art, and electronics. Thematically, she addresses a wide range of issues such as colonialism, slavery, diasporic displacement, racism, sexism, police violence, immigration, homelessness, and class divide. In Cooper's poetry, history is written large and juxtaposed and fused with personal life stories. Dub poetry, accordingly, represents an individual and collective way of telling history(ies). Similar to African American poets in the U.S. and dub poets in Jamaica, Cooper employs call-and-response patterns with a recurrent chorus that also rhythmically structures the poems and invites a dialogue between poet and community. In an interview with Emily Allen Williams she insists, "I am in communion with the audience. I am creating a dialogue – a discursive space" (323). Performing poetry becomes a sacred act: "We – the audience with me – are 'breaking bread together'" (323).

Cooper has made her mark in African Canadian culture and politics as a poet, historian activist, and cultural worker. She has challenged the Canadian myth of the "Two Solitudes" – the French and the English and their conflicted relationship (Knopf 2005, 38). In her work, she unearths silenced black Canadian history and draws attention to the lot of First

Nation people in Canada as well as the Caribbean. According to her, "slavery in Canada has been Canada's best-kept secret" (304), and she makes it her objective to recover and discover the history of black people in Canada and their transatlantic and inter-American diasporic links from colonial times to the present. From the very beginning of her career as poet music has played a central role. Hand-clapping and singing from church services and roadside preaching practices in Jamaica formed her first musical influences. In an interview with H. Nigel Thomas (2006), Cooper remembers: "We were discovering who we were as Africans and making it central to our identity" (74). To her, heritage and music became a firm bond: "Popular music – reggae music especially, dub poetry with drums in the background – and theatre with a focus on African style and issues of African identity were all ways we used to reclaim that heritage" (74).

For her early poems from *Breaking Chains* she worked with an African percussion group in the style of spoken word (Williams 1995, 317). Having grown up in the 1970s, she belongs to a generation with a new consciousness of black historiography. Rastafari was prominent, reggae music blossomed in Jamaica, Black history and Black power ideas circulated among the younger generation, and Walter Rodney became a source of inspiration for black struggle. Already before Cooper's move from Jamaica to Canada, the ideas of anti-apartheid and Black Power crisscrossed the Americas. The Toronto dub community emerged out the Black political struggles of the 1970s and 1980s. In Cooper's memories, demonstrations and marches would end in public places and parks where people would talk, dance, sing, perform, and make music. An artistic movement accompanied the political movement, and "the arts were central in every way" in the black struggles against discrimination and apartheid (Williams 1977, 319).

Cooper's poems in many ways pay homage to black musical expression, celebrating the musical achievements of Bob Marley and Mahalia Jackson, among others. Music to Cooper represents a rhythmic and spiritual force. The content, structure, and performance of her poetry have musical roots. Politically she is anti-colonial and a black feminist. Her poems let female bodies in particular move, dance, and transcend. Bodies give birth, die, and rise up again. Music and movement are conceived as fundamental to the liberation of spirit, body, and society at large. Jamaican Creole/Patois adds a rhythmic tonality to her voice in "She Dance," when she molds the social poetically:

> She dance wid di wind
> fi di wind
> against di wind
> har hands held high in supplication to God
> she dance and dance
> now is like Damballah possess har. (Cooper 1992, 99)

The female dancer's moves are multidirectional. She goes with and against the wind. Cooper suggests both affirmation and resistance in the short poetic lines. The woman's dance expresses a Pan-African consciousness. Music, rhythm, and dance from the African west coast join with black diasporic moves. Music is celebrated as a life force. Many of the poems in *Memories Have Tongue* like "Stepping To Da Muse/Sic" and "The Upper Room" are expressions of transcendence. Black music and rhythms pave the way to uplift and ascent. Inspired by the voice of Mahalia Jackson, icon of African American gospel music, the poetic voice in "The Upper Room" declares:

> You crown me with your chants
> And I spin, yes
> I stumble and then
> I rise … .
>
> As you take me to the Upper Room. (Cooper 1992,101)

Cooper's poetic women are women in the whirlwind of history. As Keith B. Mitchell puts it, "Cooper is especially interested in recuperating and revising forgotten and submerged histories of African-Canadian women" (2008, 38). For her, it is essential to address different generations, from the very young to the very old, to remind them of the bonds and ties of past and present African diaspora. In her historic imagination she resurrects Marie Joseph Angélique, a slave woman who put fire to her master's house and burned down most of Montreal as a consequence, and she does so in different types of texts, for different age groups and audiences. Cooper starts off with a children's poem, "Marie Joseph Angélique." A longer, more elaborate version occurs in "Confessions of a Woman Who Burnt Down a Town" and the historical biography *The*

Hanging of Angélique: Canada, Slavery, and the Burning of Montréal (2006b), which became a bestseller and award-winning historical book.

Cooper wants to make unheard voices heard. She is especially interested in filling the gaps in Canadian history, pointing to slavery and racism in colonial and contemporary Canada, which enables her to create a new sense of the social. Remembering for her is an act of knowledge production; at the same time it is an important step toward raising consciousness and fueling social action. In all three texts by Cooper about Marie Joseph Angélique, she humanizes her protagonist beyond questions of class, citizenship, gender, and race. She firmly establishes her as a model freedom fighter, as a feminist abolitionist of time past, and an inspiration for black immigrant women in Canada today. By resurrecting a freedom-seeking woman from colonial times, she lifts the veil from race and colorblindness in Canadian history writing and conscience. Her rhetoric reveals her to be the poet-as-historiographer and the historiographer-as-poet. She writes history with sounds and rhythms that are intricately connected to content, creating a holistic historiography, one that embraces the oral and written discourse through the performative. Her texts appear "oraliterary" (Mitchell 2008, 40). Her prose and poetry have a chant-like quality that turns her scholarship into a public text to be shared, spread, and appreciated far beyond the academic discourse – another side of her creativity which shows that she envisions a more inclusive vision of the social. She extends African griot traditions and brings old African ways of storytelling and history-making into the discourse of African Canadian historiography.

Through the fusion of contemporary rhythm (reggae in particular) with the unearthing of unnoticed historical data of African Canadian history, she adds new pieces of knowledge to the tapestry of African diaspora history. One such example is her poem about Richard Pierpoint, "Revolutionary Soldier (a poem in three voices)" (Cooper 2006a). In this poem from *Copper Woman*, Richard Pierpoint, who was born in Africa, enslaved, and brought to the Americas, and who served in the Revolutionary War and the War of 1812 "in a corps of colour raised on the frontier of Niagara" (57), writes the king's governor a letter requesting permission to return to his homeland. In her poetic rendering of the letter, Cooper retells Pierpoint's entanglement in the history of the slave trade, the independence movements in the Americas, and the establishment of early settlements. One of the voices in the poem is the migratory subject Pierpoint himself, writing, "at the age of sixteen I was made prisoner/sold as slave/conveyed to America in the year 1760 … I wish to see again the Senegal waters flow" (56, 58). A second voice belongs to Cooper's envisioned public, voicing support for Pierpoint's plea: "So please your Majestic/Listen to the petitioner's plea/He yearns to return/To the land of his family" (58). The third voice is that of Cooper herself, the dub poet, chanting "Revolutionary soldier" to reggae rhythms with reference to Bob Marley's song "Buffalo Soldier." Marley's song laments the conscription of freed slaves by the government to fight Native American tribes. Cooper transfers the historical setting to Upper Canada:

> Revolutionary soldier
> revolutionary soldier
> stolen from Africa
>   brought to Upper Canada
> revolutionary soldier
>   Revolution (2006a, 59)

Cooper discovers historical sources and chants history so that black diasporas in the Americas get entangled with the African homeland. Thus she establishes a model for black historiography as an alternative knowledge to the established historical discourse. Cooper's objective is "to revise English and French Canadian historiographies" (Knopf 2005, 38). Just like the actors in her poem "Negro Cemeteries" in *Copper Woman*, Cooper unearths the silenced (his)stories and songs of black people in Canadian society:

> "Negro" cemeteries are surfacing all over Ontario
> Ancestors rolling over
> Bones creaking
> Skeletons dusting themselves off
> Dry bones shaking in fields of corn. (2006a, 25)

In the poem, black history awakens and infuses the social. Dead black bodies turn into agents who expose the cracks in Canadian myth-making and the silences in Canadian history writing. In "500 Years of Discovery," Cooper admits that she, a "Black African Jamaican woman whose ancestry sprang from another continent, another hemisphere," is "still trying to understand her place in these Americas" (2006a, 29). To unearth uneven temporalities and their connectedness, to connect body, history and place is at the core of Cooper's poetic vision. And it is through musical voice and rhythm that she performs the act of bringing silenced and forgotten history to social consciousness, so that a better Canada can emerge.

6.5 Lillian Allen's body politics: dub poetry as a social force

Born in Jamaica, Lillian Allan has crisscrossed the Americas with stays in the U.S., the Caribbean, and Canada. She emigrated from Jamaica to Canada in 1969 and first got into a vital dub poetry scene in New York City in the 70s. Arguably Canada's most prominent dub poet, she performs verses on cultural, social, and political topics. Her performances include a distinct rhythmic and declamatory vocal style that is in dialogue with reggae and calypso accompaniment. Allen has consistently published in both sound and print, as is common in dub poetry. Since the 1980s, she has performed at cultural, literary, music, and political festivals and events in Canada, the U.S., the Caribbean, England, and Europe. She published her first book of poems, *Rhythm an' Hardtimes*, in 1982, and as a performance artist she recorded *Dub Poet: The Poetry of Lillian Allen* (1983) and *De Dub Poets* (1984), the latter including the voices of Toronto poets Clifton Joseph and Devon Haughton. Collaborating with various musicians, she later recorded *Revolutionary Tea Party* (1986) and *Conditions Critical* (1988), the former including songs like "I Fight Back" and "Riddim an' Hardtimes," which reached a broader public in Canada and Jamaica. Both records were released and distributed by Allen's label, Verse to Vinyl, and received Juno Awards for best reggae/calypso album in 1986 and 1989 respectively (Roberts 2010).

As poet and recording artist she has shown that "dub poetry has continued to inspire and sustain struggle in the many locales where it has been rerouted/rerooted in the Caribbean diaspora" (Gingell 2005, 220). Allen resorts to reggae to fuse rhythm, body, and voice as political media. "Though Allen asserts the transformative pleasure of the body through reggae and dance-hall rhythms," Carr explains, "she does so without inversions of male-originated strategies of sexual boasting" (1998, 24).

She replaces these strategies by adopting a "griot-inspired, broad-based social commentary central to the African-Jamaican national liberation struggle" (24). Inspired by a trans-American expansion of Black Power, the "Black is Beautiful" cultural movement, and Rastafarian spirituality, Allen's dub poetry gives voice to women's experiences in the Caribbean diaspora. It is through the musical framing of her political messages that she reaches subaltern and dominant groups "through the backdoor of mainstream cultural establishment" (Knopf 2005, 80). Carolyn Cooper observes that "reggae business is also a magical enterprise in which poor ghetto youths, identifying with the heroes of Hollywood fantasy, can rise to international fame and fortune" (2004, 153). At the same time, dub poetry has continued to sustain struggle in the many locations "where it has been rerouted/rerooted in the Caribbean diaspora" (Gingell 2005, 220).

Allen addresses the physical pleasures of rhythm and dance in her performances, yet she channels body politics away from eroticism to express a collective movement whose aim is social change. She links the imaginaries of the Black Power and other African American movements with Rastafarianism, thus creating a black diasporic matrix for affirmation and resistance.

Her reflections on black experience are often embedded in immigration settings that loom large in her poetry. Color as metaphor is omnipresent in *Women Do This Every Day*. Black as color and marker of identity is important in the aesthetic and communicative intent of poems like "Jazz You." The poem begins,

> Molten shimmer red
> charcoal roasting
> like hot, burn
> burn black, burn sax
> burn blue
> burn into my flesh
> brewing a potpourri of a storm
> ablowing waves of hues. (Allen 1993b, 120)

But in the refrain of this dub, *black* has a different significance, tied to oppression:

> what the people have to do today mi say
> just a juggle fi get a little peace. (120)

As the dub poem expresses in diasporic Jamaican, transculturation is complex, presented as conflicted, contested, and promising. Rethinking the social, she reflects immigrant experiences in multiple perspectives. In the poem "In these Canadian Bones" (1987), Allen performs a more positive view on transformative processes. In the course of the poem, the Caribbean immigrant becomes a cultural and political agent who shapes the social within a multigenerational diasporic experience. Music, in its reggae and calypso expressions, represents the matrix for shaping new cultural landscapes in Canada. Poetic body politics unfold, as collective imagination, musical rhythm, and personal voice fuse in the poetic voice of the immigrant persona: The lines "In these Canadian bones/where Africa landed" mark the beginning of a multilayered and multitemporal diasporic agency. The words "and Jamaica bubble inna reggae redstripe and calypso proddings of culture" expose the musical flows within the Americas that led to new cultural production. The immigrant persona is equipped with power and is perceived as mobile and productive: "We are creating this very landscape we walk on" (1993, n. pag.).

In Allen's vision of the social, it is the act of musical and cultural creation that facilitates the immigrant's immersion into Canadian society. Evidently, the immigrant's voice is full of diasporic history and a global black cultural consciousness that empowers the immigrant to take a creative role in shaping Canadian culture and society. The poem unfolds a generational narrative that highlights different temporalities within migration and immigration. Where the immigrant persona stands for arrival, first contact, and orientation in the opening of the poem, the second stanza celebrates a positive second-generation transculturation in the presence of the immigrant persona's daughter. Again, it is through musical tropes that Allen lets the immigrant persona reflect immersion and integration: "My daughter sings opera/speaks perfect Canadian" (1993, n. pag.). The immigrant persona herself is aware of difference and tension: "And I dream in dialect/grown malleable by my Canadian tongue" (n. pag.). Yet, music also remains a consolation and inspiration for a future vision: "I dream … of a world where all that matters is the colour of love/compassion/heart and music that grooves you" (n. pag). The immigrant persona "dreams in dialect," seeking to make the utopia of a true Canadian transnationality and transethnicity a reality. The power to achieve utopia is located in music, be it opera, reggae, or calypso. For her, transculturation is in process, never to be completed, and is full of ruptures. While the daughter's experience provides hope, the poem does not negate her continuous marginalization in Canadian society.

Allen is conscious of the conflicted temporalities involved in an imaginary nation-building. Her poems traverse several space and time zones to capture the diasporic sentiment of her own Canadian experience. Being in diaspora often challenges linear modes of time that are connected with homogeneous progression. Alternative expressions of temporality frequently shape the cultural and social rituals and practices in diasporic communities. A co-existence of different real and imagined worlds emerges; ancestors, homeland, and diasporic location – with its historical roots and routes – inhabit an imagined spatiotemporal world in motion. Similar to Walter Benjamin's "messianic time," these "ancestral chronotopes" suspend clear-cut temporal differences and priorities (Eisenlohr 2018, n. pag.). "We are Hurons, and visitors and traders/Adventurers and underground railroaders," Allen's poetic voice announces in pOetic gEsture from a series of Toronto poems (Allen 2014). First nation people, colonial traders, and fleeing slaves merge in a diasporic conception of time and space.

The line "We are the Iroquois's promise of unity" signals that this conception of the social can be reached only through an embrace of difference and change. The diasporic self continues in a process of becoming: "Making us larger than we are becoming." Transcendence is found in social and artistic creativity: "Dub Poetry, Hip Hop, Opera, Visual smarts and Community Arts" (n. pag.).

Allen sees poets, artists, and cultural workers as crucial players in the making of a diasporic world and a historically multilayered Canada. For her, specificity of sound, expression, and rhythm is part of Jamaican speech and lends a sonic particular quality to her poetic vision in which every syllable and words matters. "The rhythms of Jamaican speech, sustained by and reflected in the musical beat, constitute the dub experience," as Haberkost emphasizes (1993, 92).

The intimate connection between voice, speech, and beat enhances poetry as a medium for both reflecting and promoting activism. "I Fight Back" is in the style of "signifyin'" and the "cuss poem" (Carr 1998, 10, 25), and one of Allen's poems from *Women Do This Every Day* that shows precisely this empowering synthesis. Allen reflects the in-between-experience through diasporic motherhood. Her poem links generations and invokes motherly ties that are threatened by and challenge the experience of displacement and political exclusion in Canada. The lines “My Children Scream/My Grandmother is dying” set the emotional tone before the lyrical I as mother reflects her migration experience: “I came to Canada/And Found the Doors/Of Opportunities Well Guarded” (1993b, 139–140). Space and time are multiplied in the exploitative working system. “I Scrub Floors/Serve Backra’s Meals on Time … .” “Spend two days working in one/And Twelve Days a Week” (n. pag.). Allen intensifies the time-space compression of diasporic experience by relating it to a work load that makes lived time more intense than real time. In addition, motherhood takes on dual bonding and care: “Here I Am in Canada/Bring Up Someone Else’s Child/While someone Else and Me in Absentee/Bring Up My Own” (n. pag.). The mother figure stands for a double agency that keeps ties strong between homeland and Canada and within (extended) family circuits. The chorus in capital letters that repeat the poem’s title, “AND I FIGHT BACK,” expresses the endurance, resistance, and, here, triple agency of the female poetic person: working, caring, taking political action. The poem provides a critical reflection on Canadian immigration myths and takes a critical stance against neocolonial practices in the Canadian labor system. In performed and recorded versions of “I Fight Back,” the speech-beat dialogue underscores the urgency of Allen’s plea to revise immigration policies.

Clearly, then, as a dub poet, Allen relies on the spoken Jamaican word for many of her effects. When she writes her poems down, she uses alliterations, repetitions, and elliptical phrasing to translate the sound effects on the page. Next to the speech-beat dialogue, performativity of words plays a crucial role in her poetic work. Many of her poems put to music such as “For Billie Holiday” show a complex dialogical relationship between music and text through which Allen reflects the social and proposes betterment. These performances ask the listener for an intense and concentrated engagement with the play between words, sound, and music. However, Allen also uses her chants and slogans in performances in political demonstrations to create a common voice among participants; music and poetic chant become a tool to channel protest in the diaspora communities. In Allen’s poetic practice, sound as power is a concrete physical and social force.

One example of Allen's participatory poetic approach is her poem "Colors" (1993a) that is also included in the recording titled *Family Folk Festival: A Multicultural Sing Along* (1993a). Questions like "Who thinned the colors for the atmosphere" address the audience directly. The rhetorical strategies in the poem thus support Allen's poetic performance, which in a call-and-response mode traverses the promises and fractures of a Canadian multicultural mosaic. Caribbean oral tradition and a slow-paced reggae rhythm form the basis for a musical-poetic progression that culminates in the chorus sung by children and Allen together. Her performance is an invitation for the children to join, a projection of a better future Canada. "Colors" illustrates that Allen resorts to a broad spectrum of resistance practices. While "I Fight Back," with its "cuss style," is straightforward in its argumentation and accusation, "Colors" uses modes of indirection through which Allen addresses the shortcomings of Canadian foundation myths. "Is anyone listening here?" She asks in the poem, highlighting the necessity of sounding protest and critique. She creates a metaphorical tapestry of colors that recalls Canadian ideals: "Blue tights/green overcoat/polka dot underwear/Yellow ribbon/brown bobby pin/hanging from her hair/Black belt/purple shoes/ mauve hat/striped socks/Red and white Crinoline top." A series of rhetorical questions – "Who made the sky blue/Who made the pink hot" – expresses discomfort without accusing anyone directly. The poem circles back to the opening line of colors – "Blue tights/green overcoat/ polka dot underwear" – but finishes on a note of welcome and inclusion: "Yellow ribbon/brown bobby pin/glad you are here." Individual and collective voices carry the message when she alternates with a children's choir that chants the chorus lines to a slow reggae rhythm. Like the slow groove underlying the poem's performance, the critical commentary of the poem cautiously takes shape. Allen's poem challenges Canada's self-acclaimed status as a multi-ethnic and multicultural paradise, asking "Who took day and night/Joined them back to back?" She shifts between lost utopia and utopia reimagined when she contrasts Canadian immigrant realities with high flying Canadian ideals. As a coda, the poetic voice recites the multiple colors existing side by side. Sound in Allen's poetry is persistent, expressing endurance as well as insisting on the recuperation of lost dreams and ideals. Sound for Allen and for Cooper is a popular and profound way to shape the social and express it anew.

6.6 Music and history in contemporary mural and street art in Toronto, Canada, and Kingston, Jamaica

Cooper and Allen's reggae-inspired poetic historiographies find their visual counterpart in contemporary street murals in Toronto, Canada, and Kingston, Jamaica. Even before reggae got selected as a world cultural heritage in 2018 Toronto's re-urbanization, plans to beautify public places together with the project StreetARToronto (Start) began to transform Toronto's walls, alleyways, and underpasses into murals, street art, and other visual expressions, many of them referencing reggae and other musical expressions. Enhancing cultural heritage awareness and combating negative images of graffiti, Start, in collaboration with The STEPS Initiative and local artist Adrian Hayles, launched the Reggae Lane project. "Reggae Lane" refers to a Toronto laneway located behind the storefronts south of Eglinton Avenue West and east of Oakwood Avenue. It was given this title in 2015 by Toronto Councilor Josh Colle to honor the rich musical tradition of this area also known as "Little Jamaica." On September 21, 2015, a 1200-square-foot mural was unveiled to the public. Created by Hayles and other local artists, the mural celebrates legendary Toronto reggae musicians as part of a larger urban heritage project.

Figure 18: Reggae Lane Mural (© Lami Cooper).

Together with the mural, a historical Toronto plague commemorates Toronto's reggae legacy.

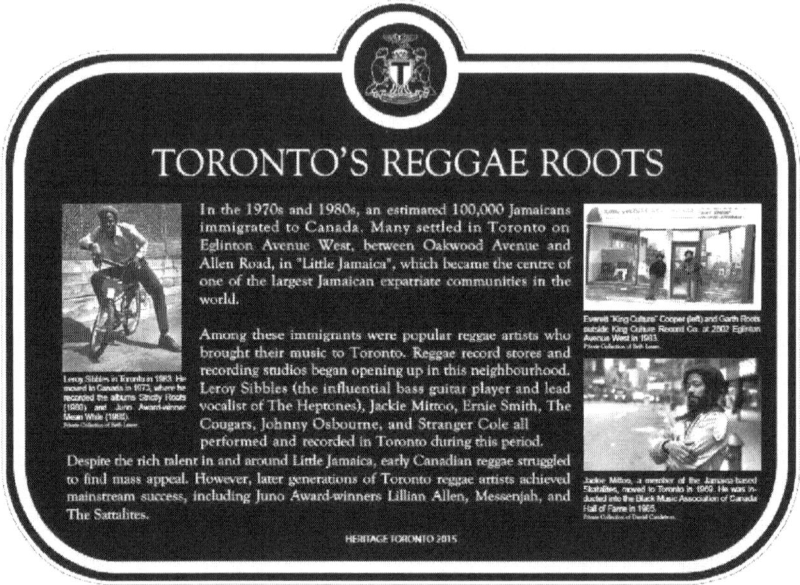

Figure 19: Reggae Roots Heritage (© Heritage Toronto 2015).

While the memorial plague "Toronto Reggae Roots" highlights the biggest wave of migration from Jamaica to Canada, the history of reggae in Toronto dates back to the 1960s, when many Jamaican musicians first settled in the city. The musicians who moved here also participated in the city's rhythm & blues scene, leading to a cross-pollination of cultures. For instance, the Studio One keyboard player Jackie Mittoo relocated to Toronto in 1969, and fellow Studio One alumni Leroy Sibbles followed him in 1973. Jamaican diasporic music performances criss-crossed many music genres, including jazz, calypso, soul, and R & B. New reggae sounds from Jamaica were soon adopted by Jamaican-Canadian musicians in the Toronto diaspora as well. A whole music culture around reggae emerged in "Little Jamaica," as record shops, music studios, little theaters, and performance venues lined Eglinton Avenue West between Marlee and Dufferin streets. Clothing, food, and music created a vibrant black Jamaican diaspora culture, as the strip became home to many West Indian clothing shops, beauty and barber shops, restaurants, grocery stores, and other businesses.

The opening of Reggae Lane remains an important marker of cultural heritage awareness, as contemporary processes of gentrification threaten to displace "Little Jamaica" into other Toronto city areas. The murals in Reggae Lane are sites of memory and identification for the Jamaican diaspora community in Toronto. At the same time, they are a significant tourist attraction. Hayles's cooperative Reggae Lane mural daily captures the attention of thousands of passers-by and global tourists. Both through its urban and new media presence it reconnects black cultures in North America, the Caribbean, and Africa, visualizing musical flows and the interconnectedness of the Caribbean diasporic experience. The creative force behind what is arguably the biggest reggae mural is Hayles, a Toronto-born visual artist with Guyanese roots. His visual art blurs the lines between graffiti and ultra-realism and is visible in Toronto on various canvasses. In collaboration with local youth and the STEPS team, he visually transformed locally sourced stories and global reggae imaginaries into what is now a cultural landmark in the Eglinton-Oakwood community. Global icons like Bob Marley appear side-by-side with local reggae artists, thus appealing to intergenerational music audiences and unrolling a transcultural tapestry of reggae continuity (Kotarba 2018, 18). The mural invites the viewer on a journey through time that highlights music's involvement with the social, from colonial freedom struggles to twenty-first century urban restructuring. Reggae's connection to religion, spirituality, political struggle, identity politics, and entertainment are aesthetically framed by colors and visuals of Jamaican reggae imaginaries. Creating the impression of figures in motion, the mural emphasizes that reggae is a traveling culture and a unifying force across temporal, spatial, cultural, and religious gaps.

While the mural gives visual representation to a global music success story, contemporary Reggae Lane crawls feature drumming workshops, dub poetry, and performances from local reggae legends like Otis Gayle, Carl Henry, Everton Pablo Paul, Bernie Pitters, and Jay Douglas, among others. Hence, sound, performance, and image collaborate and intensify reggae's cultural presence in the Jamaican diaspora and help commemorate Toronto's significance as a reggae hotspot. Both the musical and visual translations of Jamaican music into Canadian culture need to be seen in dialogue with Jamaican roots and routes. Likewise, Hayles's inspiration goes back to visualizations of reggae culture in

Kingston, Jamaica. His collaborative mural comprises images from African myth, Rastafaris, popular music icons, political leaders, and spiritual iconography, as they have been popularized in Jamaican visual arts since the 1970s.

In the visual arts in Jamaica reggae is ever-present. Cover art, poster art from annual international festivals, and, most of all, town murals and graffiti mark a strong visual presence of reggae music in the Jamaican public sphere. Especially yard art murals in Kingston combine symbols, signs, and images of Reggae music to spread social, spiritual, and political messages. Through reggae, the Rastafarian worldview filtered its way inside Africa, England, the U.S., and Canada. Like reggae, Rastafarian-influenced ideals offered youth and diasporic communities around the globe an alternative, non-Eurocentric source of meaning and identity. Undoubtedly, reggae's commitment to social justice and to the suffering of racialized, oppressed peoples has shaped youth cultures and social movements in the Americas, and has reshaped a new cultural tie to present day Africa. As the music took on the struggles of the Third World, it gradually reached the masses of young people in discotheques, parties, and other places of relaxation. In this way, reggae music has been instrumental in widening the discourse on how we conventionally perceive cultural exchange between peoples of African descent (Raussert and Tomlinson 2020).

The murals in Trench Town depict Rastafaris, popular music icons, political leaders, figures from African myth, and spiritual iconography. The murals link local politics with African diaspora experience and imagined roots in the African homelands. Musical, religious, and political expressions fuse together in transcultural imaginaries deeply rooted in Rastafarian spirituality. Just as reggae is a musical expression of political protest, the murals in Trench Town are popular artistic expressions commenting on issues such as police violence, housing evictions, social struggles, gentrification, and commodification. The iconography draws on reggae lyrics, songs, and historical figures icons to create a dialogical artistic expression to spread Rastafari thinking. Trench Town, an inner-city community of Jamaica's capital, Kingston, is similar to other neighboring communities – an urban zone with high poverty, violence, and unemployment rates. At the same time, Trench Town is culturally unique because its imaginary rests on the iconic home of Bob Marley, and the birthplace of reggae. A series of murals portray the local reggae icons like Bob Marley, Peter Tosh, and Bunny Wailer together with well-known black leaders such as Marcus Garvey. The paintings fulfill an important function in urban politics since they are situated in strategic locations. For instance, they mark the entrance to Trench Town and give a musical urban identity to the neighborhood, stretching out along the main roads. The neighborhood is considered part of the ghetto and downtown Kingston. The murals add an uplifting spirit and sense of cultural pride to the environment, which is amplified by the global success and of local heroes Bob Marley and Peter Tosh.

Along Spanish Town Road, a mural bearing the figure of Bob Marley with the caption "Welcome to Trench Town: Home of the Legendaries" welcomes visitors and tourists. Marley is depicted as smiling and strumming his guitar above a list of famous musicians, politicians and intellectuals from the community. Here, a cultural heritage monument is formed in the style of popular art. While the murals with reggae inspiration are innately political artworks, the focus on world famous reggae musicians from Kingston neglects the still wider range of local musicians, some not followers of Rastafarianism such as Ken Booth, Joe Higgs, Alton Ellis, and Leroy Sibbles.

One of the most famous murals in Trench Town shows the map of Africa behind the marijuana-smoking Bob Marley's head. The mural refers to Marley's 1977 album, *Exodus*, considered his greatest musical success.

Figure 20: Bob Marley 'Exodus' Mural, Kingston (© Lami Cooper).

The album was created in response to social and political uproar and pressing race questions in Jamaica, as well as to a politically motivated attempt to assassinate Marley in December 1976. *Exodus* was recorded during Marley's self-imposed exile in London following this attempt. Marley interrogated issues of race and class that had gained urgency in "a newly independent and postcolonial Jamaican society" (Rhiney and Cruse 2012). Other murals refer back to the charismatic Jamaican black intellectual and spiritual leader Marcus Garvey, who became a central figure in political movements of the Harlem Renaissance. The superimposition of Marley on the continent of Africa and the commemoration of the Pan-African mission of Marcus Garvey illustrate that musically inspired visual arts help preserve a vision of the African diaspora as globally connected. The same effect emerges from the representations of Ethiopian emperor Haile Selassie, whose mural stands next to those depicting Bob Marley, Peter Tosh, and Bunny Wailer, images of Africa, the colors of the Ethiopian flag in red green and gold, and the marijuana cult important for the spiritual Rastafari movement. Drenched in the visual design of popular music culture, the mural series links music, politics, and spirituality and promotes provides a Pan-African imaginary from the 1920s to the twenty-first century. The music's global appeal and the strategic positioning of murals in the streets of Trench Town also illustrate the importance of music's visual depictions to contemporary Jamaican cultural production, to tourism and cultural markets, and to local and global politics. As one more example shows, murals like "One World Is Enough For All Of Us" reflect a holistic approach to culture and politics. "One World Is Enough for All of Us," is the title of a Police song, which Sting wrote in 1981 (for the album *Ghost in the Machine*). The song itself is ska-inspired and addresses British imperialism, Irish nationalism, and sectarian hatred. With a poem celebrating Mother Nature on the left of the mural, an image of the globe in the background, a textual reference to the title of Bob Marley's song "One Love," and an appeal to black and white unity in the form of two figures touching hands, the mural translates Bob Marley's song lyrics into a visual promotion of environmentalist and racial politics. Marley's song title "One Love" is further linked with lyrics from a song written by Linda Creed and Michael Masser and performed by Whitney Houston in the concert for South Africa in 2010: "I believe the children are our are future/

Teach them well and let them lead the way." Music visually spans past, present, and future in "One World Is Enough For All Of Us," a mural that extends musically inspired local social sensibility through global ecological awareness.

Works cited

Abrahams, Roger D. 2001. "Afro-Caribbean Culture and the South: Music with Movement." In *The South and the Caribbean*, ed. Douglass Sullivan-Gonzaléz and Charles Reagan Wilson. Jackson: University Press of Mississippi, 97–115. Print.

Achtner, Wolfgang, Stefan Kunz, and Thomas Walter. 1998. *Dimensionen der Zeit: Die Zeitstrukturen Gottes, der Welt und des Menschen*. Darmstadt: Primus Verlag. Print.

Allen, Lillian. 2014. "pOetic gEsture." *Toronto in Excelsis!* https://medium.com/dub-poets/lillian-allen-e46c41b2d2bb.

——. 1999. *Psychic Unrest*. Toronto: Insomniac Press. Print.

——. 1995. "Poems are not meant to lay still." In *The Other Woman. Women of Colour in Contemporary Canadian Literature,* ed. Silvera Makeda, 262–353. Toronto: Sister Vision Press. Print.

——. 1993a. "Colors." In *Family Folk Festival: A Multicultural Sing Along*. Disco.

——. 1993b. *Women Do This Every Day*. London: Women's Press. Print.

——. 1987. *Conditions Critical*. Redwood Records. Print.

——. 1982. *Rhythm an' Hardtimes*. Domestic Bliss: Rodmersham. Print.

Baker, Houston A., Jr. *Long Black Song: Essays in Black American Literature and Culture*. Charlottesville: University Press of Virginia, 1972. Print.

——. 1991. *The Workings of the Spirit: The Poetics of Afro-American Women's Writing*. Chicago: University of Chicago Press. Print.

Bakhtin, Michail M. 1994. *The Dialogic Imagination: Four Essays by M. M. Bakhtin*. Austin: The University of Texas Press. Print.

Bauman, Zygmunt. 2000. *Liquid Modernity*. Cambridge: Polity Press. Print.

Barrett Sr., Leonard E. 1997. *The Rastafarians*. Boston: Beacon Press. Print.

Barrow, Steven, and Peter Dalton. 1997. *Reggae the Rough Guide*. London: The Rough Guides Ltd. Print.

Bernard, Emily. 2011. "The New Negro Movement and the Politics of Art." In *The Cambridge History of African American Literature*, ed. Maryemma Graham, 268–287. Cambridge: Cambridge University Press. Print.

Brim, Antoinette. 2011. "We Winter Still." In *44 on 44. Forty-Four African American Writers on the Election of Barack Obama 44th President of the United States*, ed. Lita Hooper, Sonia Sanchez, and Michael Simanga, 96. Chicago: Third World Press. Print.

Butler, Judith, and Athena Athanasiou. 2013. *Dispossession: The Performative in the Political.* Cambridge: Polity Press. Print.

Carr, Brenda. 1998, "'Come Mek Wi Work Together': Community Witness and Social Agency in Lillian Allens Dub Poetry." *Ariel* 29: 1–12. Print.

Chaar-Pérez, Kahlil. 2013. "'A Revolution of Love': Ramón Emeterio Betances, Anténor Firmin, and Affective Communities in the Caribbean." *The Global South* 7.2: 11–36. Print.

Cooper, Afua. 2006a. *Copper Woman and Other Poems*. Toronto: Natural Heritage Books. Print.

——. 2006b. *The Hanging of Angelique*. Canada: Harper Collins. Print.

——. 2000a. "Redemption Dub: ahdri zhina mandiela and the Dark Diaspora." In *Testifyin': Contemporary African Canadian Drama*, vol. I, ed. Djanet Sears, 440–444. Toronto: Playwrights Canada Press. Print.

——. 2000b. *"Doing Battle in Freedom's Cause": Henry Bipp, Abolitionism, Race Uplift, and Black Manhood, 1842–1854.* PhD thesis, University of Toronto. Print.

——, ed. 1999. *Utterances and Incantations. Women, Poetry, and Dub.* Toronto: Sister Vision Press. Print.

——. 1992. *Memories Have Tongue. Poetry by Afua Cooper*, Toronto: Sister Vision Press, 1992.

Cooper, Carolyn. 2004. *Sound Clash: Jamaican Dancehall Culture at Large*. New York: Palgrave Macmillan. Print.

Douglas, Aaron. 2002. "Letter Editorial *Fire!!*." In *Naming the Stones, Claiming the Bones: Cultural Property and the Negotiation of National and Ethnic Identity*, ed. Elazar Barkan and Ronald Bush, 289. Los Angeles: The Getty Research Institute. Print.

Eisenlohr, Patrick. 2018. "Diaspora, Temporality, and Politics: Promises and Dangers of Rotational Time." https://www.researchgate.net/publication/329061489_Diaspora_temporality_and_politics_Promises_and_dangers_of_rotational_time.

Ferris, William. 2018. *Voices of Mississippi: Artists and Musicians Documented by William Ferris*. Box Set. CD.

——. 2009. *Give My Poor Hear Ease. Voices of the Mississippi Blues.* Chapel Hill: The University of North Carolina Press. Print

Gilroy, Paul. 1993. *The Black Atlantic – Modernity and Double Consciousness*. London: Verso. Print.

Gingell, Susan. 2005. "Rooting and Routing Caribbean-Canadian Writing." *Journal of West Indian Literature* 14.1/2 (November): 220–259. Print.

Guillén, Nicolás. 1988. *Antología*. Madrid: Visor Libros. Print.

Habekost, Christian. 1993. *Verbal Riddim: The Politics and Aesthetics of African-Caribbean Dub Poetry*. Amsterdam, Atlanta: Rodopi. Print.

Hughes, Langston. 1926. "I, Too." In *The Portable Harlem Renaissance Reader*, ed. David L. Lewis, 257. 1995. New York: Penguin Books. Print.

——. 1920. "The Negro Speaks of Rivers." In *The Portable Harlem Renaissance Reader*, ed. David L. Lewis, 259. 1995. New York: Penguin Books. Print.

——. 1926. "The Negro Artist and the Racial Mountain." In *The Portable Harlem Renaissance Reader*, ed. David L. Lewis, 91–95. 1995. New York: Penguin Books. Print.

Jenkins, Henry. 2006. *Convergence-Culture: Where the Old and New Media Collide*. New York: New York University Press. Print.

Kirschke, Amy Helene. 1999. *Aaron Douglas: Art, Race, and the Harlem Renaissance*. Jackson: University of Mississippi Press. Print.

Knopf, Kerstin. 2005. "'Oh Canada': Reflections of Multiculturalism in the Poetry of Canadian Women Dub Artists." *Views of Canadian Cultures* III.2: 78–111. Print.

Kotarba, Joseph A. 2018. "The Sociology of Popular Music." In *Understanding Society Through Popular Music*, ed. Joseph Kortaba, 1–19. New York: Routledge. Print.

Lenz, Günter H. 2002. "Toward a Dialogics of International American Culture Studies: Transnationality. Border Discourses, and Public Culture(s)." In *The Futures of American Studies*, ed. Donald E. Pease and Robyn Wiegman, 461–485. Durham: Duke University Press. Print.

——. 2011. "Towards a Politics of American Transcultural Studies: Discourses of Diaspora and Cosmopolitanism." In *Re-Framing the Transnational Turin in American Studies*, ed. Winfried Fluck, Donald E. Pease, and John Carlos Rowe, 391–425. Hanover: Dartmouth College Press. Print.

Locke, Alain. 1995. "The New Negro." In *The Portable Harlem Renaissance Reader*, ed. David L. Lewis, 46–51. New York: Penguin Books. Print.

Masilela, Ntongela. 1996. "The 'Black Atlantic' and African Modernity in South Africa." In *Research in African Literatures* 27.4: 88–96. Print.

Mehring, Frank, ed. 2016. *The Mexico Diary. Winold Reiss between Vogue Mexico and Harlem Renaissance. An Illustrated Trilingual Edition with Commentary and Musical Interpretation.* Trier: WVT, Tempe: Bilingual Press. Print.

Mignolo, Walter. 2011. *The Darker Side of Western Modernity. Global Futures, Decolonial Options.* Durham: Duke University Press. Print.

Miller, E. Ethelbert. 2011. "The Day the Earth Stood Still. First President and First Lady." In *44 on 44. Forty-Four African American Writers on the Election of Barack Obama 44th President of the United States*, ed. Lita Hooper, Sonia Sanchez, and Michael Simanga, 103. Chicago: Third World Press. Print.

Mitchell, Keith B. 2008. "A Still Burning Fire: Afua Cooper's Triptych of Resistance." In *Beyond the Canebrakes Caribbean Women Writers in Canada*, ed. Emily A. Williams, 37–56. Trenton: Africa World Press. Print.

Powell, Richard J. 2002. *Black Art: A Cultural History*. London: Thames & Hudson. Print.

Raussert, Wilfried. 2017. *Diferentes conceptos de tiempo en diálogo: el blues, el jazz y la novella afroamericana.* Translation By María Luisa Arias. Guadalajara: Universidad de Guadalajara. Print.

—–, Jonathan Lantz, and Joachim Michael. 2020. "(Post)Modernism." In *The Routledge Handbook to Culture and Media of the Americas*, ed. Wilfried Raussert, José Carlos Lozano, Giselle Anatol, Sarah Corona Berkin, and Sebastian Thies, Entry 14. New York: Routledge. Print.

—, and Lisa Tomlinson. 2020. "Popular Music Flows." In *The Routledge Handbook to Culture and Media of the Americas*, ed. Wilfried Raussert, José Carlos Lozano, Giselle Anatol, Sarah Corona Berkin, and Sebastian Thies, Entry 16. New York. Print.

—, and Reinhard Isensee. 2008. "Transcultural Visions of Identities in Images and Texts-Transatlantic American Studies." In *Transcultural Visions of Identities in Images and Texts-Transatlantic American Studies*, ed. Wilfried Raussert and Reinhard Isensee, 1–12. Heidelberg: Winter. Print.

Reed, Ishmael. 1978. *Shrovetide in Old New Orleans*. New York: Doubleday. Print.

——. 1972. *Mumbo Jumbo*. New York: Avon Books. Print.

Reggae Lane Mural by Adrian Hayles. 2016. https://muralroutes.ca/mural/reggae-lane/.

Rhiney, Kevon, and Romain Cruse. 2012. "'Trench Town Rock': Reggae Music, Landscape Inscription, and the Making of Place in Kingston, Jamaica." *Hindawi, Urban Studies Research*. https://www.hindawi.com/journals/usr/2012/585160/.

Roach, Hilda. 1985. *Black American Music: Past and Present*, Vol. I. Malabar: Krieger Publishing Company Inc. Print.

Roberts, Krista L. "Lillian Allen." 2010. *The Canadian Encyclopedia*, January 7. Print.

Rosenberg, Christiana. 1995. *Handbuch für Jazz Dance*. Aachen: Meyer und Meyer. Print.

Ross, Marlon B. 2002. "The New Negro Displayed: Self-Ownership, Proprietary Sites/sights and the Bonds/Bounds of Race." In *Claiming the Stones, Naming the Bones. Cultural Property and the Nego-*

tiation of National and Ethnic Identity, ed. Elazar Barkan and Ronald Bush, 259–301. Los Angeles: The Getty Research Institute. Print.

Russell, Sandi. 1990. *Render Me My Song: African-American Women Writers from Slavery to the Present*. New York: St. Martin's Press. Print.

Shange, Ntozake. 1982. *Sassafrass, Cypress & Indigo*. New York: St. Martin's Press. Print.

Silvera, Makeda, ed. 1995. *The Other Woman. Women of Colour in Contemporary Canadian Literature*. Toronto: Sister Vision Press. Print.

Simanga, Michael. 2011. "First President and First Lady." In *44 on 44. Forty-Four African American Writers on the Election of Barack Obama 44th President of the United States*, ed. Lita Hooper, Sonia Sanchez, and Michael Simanga, 139. Chicago: Third World Press. Print.

Song of the Towers. 1934. Aaron Douglas. *WikiArt*. December 27, 2017. https://www.wikiart.org/en/aaron-douglas/song-of-the-towers-1934.

Strange, Sharan. 2011. "Inaugural." In *44 on 44. Forty-Four African American Writers on the Election of Barack Obama 44th President of the United States*, ed. Lita Hooper, Sonia Sanchez, and Michael Simanga, 94. Chicago: Third World Press. Print.

Thomas, H. Nigel. 2006. "Afua Cooper." *Why We Write: Conversations with African Canadian Poets and Novelists* (Interviews). 74–89. Toronto: Tsar Publication. Print.

Tomlinson, Lisa. 2012. "Memories Have Tongue: A Conversation with Afua Cooper." In *Jamaica in the Canadian Experience: A Multiculturalizing Presence*, ed. Carl James and Andrea Davis, 107–114. Halifax: Fernwood Press. Print.

Toronto Reggae Roots. https://read-the-plaque.appspot.com/plaque/toronto-s-reggae-roots.

Van Deburg, William. 1992. *New Day in Babylon – The Black Power Movement and American Culture*. Chicago: The University of Chicago Press. Print.

Williams, Emily. A. 1995. "Afua Cooper: An Evolving Dub Poet With Historical Foundation. An Interview with Afua Cooper." In *The Other Woman. Women of Colour in Contemporary Canadian Literature*, ed. Makeda Silvera, 317–328. Toronto: Sister Vision Press. Print.

Williams, Raymond. 1977. *Marxism and Literature*. New York: Oxford University Press. Print.

Winders, James A. 1993. "'Narratime': Postmodern Temporality and Narrative." *Issues in Integrative Studies* 11: 27–43. Print.

7 Sonic America(s): Politics of Recognition and Recent Trends in Music Documentary to Rethink the Relation between Music and the Social

From songs of enslaved African Americans to murals of Mexican modernists, from hip hop sounds to street art, sound- and imagescapes from the Americas have shaped and performed the social in the Americas. These scapes, at times, supersede language as mediators and commentators of the social. In the late twentieth century, MTV music/video culture established musical sound and image as interconnected and almost inseparable expressions of youth cultures (Edgar, Fairclough-Isaacs, and Halligan 2013). The music documentary and its growing presence in TV programs, film festivals, cinema programs, and museums of popular culture point toward the genre's increasingly important role in endorsing celebrity culture and rewriting music history. The music documentary provides a matrix to rethink music historiography in narrative forms where image, sound, and word interact intensely. It also lends itself to relocating music in history and at the intersection of entertainment, commerce, and heritage politics. Likewise, as I argue in this chapter, the music documentary reflects the interrelation of music and the social on a grander scale.

A proliferation of documentaries as well as other non-fiction or reality formats characterizes recent developments in media industry. And they reveal new tendencies in redefining the documentary mode. In global network society with its inclination toward hyperreality, simulacrum, and media saturation (Baudrillard 1994, 9ff.), the flourishing of the documentary mode responds to a newly awakened desire to come to terms with the real, the social, and with history at large. Popular documentary series for television like Martin Scorsese's *The Blues* (2003), a compilation of seven blues documentaries directed by renowned film directors from around the globe, reveal the attractiveness of the genre for fiction and nonfiction filmmakers. The documentaries highlight a new level of interaction of music and documentary film as a mix-media historiography between education and entertainment. It is safe to say that documentary filmmaking has hit the big screen and successfully rid itself of its former confinement to noncommercial distribution. Filmmakers like Michael Moore and Marilyn Agrelo have produced multi-million revenues. Documentary films like *Fahrenheit 9/11* (2004) and *An Inconvenient Truth* (2006) raised public consciousness of political and ecological issues. Music documentaries like *Searching for Sugar Man* (2012) and *20 Feet from Stardom* (2014) rose to Oscar winning fame, achieving critical and popular acclaim. Mitchell Block emphasizes that with the beginning of the twenty-first century, "theatrical exhibition of documentaries became a business" for the larger film and entertainment industry (2018, n. pag.). Documentary film not only flourishes in the contemporary digital age but adds to the creative representation of actuality through new hybrid and participatory formats. We encounter documentary modes crossed with staged performances and animation. An intensified presence of hyperreality (Baudrillard 1994) and performativity (Bruzzi 2006, 53–56) shapes the narrative modes of music documentary film and shows that the line between fiction and non-fiction film is nothing but thin and porous. Against the backdrop of these dynamics, selective approaches to truth and forms of eclectic and fragmentary narration of content and context are highlighted. Increasingly, actuality is pressed into narrative modes and patterns geared toward popular narrative and public success. "The long-cherished idea that truth in documentary film is established in a process exclusively controlled by the documentarian seems increasingly untenable," as Thies maintains (2016, 216, 168). Music documentaries are deeply embedded in the mechanisms of the cultural industry at large (Yúdice 2004, 9–39). And Sheila Curran Bernard emphasizes that, "in today's documentary marketplace, story is what commissioning editors are looking for, and training in storytelling is deemed necessary for filmmakers" (2010, 6).

Tony Palmer's 1970s TV series *All You Need is Love* may be seen as a starting point to create large span music documentaries geared toward education embedded in entertainment (Long and Wall 2013, 25–26). In the twenty-first century music documentaries like Wim Wenders's *Buena Vista Social Club* (1999) and Martin Scorsese's *Shine a Light* (2008) have popularized the genre, interweaving moments of political actuality, nostalgia, and musical history into documentary success stories. Standing out as box office successes, they illustrate the music documentary's newly gained popularity for and within the cultural industry (Yúdice 2014, 9–35).

Part of the documentary revival in recent years is the growing production of documentaries on music in the Americas. One striking tendency among filmmakers is the selection of hotbeds of social crisis and change like Havana in Cuba, Detroit in the U.S., and the U.S.-Mexican borderlands as background to the music historiography they want to present. Havana, for instance, has become a most popular site for music documentary makers. As Geoffrey Baker has documented, some dozen documentaries on the hip hop scene in Havana alone have moved the focus from traditional Cuban music to hip hop in Cuba and its relations to global subcultures (2014).

The documentary approach varies from film to film. Some documentaries pursue a high degree of objectivity and historicity in a conventional sense (*Cuban Hip Hop Desde el Principio* [2006]), others openly embrace politics and polemics (*Guerrilla Radio* [2007], *A Short Radiography of Hip Hop in Cuba* [2004]), and a third group follows artistic and symbolical patterns to create new narratives based on hip hop's cultural significance (*HavanYork* [2009]). Their differences and meanings cannot be understood without comprehending their cultural, economic, or political agendas. Many of the documentaries, such as Mexican director Luciano Larobina's *HavanYork*, are made by cultural outsiders and demonstrate the filmmaker's awareness of music's key role in performing and reflecting social change. These films not only give voice to the hip hop scene in Cuba but also shape it by narrating it anew in the mode of tourist, nostalgic or romanticizing gazes. The link between image, music, and their significance for rethinking the social in music documentaries particularly thrives in those films that create cultural narratives that transcend the notion of the musical expression or genre. *HavanYork* represents a filmic journey between New York and Havana and conveys Larobina's objective to bridge the gap between the U.S. and Cuba cinematically and musically. Oscillating between images from both cities, inserting the individual stories from hip hoppers in New York and Havana, and narrating connected subcultures beyond Cold War political divisions, the documentary creates a tapestry of interconnected Southern and Northern hemispheres. As Baker puts it, "the idea behind this film is as much to create a bridge between New York and Havana as to describe one" (2014, 12). While the desire for objectivity may fall prey to narrative vision, music in *HavanYork*'s visual and sonic representations serves as cultural memory and template for a new socio-cultural vision.

Music documentaries are increasingly present in film festivals, such as in Los Angeles and Montreal. The Guadalajara International Film Festival, one of the most influential film festivals in the Americas, started to dedicate a whole section to documentaries on music in 2009. In a rubric labeled *Son de Música*, the festival organizers presented a wide array of documentaries on music genres, individual artists, bands, and the migration of music in the Americas and extended global contexts. Among the films shown were Barbara Kopple's *Woodstock: Now & Then* (USA, 2009), Jackie Reem Salloum's *Slingshot Hip Hop* (Palestine/ USA, 2008), Guto Barra's *Beyond Ipanema* (Brazil/USA, 2009), Luciano Larobina's *HavanYork* (Mexico, 2009), and Bestor Cram's *Johnny Cash at Folsom Prison* (USA, 2008). While these films differ strikingly in their use of camera and narrative, they all mediate the representation of "otherness" in music, be it ethnic, racial, class-based or counter-cultural.

My focus in this chapter lies on a recent wave of music documentary films that have gained commercial as well as critical success. In the U.S. context, for instance, documentaries like *Standing in the Shadows of Motown* (2002), *The Wrecking Crew!* (2008), *Muscle Shoals* (2013), *Before There Was Punk There Was A Band Called Death* (2012), *Searching for Sugar Man* (2012), *Charles Bradley* (2012), and *20 Feet from Stardom* (2014) represent a fairly recent direction in music documentary of making unheard voices heard. These films are frequently linked with urban, regional, and community sites in crisis and change. They attempt to fill gaps in music history and correct standardized narratives about music genres. Unlike canonical music documentaries that take for their subject matter celebrities like Harry Belafonte, Bruce Springsteen, Neil Young, Eric Clapton, Ruben Blades, and most recently Whitney Houston, these films focus on the stories of minor figures. In spite of their historical and political interest, they unfold music historiography as entertainment; they do not hide their ambition to create narratives to reach larger audiences and popular acclaim. They seem to share what Jean-François Lyotard labels, the postmodern "incredulity toward metanarratives" (1997, 1). Looking into minor and puzzling stories of music history, they tend to produce postmodern knowledge that "refines our sensitivity to differences and reinforces our ability to tolerate the incommensurable" (1).

Knowledge production and music have long been recognized as close allies in the formation of the social. With a nod to George Lipsitz, I already pointed out in the introductory chapter that popular music plays an important role for the creation and conservation of collective memory. Songwriters frequently produce history emerging from their personal experience, memory, and reflection. Popular music, in particular, keeps collective memory a vital presence by overcoming generational gaps. Music functions as an excellent medium for representing communal values, since music can be enjoyed across the otherwise strict divisions of different languages and customs. For this very reason, music is adaptable to different cultural and social contexts, which also means that music can be appropriated for the purposes of exposing, narrating, and reflecting the social beyond local, regional, national, and generational boundaries. The music documentary, then, is an additional medium to emphasize the historicizing power of music.

The recent wave of music documentaries unravels music historiography within a complex network of education, history-making, entertainment, and politics of recognition. More intensely than ever, the topics and sites chosen are embedded in a larger politics of recognition. Certainly, recognition is a highly debated concept, but it still holds a strong position in theories of subject formation. As Winfried Fluck puts it with a nod to Althusser and Butler, "by means of interpellation … recognition remains crucial … . Recognition is not gained in reciprocal acknowledgement of others but in an act of hailing (interpellation) that turns individuals into subjects" (2014, 170–171) Current films like *Searching for Sugar Man*, *20 Feet from Stardom*, and *Before There Was Punk There Was A Band Called Death* engage with interpellation as "a performative practice whose effectiveness is based on iteration" (171). In these films, musicians, singers, and composers gain an identity (perhaps fluid) by a form of recognition. Despite their at times incomplete and eclectic narrations, these films share a desire to correct flawed representations of others and expose social, political, and cultural conditions in music history. In recent years, as Wendy Martineau, Nasar Meer, and Simon Thompson point out, "the idea of the politics of recognition has become an increasingly popular way of thinking about a wide range of political phenomena from the logic of social struggles to the nature of social justice" (2012, 1). Music history has been shaped by recognition and absence; the latter often reinforced by the misrecognition of others. Such misrecognition Richard Rorty reads as a lack of solidarity (1989, 190). The positioning of musicians in music history has also to do with certain group affiliations. That musicians from various ethnic, racial, and gender backgrounds have played a subordinate role or suffered absence in music histories has also to do with, what Charles Taylor defines as, the consequences of group entrapment and asymmetrical relations: "If a certain group is demeaned or held in contempt, its members will face forms of neglect, exclusion, and subordination" (1994, 25–26, 24).

By selecting several representative documentaries, this chapter looks at how politics of recognition shape new minor narratives in contemporary music documentary at the intersection of historiography and mass entertainment. To narrow the focus of the relation between music, music documentary, and the social, I select documentaries related to music emerging from sites of crisis like Havana, Detroit, and the U.S.-Mexican borderlands.

7.1 *Buena Vista Social Club* (1999)

Let me begin with Wim Wenders's well-known 1999 documentary, *The Buena Vista Social Club*, which arguably is not only a late-twentieth-century beginning of a wave of music documentaries feeding on nostalgia and a politics of recognition in the twenty-first century but also a striking manifestation of the politically charged mobility of music. The music documentary thematizes the long-broken ties between Cuba and the Western World through the lens of music. Many of the filmic elements serve as a reservoir to rethink music through the social and the social through music. Wenders's film is a transcultural product bringing together the musical experience of Buena Vista Social Club musicians and singers such as Compay Segundo, Eliades Ochoa, Ruben Gonzalez, Ibrahim Ferrer, and Omara Portuondo; the music ethnography and creative spirit of American musician Ry Cooder; the production talents of Nick Gold, and Wenders's cinematographic mastery of narrative progression. By providing intimate looks into the lives and minds of musicians aged 80 and more, who are seemingly far beyond the possibility of new musical success, the film narrative takes an affectionate approach to music historiography that evokes empathetic responses from the spectator.

Old age, Cuban music history, and long forgotten musicians find recompense in Wenders's narrative of Cuban *son*'s late global success. The film's title is a borrowing from the album that Ry Cooder had produced with Buena Vista Social Club in 1997. Both album and film emerged toward the end of the Cuban crisis in the 1990s, the so-called Special Period, and helped bring Cuban music and culture back into Western circuits. While Wenders's film did not rediscover the *Buena Vista Social Club* it distinctly expanded the international recognition that the above musicians had already gained from the album and show. As I argue, Wenders's film establishes central strategies for music documentaries in the twenty-first century to rethink music and the social as interrelated. His narration of Cuban music is one that tells and partly idealizes Cuba's musical emergence after a cultural freeze during the cold war period. In a nostalgic twist, Wenders reloads Cuba's music culture that had its heydays in the 1940s and 1950s before the Cuban Revolution. This nostalgia for the golden days of Cuban music that flourished in the context of a totalitarian and repressive regime, though, is paired with stories of a new cultural recognition exemplified by the Amsterdam and Carnegie Hall concert in New York and a mythic recreation of the West as arbiter of world music. Cuba is culturally reintegrated in the larger world order of Western '*gusto*.' When the Cuban musicians walk the streets of Manhattan in awe, it is not only a celebration of newly gained mobility but also of New York as the cultural hub of the modern world. Emblematically, the show window scene of the encounter of Buena Vista Social Club musicians encountering replicas of American greats like Louis Armstrong, Ray Charles, and Miles Davis, illustrates both the rupture that had characterized U.S.-Cuban relations and the lingering admiration from the South for the globally successful culture of the North.

The Buena Vista band of aging Cuban musicians, once affiliated with a prominent 1940s' social club in Havána of the same name and cast into oblivion in Castro's Cuba, provides fortunate material for a culturally and politically motivated American success story, this time, however, transnationally produced. With the release of Wenders's film, the band's global success skyrocketed. The scenes from and around the concert in New York illustrate a politically engaging story that envisions a new connectedness between Cuba and the U.S. and demonstrate that Wenders's narrative is loosely embedded in a larger context of historical conflict and change. Whereas comments of admiration for the Manhattan skyline by musicians like Ibrahim Ferrer insert a desire to embrace U.S. culture, the filmic representation of Havana evokes a sense of nostalgia for a decaying political and economic system on the brink of collapse beneath the weight of the West. The camera light surrounds the decaying colonial architecture of Havana in a shimmering vintage style. Musicians from the Buena Vista Social Club walk the streets as a public memory lane while the streets of Manhattan promise the future. Wenders's narrative stages Ry Cooder's arrival on motorbike in Havana as a friendly but firm cultural conquest. Rewriting musical history gets paired with a desire for participatory appropriation. In most concert and recording scenes Cooder takes center stage as mediator and producer. This gesture is sanctioned by also telling the story of a latent desire of Cuban musicians and artists to finally immerse their products into markets of the Western cultural industry. Wenders's fascination with Cuban and American culture is honest. His rendering of politics of recognition cannot avoid revisiting hegemonic cultural relations. Declared forgotten, Cuban music is heard again, but now channeled through Western music venues and film production.

Both album and film illustrate the political work of cultural production. In retrospect, the Buena Vista Social Group's role as messengers of traditional Cuban music and culture played a significant cultural part in the improvement of political relations between Cuba and the U.S. The fact that the musicians finished their Carnegie Hall concert with a proud presentation of the Cuban flag in the midst of one of the cultural cathedrals in the U.S., underscores the film's desire to create a relational narrative for a future U.S.-Cuban connectedness. The documentary film as box office success revealed that the culture industry, too, had recognized the image-sound connection as a gateway for Cuban traditional music to enter global music circuits. It is significant that these political and economic opportunities were made possible by a musical and cultural exchange between Cuba, the U.S., and Europe, leading to a Cuban musical success story on a global scale. Wenders's example shows that the documentation of music in the late twentieth and early twenty-first century is inextricably related to nostalgia and a politics of recognition, as well as to the production of knowledge for consumption in Western markets. The *Buena Vista Social Club* also demonstrates that the visual documentation of music can go beyond furnishing a subject matter and soundtrack; it can serve as a way to reinvent the social, as we see with this film's reappropriation of music for new historiographies of Cuban-U.S. American cultural entanglements.

7.2 *Standing in the Shadows of Motown* (2002)

Detroit, the first U.S. American city that ever had to declare bankruptcy, is home to an increasing number of music documentaries. With its historical cycles of social and political crisis on the one hand, and of tremendous music output on the other, Detroit represents an ideal matrix for dynamic and tension-driven documentaries that rethink music historiography in a larger context of social relations and development. Music documentaries like *Standing in the Shadows of Motown*, *20 Feet from Stardom*, *Before There Was Punk There Was A Band Called Death*, and *Searching for Sugar Man* create soundscapes as cityscapes, providing a strong identification between city, music, and musicians. Twenty-first century U.S. music documentaries tend to follow templates that translate politics of recognition into a creative process of rewriting of music historiography, while at the same time, presenting carefully crafted storylines to keep the audience entertained. These templates bring musicians, background singers, and performers, largely ignored by the music industry, into the spotlight.

Allan Slutsky's book, *Standing in the Shadows of Motown: The Life and Music of Legendary Bassist James Jamerson* (1989), forms the basis for the Grammy award winning music documentary, *Standing in the Shadows of Motown* (2002), directed by Paul Justman. The film's mode is predominantly poetic, the script written by Walter Dallas and Ntozake Shange. The film is set in Detroit, the home of Motown and witness to many Civil Rights marches and street dances inspired by Martha and the Vandellas. The film adds alternative historiography to the cultural music histories told by critics like Suzanne Smith in *Dancing in the Street: Motown History and the Cultural Politics of Detroit* (2009). Smith portrays

Motown's evolution from a small local record company in Detroit's black community to a global player in the music industry and establishes Motown music as cultural agent in politically turbulent times. The story of Motown, as a music industry and successful sound enterprise, is also a story of black Detroit and a microcosm of black America. Complementary to Smith's narrative, the music documentary places minor stories within this larger picture by highlighting the talents and fates of lesser known musicians involved.

Justman's music documentary tackles the Motown music history from the economically privileged position of a budget film production. The film's agenda is to create a counter-narrative to the standardized success stories of 1960s music history and expose a band of largely ignored black studio musicians as local cultural heroes. High production values are enlisted to present a highly entertaining cinematographic historiography. The documentary represents and elevates the skills of studio musicians and their significant role in shaping the sound of Motown. The film's protagonists comprise the Motown studio musicians Earl Van Dyke, Joe Hunter, Johnny Griffith, Eddie Willis, Joe Messina, Robert White, William Benjamin, Uriel Jones, Richard Allen, James Jamerson, Bob Babbitt, Jack Ashford Bass, and Eddie Brown, a group also known as The Funk Brothers. Adopting strategies used by Wenders in *Buena Vista Social Club*, Justman's documentary unites many of the former Funk Brothers with the purpose of unraveling their musical grandeur and releasing them from long-time oblivion. The documentary stages the musicians' iteration of masterful performance skills. Exaltation follows iteration in the film's progression so that the storyline moves back and forth between documentation and celebration.

Most of the musicians portrayed had been gathered by Berry Gordy from many jazz and blues clubs in Detroit from the late 1950s to the early 1970s to record the musical tracks for his Motown label. According to the film's narrative, The Funk Brothers' studio performances were the key to the success of Motown music. They accompanied Motown luminaries, only to be all but abandoned when the label moved to L.A. in the early 1970s. At the time of filmmaking many band members, including Benjamin, Jamerson, Brown, Van Dyke, and others had experienced bankruptcy and oblivion; some had already died. City and music historiography complement each other seamlessly. Race riots, class struggle, and exploitative practices in the Detroit music industry form the backdrop to the marginalization of Motown studio musicians. *Standing in the Shadows of Motown* allows the surviving Funk Brothers to tell their own story against the social reality of city decay and Motown's dubious business dealings.

The music documentary installs voiceover commentary as a bridge to line up historical reenactments. It includes several interviews of the Funk Brothers' members, the reunion concert as an assemblage, and the final climax of recognition. The film is a blend of archive footage, oral history, vivid reenactments, and concert film. The voiceover by Andre Braugher addresses the audience directly with the "recount history" of Motown Records and a brief introduction of the Funk Brothers (Nichols 2001, 105). In the opening scenes, the documentary unfolds the history of the Funk Brothers in its relation to larger social and economic developments in the industries of Detroit. The story line emblematically situates the origin of the Funk Brothers within the migration of tens of thousands of workers to Detroit after World War II. Images of migrant workers and the blossoming car industry form the backdrop to an intersectional narrative addressing race and class. Interviews with musician Joe Hunter, about his original jobs in the car factory and his motivation to play music emerging from the working experience, provide a master narrative that establishes a close link between the socio-economic context, musical expression, and the evolving music business in Detroit.

Beyond the "argumentative frame" of documentary making (Nichols 2001, 105), *Standing in the Shadows of Motown* adopts poetic as well as performative patterns to tell a story of resurrection and recognition (Renov 1993; Bruzzi 2006). In Nichols's reading of documentary practice, the poetic mode permits the exploration of "associations and patterns that involve temporal rhythms and spatial juxtapositions" (2001, 102). Justman fuses recent musical material by the Funk Brothers with archive footage of dead band members to create the impression of a cultural continuum. The reunion concert in the present gets intersected by band members' memories and archive footage. Thus, the music documentary fuses the storytelling function of Braugher's voiceover with the performativity of the concert, creating a mix of telling and performing the social history behind the Motown sound.

The storyline emerging around the deceased bass player James Jamerson is, arguably, the most illustrative for the generational narrative of *Standing in the Shadows of Motown.* The voiceover about James Jamerson's boyhood emerges against the background of a short video clip of the bass player's former school site. A reenactment scene of a little boy playing a self-made instrument follows the archive footage before the interview of James Jamerson Jr. telling his father's story takes center stage. In the reenactment scene, Jamerson is shown as a little boy creating a makeshift bass out of a stick strung with a rubber band. Jameson Jr. is shown reenacting the one-finger plucking that marked the late bass player's unique and captivating style. Among its other stories, the film here provides an uplifting story of a little-known bass player legend through family narrative, replacing the musician's actual decline into alcoholism and oblivion with a story of a musical continuum from father to son. This is a major storyline among many other minor ones that give voice to the sounds, rhythms, and people behind the globally successful Motown sound.

Similar to Wenders's *Buena Vista Social Club*, Justman's music documentary is driven by a strong nostalgia for the past and a desire to perform music history anew. The documentary film celebrates the Funk Brothers as principal creators of the Motown sound behind seemingly endless number one hits in the U.S. charts. With the Funk Brothers as the mastermind of one the greatest soundtracks in music history, the film uplifts working class and race in an alternative historiography and rethinks the social from the perspective of the dispossessed (Butler and Athanasiou 2013, 4–5).

7.3 *20 Feet from Stardom* (2014)

A decade later, aspects of Motown and Detroit music history, within a larger context of rock music history, were revisited from a transcultural and gender perspective in the Oscar award winning music documentary and box office hit *20 Feet from Stardom* by Morgan Neville, one of the most prolific documentary producer/directors of American pop culture, credited with documentaries on Muddy Waters, James Brown, and James Taylor among others. The music documentary mixes archival material, TV footage, concert clips, recent interviews, recording scenes, and private as well as public scenes from the lives of the portrayed female vocalists. Beginning with the story of Darlene Love, who, with her trio The Blossoms, helped tear down the color barrier for black backup singers in the early 1960s, the film revisits black female artists in the context of rock music but looks at musical history through a sharpened lens of gender and race. Arguably, background singers in rock music historically contributed to "politics of racial alterity" (Fast 2009, 170ff.). A great number of black female background singers performed aside or behind white male rock icons like Bruce Springsteen, Mick Jagger, Sting, Joe Cocker, and African American icons like Ray Charles, Ike Turner, and Stevie Wonder. As Susan Fast reminds us, the stage scenario reinforced persisting patterns of "heteronormativity and whiteness" (2009, 174) even at a time when the feminist movement took full speed in the 1960s. With reference to the title '*20 Feet from Stardom*,' David Scott Diffrient maintains that "those … twenty feet also hint at the larger history of race relations and sexual politics in twentieth-century America" (2017, 26). Concert venues and recording sessions frequently reproduced "divisionist discourses and segregationist policies" from larger society in the realm of music (26). *20 Feet from Stardom* clearly addresses the power structures visible in the performance culture of popular music along the lines of gender and race and presents itself as a revisionist documentary to bring this issue to the foreground. Similar to music documentaries, such as *Muscle Shoals* and *The Wrecking Crew*, all of which narrate the histories of largely unknown instrumental backing groups, *20 Feet from Stardom* seeks to tell the silenced history of female background vocalists and their respective roles in concert performances and recordings of R&B and rock since the early 1960s.

20 Feet from Stardom's proclaimed protagonists are primarily African American female background singers, such as Mable Merry Clayton, Darlene Love, and Lisa Fischer. While their stories stand in the foreground, they equally serve as gateway to introduce other female vocalists, including Afro Caribbean Tata Vega, who tours with Elton John; Cindy Mizelle, who backs up Bruce Springsteen; and Janice Pendarvis, who collaborates with Stevie Wonder. Against the backdrop of skyrocketing music careers like those of Ray Charles, Ike and Tina Turner, and others, the film thus brings out previously marginalized members of rock music groups and provides a generational panorama of female back-up vocalists whose overlapping careers span a roughly sixty-year period (1950s–2010s). Many of these performers share similar histories of starting out as singers in gospel choirs, mastering the call-and-response techniques essential to background performance, and eventually pursuing their own musical careers in the realm of R&B and rock music. The film permits them to recount their own stories and add histories to counter the standard historiography of R&B and rock music. Concert and recording clips, and interviews that offer insights into the female vocalists' everyday lives, fuse the public and private persona to create a series of minor portrayals.

Admittedly, the film chronicles a shift from white to black female back-up vocalists in the 1960s and also addresses the consequences of complex racial politics in the musical industry. One of the female protagonists in the film is Tata Vega, whose ethnicity and multiracial background (her family hails from Puerto Rico and the Dominican Republic) complicated her access to contracts and performances. Zaineb Mohammed cites Vega in her film review: "I did have a hard time finding gigs because of the way I looked. Either I was too white, not white enough, too black, not black enough" (2013, n. pag.). As this example shows, the film does not shy back from highlighting the complexity of changing racial and gender politics in the 1960s. Still, its take on the social dimension of musical performance remains framed by heteronormative patterns of recognition. Orthodox music historiography keeps creeping into the film's overall narrative when voices of rock icons complement the female histories, applauding the singers through a male gaze and voice. The talking-head interviews with rock stars such as Bruce Springsteen, Mick Jagger, and Sting effectively provide recognition of the women's histories by male authority figures. Their voices overlay archival footage and frame recently recorded studio performances in which the female backup vocalists now take center stage.

With a nod to Andrew Flory, I argue that while questions about gender differences, inequalities, and power asymmetries are raised by the music documentary, thus pointing toward the imbrication of musical performance with the social, numerous questions – "Why did rock musicians, who were mostly white and male, start to value the 'insertion' of female vocal blackness (or a 'gospel vocal sound') into their music? How did this 'syncretic sound' represent the changing cultural identity of rock during the 1960s and 1970s? Finally, what are we to make of the issues of race, gender, and power implied by this characteristic representation?" (2014, n. pag.) – remain largely unanswered. Instead, the music documentary drifts off in domestic stories, explores gender issues in relation to career making, addresses racial issues in a predominantly personal context, and plays with personal erotic attractions between black female vocalists and white male front singers.

It is fair to say that the documentary uncovers neglected and largely unknown voices whose musical power and expressivity get full aesthetic recognition. The film also shows that linking gender, race, and music reveals new historiographies, thus making us see the interrelatedness of social developments and music history in a more complex light. Still, historiography in *20 Feet from Stardom* gets framed, limited, and controlled by the film's high-budget necessity to appeal to an imagined, predominantly heteronormative mainstream. The film demonstrates that despite their best intentions, alternative music historiographies struggle to come to terms with the asymmetrical power hierarchies deeply inscribed in the market policies of the music industry, which encourages narratives of music history that maximize profit.

7.4 *Searching for Sugar Man* (2012)

Oscar award-winning music documentary *Searching for Sugar Man*, directed and written by the late Malik Bendjelloul, tells a story of transnational music flows with the songs of Sixto Díaz Rodríguez and their countercultural impact on white South African middle-class youth culture in the 1970s and 1980s. In 2012, the film premiered at the Sundance Film Festival. The documentary, produced by Simon Chinn and John Battsek as a Swedish-British transnational project, gained further fame by winning the World Cinema Special Jury Prize and the Audience Award for World Cinema Documentary. A year after its release, the documentary won the Award for Best Documentary Feature at the 85th Academy Awards.

Searching for Sugar Man is a multifaceted documentary that is more about music and social relations than music itself. The music documentary catapults imaginaries of Detroit working class hardships in the late 1960s and early 1970s and glimpses into white youth protest culture in apartheid-era South Africa in the late 1970s and 1980s into the figure of Sixto Díaz Rodríguez, a musician born in Detroit of Mexican and Native American descent. He recorded two albums with Sussex, *Cold Fact* in 1970 and *Coming from Reality* in 1971. Combining the story of Rodríguez's minor music career with Detroit's working class history and a changing South African social and historical landscape, the documentary links three thin narratives in an aesthetically crafted plotline that stylizes and mystifies Rodríguez as an icon for white youth protest in South Africa and socially active artist-citizen of the Detroit working class. The documentary reads like a "fairytale of a Mexican American working class hero finding recognition amongst his unknown fans in far-away South Africa" (Hyslop 2013, 491) and "derives its appeal, in large part, from the way it allegorizes and dramatizes South Africa's emergence from an isolated, censorious pariah state to a participant in an increasingly globalized world" (Lewsen 2013, 456). In the figure of Rodríguez, recognition becomes threefold: first, there is a personal recognition for him as musician with the climax of his first concert in Cape Town in March 1998, second, there is a recognition of Rodríguez as embodiment of the enduring spirit of the Detroit working class, and, third, there is a recognition of South Africa as member of a global society exemplified by its participation in cultural exchange.

In a highly eclectic manner, the film not only connects these three narratives but builds a postmodern minor success story in which a lot of idealizing and mystifying takes place around a few 'cold facts' about Rodríguez's life. The spectator learns about his different jobs as hard-working laborer in Detroit, his role as a caring father, his political engagement in his Detroit community, and his performances in run-down local clubs. As the story puts it, it was the combination of voice and lyrics that opened the doors to the recording industry. However, his two albums sold few copies in the U.S., and, consequently, Sussex dropped Rodríguez before he could release a third album. Sussex itself closed shortly after in 1975.

While Rodríguez never gained recognition by the American public and larger music industry in the U.S. during the 1970s, the film and earlier re-release of the albums *Cold Fact* and *Coming from Reality* by Light in the Attic Records brought Rodríguez to the attention of critics and fans in the U.S. and Europe in the twenty-first century. The film's unusual American success story created prominent news coverage and ushered in a new fan culture around a musician whose modest and humble personality made him an uplifting representative for the working class of the economically battered Detroit. Arguably, his songs of working-class experience and urban melancholia finally found better hearing in the twenty-first century U.S., a time when the U.S. myth of a classless society continues to be heavily challenged by social reality.

Like *Buena Vista Social Club* and *20 Feet from Stardom*, *Searching for Sugar Man* proves that, while the American Dream may have lost some of its appeal, new transculturally produced success stories in the 'American style' continue to sell well. The story reads like a modern myth, inserting elements of suspense, enigma, and animation to create a poetic and performative mode of documentary. Roe detects in the combination of animation and documentary "an odd couple" (2013, 1). Their opposite positions in portraying the real, however, offer a unique perspective in how we view the world, she argues. This odd coupling, in particular, underscores the cinematic power to construct and perform the social within a documentary mode that seeks to expose, convince, and entertain. The film reflects and performs the social by connecting working class endurance in the U.S. with countercultural politics in anti-apartheid South Africa through global music circuits. It is the traveling of sound and word as means for identity and resistance that crosses barriers between classes and nations, and that exposes the social as flexible and fluid (Bauman 2000, 2–3).

Bendjelloul's film explicitly treats the medium of documentary as "not being reality but a construct" (Rabiger 2004, 68). The search for the true story behind Rodríguez, as it unfolds in the film, permits "the possibility of alternative forms of knowledge to the straightforward transfer of information, the prosecution of a particular argument or point of view" (Nichols 2001, 103). And for the film director mythmaking appears to be an appropriate means for coming closer to the truth to be conveyed. Drawing upon a well-structured mix of talking-head interviews, archival footage, and several melancholic animation scenes, Bendjelloul creates a narrative based upon unity of tone and effect. The opening narrative announces the potentially greatest suicide story in the history of rock about a musician who presumably had put himself on fire while on stage. The camera shifts from distant views of Cape Town, South Africa to night shots of Detroit in thunder and lightning. Dramatic music, narration, and image create a spooky atmosphere to open the film's narrative of rediscovery and recognition. Every piece of information from various interviews adds new mystery to the puzzle and holds the viewer in suspense about who was or is Rodríguez. While his persona is initially kept a mystery, the songwriter's mournful urban laments accompany the mythmaking storytelling of the compiled interviews as background music. The tone of mystery is confirmed by interviews with the producers of Rodríguez's record and a bartender who vaguely remembers the protagonist as a peculiar musician wandering the streets of Detroit and performing with his back to the audience.

Since the documentary holds back and then reveals information only step by step, it also narrates bits and pieces of the archival work behind documentation on a meta-level, spicing it with elements of suspense and mystery. The rumors of Rodríguez's suicide, for instance, are encouraged rather than questioned by the wave of early interviews. Driven by the melancholy mood of Rodríguez's songs, the film unfolds a quest story whose narrative elements are the selected interviews with music producers, music fans, Rodríguez's daughters, and Rodríguez himself. Going through a timespan of over thirty years, *Searching for Sugar Man* portrays a romanticized search for the true history behind Rodríguez. The music documentary moves back and forth between South Africa and Detroit, revolving around the archival work of the two Cape Town music fans, Stephen "Sugar" Segerman and Craig Bartholomew Strydom, who embark on a voluntary mission to find out whether the rumored death of Rodríguez is true. Segerman and Strydom are ultimately led to the daughter of Rodríguez and a phone call with the musician himself. The film follows a carefully crafted storyline of Rodríguez's emergence from putative death to an animated and, eventually, real flesh and blood musician. From rumors to a scene of reenactment, from animated images of Rodríguez walking in the snow to his voice on the phone, from his voice in the songs to the final physical presence of Rodríguez, the film slowly unveils the secrets about the composer and musician behind the songs "Sugar Man" and "I Wonder." We learn later in the film that Rodríguez spent most of his life as a construction worker in Detroit who was active in local politics; interviews with selected locals build the narrative of an 'inner-city poet,' a 'wandering spirit,' and even a 'prophet' in the local community of Detroit.

The documentary, on different levels, moves from invisibility to visibility. In many ways it unfolds a narrative of the dispossessed and alienated (Butler and Athanasiou 2013, 5), linking examples from industrial Detroit with anti-apartheid Cape Town with a clear appeal to all those who share similar social and economic experiences. Rodríguez's lyrics and melancholic tone reflect harsh living and working conditions for the lower classes in Detroit. His music appeals to a younger white generation of South Africans disenchanted with mainstream control and conservatism and appalled by apartheid politics that are dividing society, and oppressing the black population. As Peter Bradshew puts it, the film functions partly as an "interesting footnote to a species of secret or denied cultural history: the history of South Africa's white liberal classes, the fabric of whose lives may be overlooked by social historians … . Many were trapped by history and fate and the apartheid laws they detested" (2000, n. pag.).

According to the film's narrative, a bootleg copy of *Cold Fact* found its way to apartheid-era South Africa where it became a hit among the white liberal classes and a soundtrack for the white anti-apartheid movement. South African record labels picked up distribution rights from Rodríguez's U.S. label, Sussex Records, and while some songs were banned on South African radio the record sales, according to witnesses interviewed, equaled the success of Simon and Garfunkel's *Bridge over Troubled Water* and the Beatles' *Abbey Road* album in South Africa.

Rodríguez himself is portrayed as a victim of the corrupt music industry, Sussex never sharing royalties for high record sales in South Africa and other African countries. The documentary reflects, on different levels, inequality and social injustice, linking class, race, youth issues, and music industry politics loosely and transnationally. While all this provides material for empathy, it is the story of redemption and recognition that touches the spectator. While it is not a classical story from 'rags to riches,' it is still conceived as an uplifting story that moves the protagonist from oblivion to recognition. Recreating the social transnationally, the music documentary shows Rodríguez's communal presence and impact in two geopolitically and geographically distant locations characterized by uneven temporalities. The reflection and the transformation of the social, as *Searching for Sugar Man* wants us to convince, is possible through the power of music to cross national, cultural, and class boundaries both by music industry channels and idiosyncratic underground music circuits.

7.5 *Flor de Muertos* (2011)

Flor de Muertos [Flower of the Dead] performs and narrates the interrelation of music and the social in and against the background of the U.S.-Mexican American borderlands. Danny Vinik – film director, film producer, film distributor, writer, web developer, and founder of BrinkMedia – thoroughly remolded an original set for a concert film into a performative documentary that contains a wide range of interviews: for example, journalist Charles Bowden observes social issues on the U.S.-Mexican border, community worker Gustavo Lozano attributes the heightened risk of death to the border fence, writer Margaret Regan explores immigration issues, and visual artist Salvador Duran paints to mourn the loss of life.

Most interviewees express their opinions of the United States immigration policies, the violence and destruction from a seemingly ceaseless drug war, and the search for spiritual comfort in the *Santa Muerte* [Saint Death] religion, the growth of which can be observed on both sides of the border. Voices of interviewees take turns with Calexico's music and thus create an aesthetically and musically multifaceted documentary film that exposes social injustice while, at the same time, celebrating contemporary spectacle culture as a venue for performing cross-border flows of culture, music, and religion. The film revolves around a concert performance by Calexico in the historic Rialto Theater in Tucson, Arizona. Calexico is a Tucson-based band named after a small border town in rural California. As a loosely knit, constantly changing collective of musicians, they adopt and assemble a great variety of musical styles like indie rock, Portuguese *fado*, Cajun jazz, and Southern folk ballads. Additionally, they incorporate elements of *mariachi* sounds, *cumbia* waltzes, and a broad range of other Latin American musical forms (Roddy 2008; Schacht 2003; Engelschalt 2018) into what can be called a truly trans-American musical vision. Their hybrid approach to cultures is also reflected in their use of English and Spanish in their lyrics. Their songs are politically conscious and address issues of social, economic, and environmental crisis. Many of their songs express an activist standpoint that is critical of U.S. foreign and social policies as well as of the treatment of migrants and political activists in Latin American countries. For example, songs cover the disastrous impact of hurricane Katrina on the U.S. and Mexican Gulf Coast, human rights issues of indigenous tribes in the borderlands between Mexico and the U.S., issues of drug and human trafficking in the Americas, and the violence and oppression used against activists like the assassination of protest singer Victor Jara by CIA agents in Chile (Schacht 2003; Engelschalt 2018).

Calexico's concert performance in the Rialto Theater represents the point of departure from which Vinik expands the original set for a concert film to include documentary footage about the Mexican Day of the Dead (Thomas 2016, n. pag). The film reflects the liminal experience of the social and the cultural in the borderlands, sonically and rhythmically through the fusion music of Calexico, visually through vivid images from the All Souls Procession in Tucson, Arizona in honor of the dead and Day of the Dead cultural practices in Mexico, and discursively through various borderland expert interviews. By inserting and editing seven performances from the Calexico concert, including the songs *Roka*, *Faker Fur*, *Inspiración*, *Victor Jara's Hands*, *Guero Canel*, *None of This is Mine*, and *Fronter/Trigger*, Vinik keeps the emphasis on a primarily performative mode to relate a hybrid musical world from the borderlands – whose contribution to popular music frequently goes unacknowledged – to a conflicted social world at the U.S.-Mexican border. The documentary makes use of music as spectacle and part of spectacle culture to reflect on violence, disappearance, and death in the borderlands.

Vinik's documentary highlights that "[p]erformative documentary underscores the complexity of our knowledge of the world by emphasizing its subjective and affective dimensions" (Nichols 2001, 131). The film effectively draws viewers into "subjective qualities" (131) and underscores that "[p]erformative documentaries primarily address us, emotionally and expressively, rather than pointing us to the factual world we hold in common" (132). The musical pieces from the concert function as a bridge to connect images, scenes, and cultural expressions from both sides of the border. The border itself holds an omnipresence in the film, as the camera repeatedly inserts images of it in the narrative. *Flor de Muertos* commences with the Mexican celebration of the *Dia de los Muertos* [Day of the Dead] and ends with the All Souls Procession, an annual spectacle in which thousands of locals turn out in skull face to parade through the streets of downtown Tucson, Arizona, to honor and dance with the dead. *Flor de Muertos* – the Aztec marigold, '*cempasuchil*'– spreads on both sides of the border and becomes the visual bond between the cultures from the natural world. Repeatedly, the film inserts images of this flower whose strong transcultural impact on religion in the borderlands appears in the resurgent *Santa Muerte* religious tradition. In this religious context, the scent of marigolds forms a path that the souls of the dead can follow back to the living on the annual Day of the Dead. Symbolically, marigolds personify the compression of time in which past and present merge. As a unifying image throughout documentary, marigolds in the fields sharply contrast with the dividing border.

7.6 Conclusion

With estimates of the border death toll climbing, *Flor de Muertos* ultimately manages to associate the Day of the Dead ceremony with U.S. immigration policies. As Nichols puts it, "[r]ecent performative documentaries try to give representation to a social subjectivity that joins the general to the particular, the individual to the collective, and the political to the personal" (Nichols 2001, 133). Individual, often anonymous fates in the South and the North gain a collective voice in the film's visual and sonic narration of the All Souls Procession and the cultural practices related to the Day of the Dead. *Flor de Muertos* is a good point to start closing the book's reflections on the interrelations of music and the social. In *Flor de Muertos*, music speaks to and about the living and the dead in the borderlands. In the film, music propels the social to stay dynamic, versatile, and hybrid beyond representation. With Calexico's sonic spectacle on the Rialto Theater stage – a performance that echoes the tones of sound sculpture artist Glenn Weyant, who turns the border fence into a gigantic percussion instrument – *Flor de Muertos* expresses music as a performance of entangled American histories that are conflictive, yet relational, and in process. The social discursively evolves in and around sound and image and is bound to keep moving even in the face of violence and death. So at least the sonic and visual performances in *Flor de Muertos* make us want to believe.

Works cited

Baker, Geoff. 2014. "Represent Cuba: Havana Hip Hop Under the Lens." *alter/nativas Latin American Cultural Studies Journal*, Vol. 2 (Spring): 1–18. https://alternativas.osu.edu/assets/files/Issue%202/ensayos/baker.pdf.

Baudrillard, Jean. 1994. *Simulacra and Simulation*. Michigan: University of Michigan Press.

Bauman, Zygmunt. 2000. *Liquid Modernity*. Cambridge: Polity Press. Print.

Block, Mitchell. 2007. "Docunomics: The Money, Markets and Business of Non-Fiction." *IDA International Documentary Association*. https://www.documentary.org/feature/docunomics-money-markets-and-business-nonfiction.

Bradshew, Peter. 2012. "Searching for Sugar Man: Review." *The Guardian* online edition. https://www.theguardian.com/film/2012/jul/26/searching-for-sugar-man-review.

Bruzzi, Stella. 2006. *New Documentary*. New York: Routledge. Print.

Butler, Judith, and Athena Athanasiou. 2013. *Dispossession: The Performative in the Political*. Cambridge: Polity Press. Print.

Curran Bernard, Sheila. 2010. *Documentary Storytelling. Creative Nonfiction on Screen*. Amsterdam: Focal Press. Print.

Diffrient, David Scott. 2017. "Backup Singers, Celebrity Culture, and Civil Rights: Racializing Space and Spatializing Race in *20 Feet from Stardom.*" *Black Camera: An International Film Journal*, Vol. 8.2 (Spring): 25–49. Print.

Edgar, Robert, Kirsty Fairclough-Isaacs, and Benjamin Halligan. 2013. *The Music Documentary: Acid Rock to Electropop*. London/New York: Routledge. Print.

Engelschalt, Julia. 2018. "Straddling the Crystal Frontier: Reworkings of the U.S.-MexicanBorder in the Lyrics of Calexico." *fiar forum for inter-american research* 11.1: 34–46.

Fast, Susan. 2009. "Genre, Subjectivity, and Back-Up Singing in Rock Music." *The Ashgate Research Companion to Popular Musicology*, ed. Derek B. Scott, 171–187. Farnham: Ashgate. Print.

Flory, Andrew. 2014. "20 Feet from Stardom: Entertainment or History." https://www.musicologynow.org/2014/02/20-feet-from-stardom-entertainmentor.html.

Fluck, Winfried. 2014. "The Concept of Recognition and American Cultural Studies." In *American Studies Today. New Research Agendas*, ed. Winfried Fluck, Erik Redling, Sabine Sielke, and Hubert Zapf, 167–208. Heidelberg: Winter. Print.

Hyslop, Jonathan. 2013. "'Days of Miracle and Wonder'?: Conformity and Revolt in *Searching for Sugar Man*." *Safundi* 14.4: 490–501. https://www.tandfonline.com/doi/full/10.1080/17533171.2013.841066.

Lewsen, Simon. 2013. "On Music, Censorship and Globalization." *Safundi* 14.4: 455–466. https://www.tandfonline.com/doi/full/10.1080/17533171.2013.841060.

Lipsitz, George. 2007. *Footsteps in the Dark. The Hidden Histories of Popular Music*. Minneapolis: University of Minnesota Press. Print.

Long, Paul, and Tim Wall. 2013. "Tony Palmer's *All You Need Is Love*: Television's First Pop History." In *The Music Documentary: Acid Rock to Electropop*, ed. Robert Edgar, Kirsty Fairclough-Isaacs, and Benjamin Halligan, 25–26. New York: Routledge. Print.

Lyotard, Jean-François. 1997. *The Postmodern Condition: A Report on Knowledge*. Minneapolis: University of Minnesota Press. Print.

Martineau, Wendy, Nasar Meer, and Simon Thompson. 2012. "Theory and Practice in the Politics of Recognition and Misrecognition." *Res Publica* 18: 1–9. Print.

Mohammed, Zaineb. 2013. "New Film Puts Back Singers in the Spotlight." *Mother Jones* online edition, June 17. https://www.motherjones.com/media/2013/06/20-feet-stardomdocumentary-backup-singers/.

Nichols, Bill. 2001. *Introduction to Documentary*. Bloomington: Indiana University Press. Print.

Rabiger, Michael. 2004. *Directing the Documentary*. London: Focal Press. Print.

Renov, Michael, ed. 1993. *Theorizing Documentary*. London: Routledge. Print.

Roddy, Nikki. 2008. "Calexico's Joey Burns – Interview." *Country Music Pride RSS*. November 1. Print.

Roe, Annabelle H. 2013. *Animated Documentary*. Basingstroke: Palgrave MacMillan. Print.

Rorty, Richard. 1989. *Contingency, Irony, Solidarity*. Cambridge: Cambridge University Press. Print.

Schacht, John. 2003. "The Musical Mixing Pot of Calexico." *Pastemagazine* online edition, February 10. https://www.pastemagazine.com/articles/2003/02/the-musical-mixing-pot-of-calexico.html.

Slutky, Allan. 1989. *Standing in the Shadows of Motown: The Life and Music of Legendary Bassist James Jamerson*. Milwaukee, WI: Hal Leonard Publication. Print.

Smith, Suzanne. 2009. *Dancing in the Street: Motown History and the Cultural Politics of Detroit*. Cambridge: Harvard University Press. Print.

Taylor, Charles. 1994. "The Politics of Recognition." In *Multiculturalism and the Politics of Recognition*, ed. Amy Gutman, 25–73. Princeton: Princeton University Press. Print.

Thies, Sebastian. 2016. "United Colors of Belonging? Participatory Culture and Diversity 2,0 in the Crowd-Sourced Documentary Life in a Day." In *Mobile and Entangled Americas*, ed. Wilfried Raussert and Maryemma Graham, 167–187. New York: Routledge. Print.

Thomas, Bryan. 2016. "'Flor de Muertos': A Love Letter to the Sonoran Desert where Life, Death and Cultures Collide with Calexico." *Nightflight*. http://nightflight.com/flor-de-muertos-a-love-letter-to-the-sonoran-desert-whose-life-death-and-cultures-collide-with-calexico/.

Yúdice, George. 2004. *The Expediency of Culture*. Durham: Duke University Press. Print.

Filmography

A Short Radiography of Hip Hop in Cuba. 2004. Directed by Ricardo Bacallao. Cubafilms.

All You Need Is Love. 1977. Directed by Tony Palmer. TV.

An Inconvenient Truth. 2006. Directed by Davis Guggenheim. Paramount Classics.

Before There was Punk There Was a Band Called Death. 2012. Directed by Mark Christopher Covino and Jeff Howlett. Drafthouse Films.

Beyond Ipanema. 2009. Directed by Guto Barra. IMDb.

Buena Vista Social Club. 1999. Directed by Wim Wenders. ARTHAUS.

Charles Bradley: Soul of America. 2012. Directed by Poull Brien. IMDb.

Cuban Hip Hop Desde el Principio. 2006. Directed by Larissa and Vanessa Diaz. IMDbPro.

Fahrenheit 9/11. 2004. Directed by Michael Moore. IMDb.

Flor de Muertos (Flower of the Dead). 2011. Directed by Danny Vinik. Brink Films.

Guerrilla Radio: The Hip-Hop Struggle Under Castro. 2007. Directed by Thomas Nybo. IMDb.

HavanYork. 2009. Directed by Luciano Larobina. Acitron.

Johnny Cash at Folsom Prison. 2008. Directed by Bestor Cram. IMDb.

Muscle Shoals. 2013. Directed by Greg Camalier. Magnolia Pictures.

Searching for Sugar Man. 2012. Directed by Malik Bendjelloul. Non-Stop Entertainment.

Shine a Light. 2008. Directed by Martin Scorsese. Paramount Classics.

Slingshot Hip Hop. 2008. Directed by Reem Salloum. IMDb.

Standing in the Shadows of Motown. 2002. Directed by Paul Justman. Artisan Entertainment.

The Blues. A Musical Journey. 2003. Directed by Martin Scorcese. Television.

The Wrecking Crew. 2008. Directed by Denny Tedesco. IMDb.

20 Feet from Stardom. 2014. Directed by Morgan Nelville. Studiocanal.

Woodstock: Now & Then. 2009. Directed by Barbara Kopple. IMDb.

INTER-AMERICAN STUDIES
Cultures – Societies – History

ESTUDIOS INTERAMERICANOS
Culturas – Sociedades – Historia

This interdisciplinary series examines national and transnational issues in the cultures, societies, and histories of the Americas. It creates a forum for a critical academic dialogue between North and South, promoting an inter-American paradigm that shifts the scholarly focus from methodological nationalism to the wider context of the Western Hemisphere.

Vol. 1
Raab, Josef, Sebastian Thies, and Daniela Noll-Opitz, eds. *Screening the Americas: Narration of Nation in Documentary Film / Proyectando las Américas: Narración de la nación en el cine documental.* 2011. 470 pp.

WVT Wissenschaftlicher Verlag Trier	ISBN 978-3-86821-331-7	€ 29,50
Bilingual Press / Editorial Bilingüe	ISBN 978-1-931010-83-2	$ 29.50

Vol. 2
Raussert, Wilfried, and Michelle Habell-Pallán, eds. *Cornbread and Cuchifritos: Ethnic Identity Politics, Transnationalization, and Transculturation in American Urban Popular Music.* 2011. 292 pp.

WVT Wissenschaftlicher Verlag Trier	ISBN 978-3-86821-265-5	€ 29,50
Bilingual Press / Editorial Bilingüe	ISBN 978- 1-931010-80-1	$ 29.50

Vol. 3
Butler, Martin, Jens Martin Gurr, and Olaf Kaltmeier, eds. *EthniCities: Metropolitan Cultures and Ethnic Identities in the Americas.* 2011. 268 pp.

WVT Wissenschaftlicher Verlag Trier	ISBN 978-3-86821-310-2	€ 29,50
Bilingual Press / Editorial Bilingüe	ISBN 978-1-931010-81-8	$ 29.50

Vol. 4
Gurr, Jens Martin, and Wilfried Raussert, eds. *Cityscapes in the Americas and Beyond: Representations of Urban Complexity in Literature and Film.* 2011. 300 pp.

WVT Wissenschaftlicher Verlag Trier	ISBN 978-3-86821-324-9	€ 29,50
Bilingual Press / Editorial Bilingüe	ISBN 978-1-931010-82-5	$ 29.50

Vol. 5
Kirschner, Luz Angélica, ed. *Expanding* Latinidad*: An Inter-American Perspective*. 2012. 292 pp.
WVT Wissenschaftlicher Verlag Trier ISBN 978-3-86821-309-6 € 29,50
Bilingual Press / Editorial Bilingüe ISBN 978-1-931010-84-9 $ 29.50

Vol. 6
Raussert, Wilfried, and Graciela Martínez-Zalce, eds. *(Re)Discovering 'America': Road Movies and Other Travel Narratives in North America / (Re)Descubriendo 'América': Road movie y otras narrativas de viaje en América del Norte*. 2012. 252 pp.
WVT Wissenschaftlicher Verlag Trier ISBN 978-3-86821-384-3 € 29,50
Bilingual Press / Editorial Bilingüe ISBN 978-1-931010-91-7 $ 29.50

Vol. 7
Kaltmeier, Olaf, ed. *Transnational Americas: Envisioning Inter-American Area Studies in Globalization Processes*. 2013. 278 pp.
WVT Wissenschaftlicher Verlag Trier ISBN 978-3-86821-415-4 € 29,50
Bilingual Press / Editorial Bilingüe ISBN 978-1-931010-92-4 $ 29.50

Vol. 8
Raab, Josef, and Alexander Greiffenstern, eds. *Interculturalism in North America: Canada, the United States, Mexico, and Beyond*. 2013. 312 pp.
WVT Wissenschaftlicher Verlag Trier ISBN 978-3-86821-460-4 € 29,50
Bilingual Press / Editorial Bilingüe ISBN 978-1-931010-99-3 $ 29.50

Vol. 9
Raab, Josef, ed. *New World Colors: Ethnicity, Belonging, and Difference in the Americas*. 2014. 418 pp.
WVT Wissenschaftlicher Verlag Trier ISBN 978-3-86821-461-1 € 29,50
Bilingual Press / Editorial Bilingüe ISBN 978-1-939743-00-8 $ 39.50

Vol. 10
Roth, Julia. *Occidental Readings, Decolonial Practices: A Selection on Gender, Genre, and Coloniality in the Americas*. 2014. 284 pp.
WVT Wissenschaftlicher Verlag Trier ISBN 978-3-86821-446-8 € 26,50
Bilingual Press / Editorial Bilingüe ISBN 978-1-939743-07-7 $ 32.50

Vol. 11
Thies, Sebastian, Gabriele Pisarz-Ramirez, and Luzelena Gutiérrez de Velasco, eds. *Of Fatherlands and Motherlands: Gender and Nation in the Americas / De Patrias y Matrias: Género y nación en las Américas*. 2015. 344 pp.
WVT Wissenschaftlicher Verlag Trier ISBN 978-3-86821-528-1 € 29,50
Bilingual Press / Editorial Bilingüe ISBN 978-1-939743-08-4 $ 39.50

Vol. 12
Fuchs, Rebecca. *Caribbeanness as a Global Phenomenon: Junot Díaz, Edwidge Danticat, and Cristina García*. 2014. 298 pp.
WVT Wissenschaftlicher Verlag Trier ISBN 978-3-86821-533-5 € 26,50
Bilingual Press / Editorial Bilingüe ISBN 978-1-939743-09-1 $ 32.50

Vol. 13
Andres, Julia. *¡Cuéntame algo! – Chicana Narrative Beyond the Borderlands*. 2015. 202 pp.
WVT Wissenschaftlicher Verlag Trier ISBN 978-3-86821-569-4 € 25,00
Bilingual Press / Editorial Bilingüe ISBN 978-1-939743-11-4 $ 28.50

Vol. 14
Hertlein, Saskia. *Tales of Transformation: Emerging Adulthood, Migration, and Ethnicity in Contemporary American Literature*. 2014. 228 pp.
WVT Wissenschaftlicher Verlag Trier ISBN 978-3-86821-570-0 € 25,00
Bilingual Press / Editorial Bilingüe ISBN 978-1-939743-10-7 $ 31.50

Vol. 15
Raab, Josef, and Saskia Hertlein, eds. *Spaces – Communities – Discourses: Charting Identity and Belonging in the Americas*. 2016. 382 pp.
WVT Wissenschaftlicher Verlag Trier ISBN 978-3-86821-590-8 € 29,50
Bilingual Press / Editorial Bilingüe ISBN 978-1-939743-13-8 $ 39.50

Vol. 16
Mehring, Frank, ed. *The Mexico Diary: Winold Reiss between Vogue Mexico and Harlem Renaissance. An Illustrated Trilingual Edition with Commentary and Musical Interpretation* (includes color plates and audio CD). 2016. 244 pp.
WVT Wissenschaftlicher Verlag Trier ISBN 978-3-86821-594-6 € 29,50
Bilingual Press / Editorial Bilingüe ISBN 978-1-939743-14-5 $ 39.50

Vol. 17
Raussert, Wilfried, Brian Rozema, Yolanda Campos, and Marius Littschwager, eds. *Key Tropes in Inter-American Studies: Perspectives from the* forum for inter-american research (fiar). 2015. 374 pp.
WVT Wissenschaftlicher Verlag Trier ISBN 978-3-86821-627-1 € 29,50
Bilingual Press / Editorial Bilingüe ISBN 978-1-939743-16-9 $ 39.50

Vol. 19
Rehm, Lukas, Jochen Kemner, and Olaf Kaltmeier, eds. *Politics of Entanglement in the Americas: Connecting Transnational Flows and Local Perspectives*. 2017. 226 pp.
WVT Wissenschaftlicher Verlag Trier ISBN 978-3-86821-675-2 € 27,50
Bilingual Press / Editorial Bilingüe ISBN 978-1-939743-17-6 $ 32.50

Vol. 20
Britt Arredondo, Christopher. *Imperial Idiocy: A Reflection on Forced Displacement in the Americas*. 2017. 194 pp.

WVT Wissenschaftlicher Verlag Trier	ISBN 978-3-86821-706-3	€ 26,50
Bilingual Press / Editorial Bilingüe	ISBN 978-1-939743-20-6	$ 30.00

Vol. 21
Schemien, Alexia. *Of Virgins, Curanderas, and Wrestler Saints: Un/Doing Religion in Contemporary Mexican American Literature*. 2018. 218 pp.

WVT Wissenschaftlicher Verlag Trier	ISBN 978-3-86821-724-7	€ 27,50
Bilingual Press / Editorial Bilingüe	ISBN 978-1-939743-22-0	$ 32.50

Vol. 22
Fulger, Maria Diana. *The Cuban Post-Socialist Exotic: Contemporary U.S. American Travel Narratives about Cuba*. 2020. 266 pp.

WVT Wissenschaftlicher Verlag Trier	ISBN 978-3-86821-769-8	€ 32,50
Bilingual Press / Editorial Bilingüe	ISBN 978-1-939743-27-5	$ 36.00

Vol. 24
Kaltmeier, Olaf, Mirko Petersen, Wilfried Raussert, and Julia Roth, eds. *Cherishing the Past, Envisioning the Future. Entangled Practises of Heritage and Utopia in the Americas*. 2021. 176 pp.

WVT Wissenschaftlicher Verlag Trier	ISBN 978-3-86821-804-6	€ 23,50
UNO University of New Orleans Press	ISBN 978-1-60801-206-0	$ 27.50

Vol. 26
Raussert, Wilfried. *'What's Going On': How Music Shapes the Social*. 2021. 224 pp.

WVT Wissenschaftlicher Verlag Trier	ISBN 978-3-86821-811-4	€ 28,50
UNO University of New Orleans Press	ISBN 978-1-60801-199-5	$ 34.00

Vol. 27
Frank-Job, Barbara. *Immigration as a Process: Temporality Concepts in Blogs of Latin American Immigrants to Québec*. 2021. 138 pp.

WVT Wissenschaftlicher Verlag Trier	ISBN 978-3-86821-820-6	€ 20,00
UNO University of New Orleans Press	ISBN 978-1-60801-215-2	$ 24.00

Vol. 28
Roth, Julia. *Can Feminism Trump Populism? Right-Wing Trends and Intersectional Contestations in the Americas*. 2021. 166 pp.

WVT Wissenschaftlicher Verlag Trier	ISBN 978-3-86821-821-3	€ 23,00
UNO University of New Orleans Press	ISBN 978-1-60801-205-3	$ 26.00

Vol. 30
Buitrago Valencia, Clara. *Missionaries: Migrants or Expatriates? Guatemalan Pentecostal Leaders in Los Angeles.* 2021. 236 pp.
WVT Wissenschaftlicher Verlag Trier ISBN 978-3-86821-818-3 € 28,50
UNO University of New Orleans Press ISBN 978-1-60801-210-7 $ 34.50

Vol. 31
Schwabe, Nicole. *De-Centering History Education: Creating Knowledge of Global Entanglements.* 2021. 92 pp.
WVT Wissenschaftlicher Verlag Trier ISBN 978-3-86821-828-2 € 18,00
UNO University of New Orleans Press ISBN 978-1-60801-214-5 $ 21.00

Vol. 32
Manke, Albert. *Coping with Discrimination and Exclusion. Experiences of Free Chinese Migrants in the Americas in a Transregional and Diachronic Perspective.* 2021. 162 pp.
WVT Wissenschaftlicher Verlag Trier ISBN 978-3-86821-829-9 € 23,00
UNO University of New Orleans Press ISBN 978-1-60801-207-7 $ 27.00

Vol. 33
Rohland, Eleonora. *Entangled Histories and the Environment? Socio-Environmental Transformations in the Caribbean, 1492-1800.* 2021. 92 pp.
WVT Wissenschaftlicher Verlag Trier ISBN 978-3-86821-833-6 € 18,00
UNO University of New Orleans Press ISBN 978-1-60801-208-4 $ 21.00

Vol. 34
Kaltmeier, Olaf. *National Parks from North to South. An Entangled History of Conservation and Colonization in Argentina.* 2021. 210 pp.
WVT Wissenschaftlicher Verlag Trier ISBN 978-3-86821-834-3 € 27,50
UNO University of New Orleans Press ISBN 978-1-60801-204-6 $ 32.50

Vol. 35
Raussert, Wilfried. *Off the Grid. Art Practices and Public Space.* 2021. 232 pp.
WVT Wissenschaftlicher Verlag Trier ISBN 978-3-86821-835-0 € 29,50
UNO University of New Orleans Press ISBN 978-1-60801-213-8 $ 34.50

Vol. 36
Ravasio, Paola. *This Train Is Not Bound to Glory. A Study of Literary Trainscapes.* 2021. 114 pp.
WVT Wissenschaftlicher Verlag Trier ISBN 978-3-86821-836-7 € 18,00
UNO University of New Orleans Press ISBN 978-1-60801-216-9 $ 21.00

Vol. 37

Schäfer, Heinrich Wilhelm. *Protestant 'Sects' and the Spirit of (Anti-)Imperialism. Religious Entanglements in the Americas.* 2021. 242 pp.

WVT Wissenschaftlicher Verlag Trier	ISBN 978-3-86821-855-9	€ 29,50
UNO University of New Orleans Press	ISBN 978-1-60801-209-1	$ 34.50